T0305084

Asset Liability Management Optimisation

Asset Liability Management Optimisation

A Practitioner's Guide to Balance Sheet Management and Remodelling

BEATA LUBINSKA

WILEY

Registered office
John Wiley & Sons Ltd, The Atrium, Southern Gate, Chichester, West Sussex, PO19 8SQ, United Kingdom

For details of our global editorial offices, for customer services and for information about how to apply for permission to reuse the copyright material in this book please see our website at www.wiley.com.

Library of Congress Cataloging-in-Publication Data

Names: Lubinska, Beata, 1973- author.
Title: Asset liability management optimisation : a practitioner's guide to balance sheet management and remodelling / Beata Lubinska.
Description: First edition. | Hoboken : Wiley, 2020. | Series: The wiley finance series | Includes bibliographical references and index.
Identifiers: LCCN 2019041408 (print) | LCCN 2019041409 (ebook) | ISBN 9781119635482 (hardback) | ISBN 9781119635499 (adobe pdf) | ISBN 9781119635512 (epub)
Subjects: LCSH: Asset-liability management. | Banks and banking.
Classification: LCC HG1615.25 .L83 2020 (print) | LCC HG1615.25 (ebook) | DDC 332.1068/1—dc23
LC record available at https://lccn.loc.gov/2019041408
LC ebook record available at https://lccn.loc.gov/2019041409

Cover Design: Wiley
Cover Images: Chart board © golero/Getty Images, London Tower © fotoVoyager/Getty Images

Set in 10/12pt SabonLTStd by SPi Global, Chennai, India

Printed in Great Britain by TJ International Ltd, Padstow, Cornwall, UK

10 9 8 7 6 5 4 3 2 1

To my Family.

With special gratitude to Lidia, the best daughter I can imagine and to Daniele, my husband, who has a special place in my heart

Contents

Foreword

Banking is an age-old art. As a commercial discipline, modern banking dates from the fifteenth century but there is evidence of practice uncannily similar to 'modern' banking dating from Roman and even Babylonian times. If by banking we mean an independent enterprise that accepts deposits from customers, which it promises to keep safe and repay (with interest) on demand, whilst at the same time lending funds to borrowers who agree to repay (with interest) at a set date in the future, then banking is indeed an ancient art.

Of course, that makes asset liability management (ALM), as a discipline linked hand-in-glove with banking, a fairly time-honoured practice as well. Because to practise banking is to practise ALM. Every bank operates an ALM function, for the simple reason that to undertake banking requires the institution to manage its assets and liabilities efficiently. An ALM desk is as vital to a bank as the engine and wheels are to a motor car. Deposits and loans have different cashflow profiles, they behave differently at different times, and they represent different risks on the balance sheet. Managing these various differences is what banking and ALM, or at least long-term sustainable banking, are all about.

It seems, however, that ALM as a formal discipline, codified into formal text, is a rather more recent thing. I can find no trace of the use of this expression, in the context of banking, in any academic or practitioner text that dates before the early 1970s. This is curious, to put it mildly, because it is such a vital part of the art of banking. I surmise that the reason for this is twofold: one, as a process, it was traditionally part of the Treasury function, a desk well-known for its 'learn on the job, in-at-the-deep end' approach to its duties; and two, it is an area of finance that has never attracted overmuch attention from academia. And if academics aren't writing technical papers about your art, then usually precious few Treasury practitioners are going to either.

No matter, one of the many impacts of the 2008 global financial crash was the new emphasis on ALM, or I should say the importance of ALM. No longer was it the chap at the conference in the dull grey suit who stood in the corner looking at his (it was generally a he, in the UK anyway) shoes. Now it was the rock star, a prime focus for attention. Why? Because capital and liquidity were now, for banks, more constrained, more expensive. Having too much of either was unbearably inefficient, whilst having insufficient of either was now going to bring the wrath of the regulator down on one's head. However relaxed one might have been about ALM before, overnight it became urgent business, deserving of the C-suite's undivided attention.

Thus, the buzzword since 2008 has been balance sheet *optimisation,* what I've been calling *strategic ALM* for as long as anyone has cared to listen. I like to think of ALM optimisation as meaning structuring the balance sheet, at the loans and deposits origination stage, in a way that meets the competing needs of regulator, customer, and shareholder as efficiently and as effectively as possible. This is, in essence, strategic ALM. Considering the needs of all three key stakeholders and practising proactive, as opposed to reactive, ALM.

The author of this fine book defines optimisation slightly differently, although to me her definition follows on logically from mine. Whereas I define the 'what?', Ms Lubinska defines the 'how?'; to wit, optimisation is *'a process which involves the application of optimisation techniques (described in this book) and definition of the optimisation criterion (which metric do we want to prioritise), objectives (what do we want to optimise), and constraints (conditions which need to be taken into account in the optimisation process).'*

As she notes further,

One of the objectives of this book is to walk the reader through the optimisation process in detail, from the practical perspective, in order to quantify the economic benefits coming from this exercise.

This is, quite simply, solid gold. In the post-crash era of onerous banking regulation and constrained capital and liquidity, undertaking a more disciplined, formal approach to ALM becomes as important as cyber security, as important as treating customers fairly, of pursuing the right strategy to compete. It is the key to a sustained and viable balance sheet over the long term. And as I am fond of saying, the balance sheet is everything.

This is a book to be studied carefully, to read and re-read and then to assess for application to one's own bank. The tools described herein, illustrated with case study examples, are not necessarily transferable verbatim to every bank. Rather, it is the discipline that is being demonstrated that needs to be adopted, and the techniques tweaked, to ensure that the right approach is tailor-made for each specific case. This isn't a trivial subject. But if one gets it right, the simultaneous reward for all of a bank's stakeholders will be plain to see.

Professor Moorad Choudhry
Surrey, England
31 October 2019

About the Author

Dr. Beata Lubinska is a financial engineer with over 15 years of practical experience gained in international financial institutions such as GE Capital, Deloitte, and Standard Chartered Bank based both in Milan and London. Currently, she leads BL Advisory & Consulting, a small boutique consulting company based in London.

Previously, she was a Head of Market Risk Department in MeDirect Group in London with the main focus on IRRBB, Market Risk and Balance Sheet Management. Aside from being a member of BTRM Faculty, which was founded by Professor Moorad Choudhry in London, she also provides trainings for professionals from banking industry across the globe (including Kuwait, London, USA, Oman, Qatar, and Turkey).

Her main areas of specialisation include: Funds Transfer Pricing, Interest Rate Risk in the Banking Book, Asset Liability Management, and Balance Sheet management through FTP and optimisation.

Beata holds a PhD from Wroclaw University of Economics in Poland. In her PhD thesis, she introduces the hypothesis that the application of the optimisation techniques improves the management of the banking book in terms of quantifiable economic impact on the P&L of the bank and that there is clear benefit from the integrated treatment of the interest rate risk and liquidity risk under one approach. She strongly promotes the proactive management of the balance sheet of a bank. The results of her research are published in *Financial Sciences, Springer Proceedings in Business and Economics* and *Research Papers of Wroclaw University of Economics*. Her recent publications include:

- 'Review of the static methods used in the measurement of the exposure to the interest rate risk' – Financial Sciences 2014.
- 'Balance Sheet Shaping Through Decision Model and the Role of the Funds Transfer Pricing Process' – Springer 2017.
- 'Balance Sheet Shaping through a Decision model and Funds Transfer Pricing' – Research Papers of Wroclaw University of Economics, 2017.
- 'Contemporary challenges in the Asset Liability Management' – Springer 2018.
- 'Contemporary challenges in the Asset Liability Management' – Research Papers of Wroclaw University of Economics, 2018.
- 'Modern Asset Liability management (ALM) needs to operate in the multidimensional world' – ALCO magazine, August 2018.
- 'Interest Rate Risk in the Banking Book (IRRBB) – key challenges in the implementation of the revised European Banking Authority Guidelines and why it is so important' – ALCO magazine, November 2018.

Introduction

The role of the Asset Liability Management function (ALM) in the management of the banking book of a bank is constantly growing. A clear evolution can be seen as ALM managers realise that a reactive approach, which consists of the management of the banking book as a passive structure resulting from the commercial and funding strategy of a bank, should be replaced by a proactive approach where the banking book structure is decided in a conscious and active way in order to come up with the desired target structure of the banking book.

The intention of this book is to promote a change in the role of ALM and, in general, in the approach towards financial risk management practice in modern finance. It will show that the proactive role of ALM through an integrated approach for the management of two main financial risk categories, i.e. interest rate risk (IRR) and liquidity risk under one approach, and interrelation with the commercial strategy that a bank wants to adopt, brings significant benefits. Those benefits are mainly economical and can be quantified. The need for change seems to be driven by a number of challenges, such as a heavily regulated landscape, low or negative rates (in the eurozone), and margin compression, which the banking industry has been facing since 2008.

This is why the word 'optimisation' is commonly used in banks these days as an attempt to address the aforementioned challenges. However, I quite often wonder what this word means in practice. What in reality should be optimised, and how it should be optimised. I believe that often the word 'optimisation' just means to make better allocation of resources such as liquidity or capital in order to align a bank with the regulatory requirements. In my view, optimisation is a process which involves the application of optimisation techniques (described in this book) and definition of the optimisation criterion (which metric do we want to prioritise?), objectives (what do we want to optimise?), and constraints (conditions which need to be taken into account in the optimisation process). It also needs a practical implementation tool (method). One of the objectives of this book is to walk the reader through the optimisation process in detail, from a practical perspective, in order to quantify the economic benefits coming from this exercise. At the end, the reader is provided with two business cases on which the optimisation process is tested.

Additionally, the book sheds light on another aspect: the *silo-based* approach adopted for the management of financial risks still commonly used as a *day-by-day* practice in banks. The *silo-based* approach consists of separated management of financial risks, in particular interest rate risk in the banking book and liquidity risk. The consequence of this is taking suboptimal decisions regarding the funding strategy (and consequently liquidity and funding risk) and suboptimal hedging strategies (and consequently mitigation of the interest rate risk in the banking book). In my experience, I have always seen these two risk categories treated separately and not interrelated in the daily measurement and management process. For example, in the risk management department there was a person (or team) focused on the calculation of liquidity metrics and another person (team) responsible for analysis of the interest rate risk in the banking book (IRRBB) metrics. The treasury department, in each bank, had its own set-up and targets designed for this function. As such, in some banks you will see the ALM function operating within the treasury department, with the main objective being to focus on taking an active positioning on the interest rate curve and benefiting from the expected movements of the curve in line with the market forecast. Quite often the size and components of the liquidity buffer (also within the responsibilities of the treasury department) are decided separately and the impact on IRRBB metrics is assessed only after the whole process of building the liquidity buffer is already finalised. One of the most important tasks of a bank's treasurer is to come up with the funding strategy. This is the process where all available funding sources are assessed, and their composition is decided. Again, there is still quite often little interaction with IRRBB. Instead, my experience and academic research lead towards the conclusion that such an interaction should be imperative.

Let's analyse this aspect in detail.

The crucial task of the treasury department is to maintain a heathy balance between the profitability of the banking book and its exposure to financial risks altogether. There is a clear trade-off between the riskiness of the banking book and its profitability. In this book, I call it a *target position*. Finding such a target position (or target profile) is the real challenge of ALM analysis because it requires the analytical tools and framework to be put in place. Herein, the target profile means the definition of a composition of assets and liabilities so that the profitability of the banking book reaches its maximum, taking into account a number of regulatory and internal risk constraints. I will come back to this definition later. For now, my main objective is to show that there is a strong interrelation between those two risk categories, i.e. interest rate risk in the banking book and liquidity risk (the two main risk categories which the ALM department has to manage), which becomes very evident when looking at the projection of outstanding stocks according to interest commitment dates (interest rate risk view) and liquidity commitment dates (liquidity risk view).

In order to present this argument in detail, let's analyse a very simple case, in which the banking book of a bank is composed of the fixed rate loan funded by a floating rate note with a 3-month reset. Their financial characteristics are shown in Figure I.1.

In analysing the ALM profitability, we need to first define some terms. First of all, there is a positive margin resulting from the interest rate risk management which is attributed to ALM (the allocation of profits between business units and ALM is described in this book later on) if the spread of assets is higher than the spread of liabilities. If this margin is already crystallised and attributed, we call it *margin locked in*. If there is uncertainty about the future spread because the position, at some point of time, is exposed to the risk of changes in interest rates, we call it *margin at risk*. The same applies to the funding spread on the position as it fluctuates over time.

In the case of the analysed example, the banking book shows exposure to the IRR on 31 March 2019 due to the refixing of the floating rate liability. Starting from that date, the refixed asset will be funded by the refixing liability, causing the interest rate gap and

ASSET – Fixed rate loan at maturity 100

Repayment type: bullet
Next (capital) payment date: 31/12/2019
Next repricing date: 31/12/2019
Customer Rate: 3.50%
FTP Base Rate: 2.00%
FTP Liquidity Spread: 0.50%

LIABILITY – Floating rate note 3m reset 100

Repayment type: bullet
Next (capital) payment date: 30/09/2019
Next repricing date: 31/03/2019
Customer Rate: 1.50%
FTP Base Rate: 1.25%
FTP Liquidity Spread: 0.25%

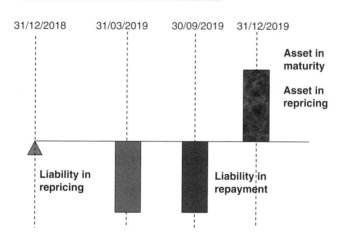

FIGURE I.1 IRR and liquidity profile in the banking book.
Source: own elaboration.

the impact on net interest income known as *NII sensitivity*. As regards the profitability of this position, due to the interest rate risk component, the locked-in ALM margin is equal to 0.75%, while the ALM margin at risk is equal to 1% under the assumption of a decrease in EURIBOR 3 M by 25 bps (from 1.25% to 1%).

This situation is presented in Figure I.2.

The same situation analysed from the liquidity standpoint looks slightly different. The bank begins to be exposed to the liquidity risk on 30 September 2019 when the liability expires and needs to be rolled over. Starting from that date, the funding gap creates the NII sensitivity. It can be clearly seen in Figure I.3.

The ALM locked-in margin deriving from this position is equal to 0.25% (the difference between the liquidity spread of the asset and the liability). However, the ALM margin at risk depends on the new liquidity spread related to the liability which needs to be rolled over.

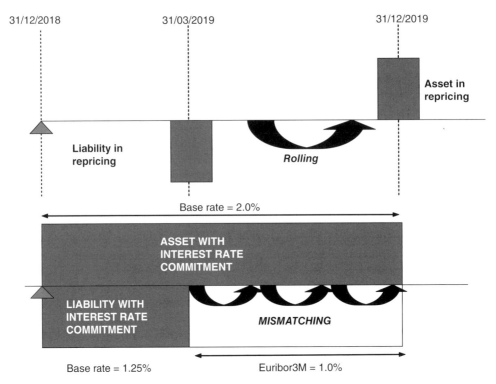

31/12/2018   31/03/2019   31/12/2019

Asset in
repricing

Liability in
repricing

Rolling

Base rate = 2.0%

ASSET WITH
INTEREST RATE
COMMITMENT

LIABILITY WITH
INTEREST RATE
COMMITMENT

MISMATCHING

Base rate = 1.25%   Euribor3M = 1.0%

FIGURE I.2 Exposure to IRR in the banking book.
Source: own elaboration

Arriving at the total profitability of the bank, in this particular example, we need to sum the NII margin obtained by the positioning of the bank in terms of both interest rate risk and liquidity risk.

Consequently, the total net interest margin in the period until 31 March 2019 is equal to 1% (0.75% + 0.25%) and will be assigned to the ALM book within the treasury department. From 31 March 2019 to 30 September 2019 it gives 1.25%, but due to the fact that the component related to the IRR is uncertain, this result is unrealised. The same situation appears from 30 September 2019 onward. The unrealised ALM profit depends on the new liquidity spread of the liability in maturity and the movement of the EURIBOR 3 M pillar of the interest rate curve.

It is up to the treasurer to decide how to minimise the NII sensitivity derived from the interest rate risk and liquidity component of the banking book, and what profitability needs to be provided by the ALM unit to the bank. Therefore, the real challenge consists in understanding the trade-off between profitability and risk.

The realised profitability of the bank in terms of P&L impact is determined both by past hedging strategies concerning the interest rate management in the banking book and maturity transformation performed by the treasury with reference to its funding strategy. While the unrealised P&L results will be a function of the magnitude of the margin at risk due to both IRR and the funding strategy for the future accounting periods and the trade-off between expected P&L and its volatility (sensitivity), the riskiness

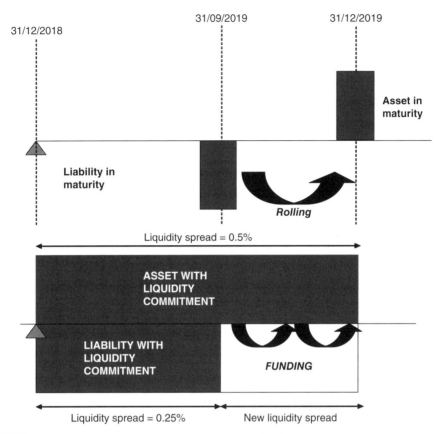

FIGURE I.3 Exposure to the funding risk in the banking book.
Source: own elaboration

embedded in the banking book structure is determined by the risk tolerance of a bank and regulatory requirements. It is obvious that the level of uncertainty and the capability of the bank to predict the direction of the market in terms of the interest rate curve and funding spread are the main impact factors in this exercise, but this is not sufficient.

There are other important factors, such as the unpredictable behaviour of customers of a bank both from the assets and liabilities side, which define the final composition of the banking book. The behavioural assumption related to the assets side is mostly defined by the prepayment rate of mortgages or personal loans which can be prepaid before their contractual maturity date. This factor introduces significant uncertainty into the banking book, since it can change the liquidity profile of the bank within the short-term period. Also, the hedging strategies undertaken in the past might turn out to be inefficient and might need to be adjusted.

As a consequence of the above, the main challenge of the ALM function is to find the banking book target position in terms of the exposure to financial risks, in order to boost its profitability and to minimise the cost of funding being subject to the limits dictated by internal policies and regulatory requirements. Another challenge of ALM is to cooperate in a proactive way with the business units (BUs) over the definition of the target position of assets in the banking book. There will be the return maximisation aspect and regulatory requirements which may apply to the asset side.

The problem relating to the existence of the interrelation between interest rate risk and liquidity risk and its consequent impact on the structure of the banking book is not new and has been discussed in various papers and books, for example Baldan, Zen, and Rebonato in 2012, and Choudhry in 2017 and 2018. Consequently, this book attempts to approach the integration problem from a different angle, i.e. formulation of mathematical functions and thereafter application of optimisation techniques in order to find out the most appropriate composition of the banking book. The functions are built for the objective variables which need to be optimised (asset profitability and cost of funding) and constraints which need to be taken into account in the optimisation exercise (for example the NII volatility, concentration of funding, and desirable level of liquidity buffer). The output of such a constructed optimisation problem will lead to the achievement of the target profile of a bank in terms of the composition of assets and liabilities and the quantification of the economic impact on the bank's P&L. Finally, the recent sovereign crises, interbank market illiquidity, and strengthened regulatory requirements such as Basel III have forced the banking industry to find the most appropriate position in order to maximise profitability and, at the same time, respect limits dictated by the internal policies and the regulator.

The structure of this book has been subordinated to its main purpose, i.e. the definition of the target structure both for the asset side and liability side of the banking book.

Chapter 1 presents the main concepts of asset and liability management in commercial banks and highlights the special role of the treasury department in seeking a balance between maximising profitability (which is largely derived from the selection of strategies for financing banking operations in the context of expected yield curve and maintaining the previously defined level of metrics describing the risk). From the point of view of liquidity management, the optimisation task focuses on the issue of building a sufficient buffer of liquid assets (HQLA) and maintaining an appropriate long-term liquidity ratio. The interest rate risk is limited by setting a threshold for the sensitivity of interest income (ΔNII). This part of the book presents the most important concepts of managing the banking book in commercial banks, the main financial risks it is subject to, and the concept of the funds transfer pricing process. This chapter also contains an overview of the regulatory architecture built after the global financial crisis of 2007–2009, i.e. Basel III.

Chapter 2 of the book provides the reader with a description of methods for measuring and limiting the interest rate risk and liquidity risk within the banking book. This chapter presents in detail the methods of risk measurement using the gap method and quantifying mismatch of the maturity dates of the banking book items and its impact on the economic value of capital. The subject of the analysis is also the duration method and its application in the process of managing the bank's assets and liabilities (DGAP method). The second part of this chapter presents decomposition of liquidity risk and selected methods of measurement and management in the short and long run. Particular attention is given to analysis of the mismatching risk between risk sensitive assets, liabilities, and basis risk. A separate section is dedicated to the problem of funds transfer pricing (FTP) in the banking sector and the possibility of using it to determine the price parameters of assets in accordance to the level of liquidity risk driven by the liabilities financing them. This part of the book describes the concept of FTP and the interest rate decomposition paid by the client. The FTP process plays a major role in banking book shaping techniques.

Chapter 3 focuses on the behavioural factors determining the decision of the bank's clients. This problem is presented both for the liabilities side (behaviour of depositors) and for borrowers with the option of early repayment of their liabilities to the bank. This chapter highlights the importance of behavioural factors for the stability and structure of the banking book. One of the key challenges, from the perspective of liquidity and interest rate risk management, is to model these phenomena. Among a number of existing methods, the book presents two methods for estimating the level of deposits without defined the maturity date. The first of these, classified as a quantitative approach, allows for the determination of the stability of deposits based on the growth model; the second is classified as a hybrid method. The sensitivity analysis carried out allows one to point out factors significantly affecting change in the stability of deposits; for example, the level of interest rates or macroeconomic factors. Instead, the process of modelling early repayment of loans (the asset side of the banking book) is presented in stages. The first stage describes the objective of modelling, then the types of behaviour regarding early repayments and factors affecting the decision-making process. This part of the work is descriptive and serves to present an approach to modelling the option of early repayment by the client. In particular, there is the phenomenon of financial prepayments, which is determined by macroeconomic factors and changes in interest rates, as well as statistical prepayments, which cannot be explained by the above mentioned factors.

Chapter 4 focuses on optimisation techniques and describes the optimisation process in the decision-making model. The first section introduces the concept of optimisation and the optimisation algorithm based on the Lagrange multipliers method. The second section concerns the definition of the banking book profile and the description of the initial state of assets and liabilities for which the decision model was constructed (roll-over of time deposits, volatility of current and savings accounts, amortisation profile of assets, prepaid rate of assets, and type of interest rates and pricing policy). This part presents the differences in the structure of the banking book in various countries and the supervisory constraints to which the model is subject. The next section contains a description of the model's structure and constraints imposed on the objective function in the optimisation process. The constraints are divided first into those that determine the banking book's asset side, and include liquidity risk (liquidity buffer, short-term liquidity ratio, structural liquidity ratio, including the behaviour of clients and without taking them into account), interest rate risk (income-based measures and measures of economic value), and capital absorption (capital adequacy ratio). On the liabilities side, the constraints additionally include (apart from the liquidity and interest rate risk) the risk of excessive reliance on a particular source of funding (concentration risk). The chapter also includes the derivation of the objective functions: maximisation of assets income and minimisation of funding costs (costs of obtaining liabilities). The last section of this chapter presents the model risk and its sensitivity analysis. In particular, it defines the model risk and provides some insight on supervisory requirements. Subsequently, it defines the number of scenarios on which the business cases are based.

Chapter 5 includes a practical case study and shows the impact of individual scenarios on the results obtained from the application of the optimisation model. The case study is conducted on the example of two different banks. The case study can be seen as a test of the previously designed model.

In Appendices 1 and 2, the reader can find the quantification of benefits resulting from the application of the optimisation model, both for the asset and liability side of the banking book, under a number of scenarios (described in Chapter 4).

The term decision model is used in order to emphasise the practical application of the optimisation exercise in the decision-making process. Optimisation, in the form described throughout the book, provides a benchmark for the treasurer, CFO, and CRO related to the optimal composition of the banking book. Thus, senior management can gain awareness of the banking book composition, which allows them to reduce the cost of funding for the liability side and increase income for the asset side.

The book concludes with a number of take away messages and emphasises key points delivered to the reader.

CHAPTER 1

ALM of the Banking Book

This chapter describes in detail the main concepts related to the Asset Liability Management (ALM) in a commercial bank. Several aspects are analysed and put in evidence. It highlights the evolving role of ALM and its growing importance in ensuring the healthy and profitable structure of the banking book. There is an overview of financial risks existing in the banking book and managed within the ALM function, and a reminder of the Basel Committee on Banking Supervision (BCBS) practices related to the liquidity and funding risk, known as Basel III. Quite an important portion of this chapter is devoted to the Funds Transfer Pricing process (FTP) and its role in the management of interest rate risk and liquidity risk in the banking book.

The final part of this chapter is focused on the selective review of the main literature positions which have contributed significantly to the developments in the ALM field and have ensured the progress in the ALM role, risk measurement techniques, and profitability enhancement strategies.

THE ROLE OF ASSET LIABILITY MANAGEMENT IN COMMERCIAL BANKS

Under the common definition, Asset Liability Management (ALM) means the management of the balance sheet structure with two main objectives:

- to keep risks within the limits of risk bearing capacity;
- to earn on the capital utilised for banking book risks.

Those objectives are set within a bank's treasury division by a bank's Asset Liability Committee (ALCO) in a sense that each bank has a different risk appetite towards interest rate risk in the banking book and liquidity risk, which are managed within the ALM desk. As such, banks set up their own trade-off between risk and profitability in their banking books. For example, some banks are willing to take on more exposure in terms of *riding the yield curve* strategy through funding fixed rate assets with floating rate liabilities. Other banks opt for an immunisation strategy.

Exchange rate risk and credit spread risk are also managed within ALM.

In my view, ALM also has another important objective which gained attention quite recently, i.e. after the financial crisis of 2008. It consists of the determination of the cheapest funding structure for the bank in order to optimise its resources, such as liquidity, and support the business model of the bank. In this context, ALM acts as a strategic and active connection between business units, in particular to support them in decision-making processes (this point is explained in detail later on). Additionally, it has to find the target position for a bank through minimisation of funding costs. ALM is also a game changer – it adopts an integrated view for the management of financial risks, interest rate risk, and liquidity risk in the first instance.

Quite often the role of ALM is referred to as *'a bank within a bank'* and I support this statement. This important role can be clearly seen once you introduce the FTP process into Figure 1.1.

ALM charges the asset centre (the business unit responsible for delivering products to clients who intend to borrow from the bank, for example credit cards, mortgages, commercial loans) the FTP rate and recognises the FTP rate to the liability centre (the business unit responsible for delivering products to clients who intend to invest or hold their money within the bank). In doing so, the financial risks (interest rate risk and funding risk) are stripped off the business unit and transferred to ALM to manage. This is why it adopts this 'bank within the bank' role. The whole process, which is presented in Figure 1.1, is the basis of the FTP process and we will come back to this point repeatedly.

However, it must be noted that some of risks specific to the bank cannot be transferred to the financial market through derivatives and managed within ALM. This can be driven either by inappropriate FTP set up in the bank (incorrect methodologies or

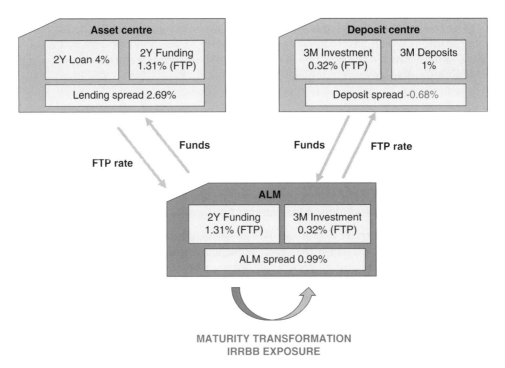

FIGURE 1.1   Maturity Matched Funds Transfer Pricing and ALM role.
Source: own elaboration.

curve construct) or an illiquid derivatives market in certain locations or currencies. By definition, credit risk cannot be transferred to ALM either.

Thus, ALM is defined as the management of balance sheet risks with financial instruments; however, not all balance sheet risks can be managed within ALM and ALCO.

Credit risk, which consumes the largest part of capital, is frequently managed by another body called the Total Bank Management Committee (in some banks managed by a Risk Committee) and is strictly linked to the commercial strategy of the bank and the products it is willing to offer.

In fact, it is still very common practice to separate credit risk management from financial risk management, although the name of the committee which governs the credit risk can differ across the banks. Again, in my view, ALM has a significant role in the balance sheet shaping and should be interlinked with the commercial units.

As already mentioned, the main task of ALM is to limit and manage risks on- and off-balance sheet. Management requires respecting internal and regulatory limits and controlling the revenue impact on the balance sheet. Thus, regulatory and internal limits are constraints. The goal of managing risk is to earn on it, to fulfil the revenue budget. In addition, it is practically impossible to mitigate all risks resulting from a bank's customer business and balance sheet. The following risks are managed by ALM:

- Interest Rate Risk in the Banking Book (IRRBB) – the risk of reduction of interest income through unfavourable interest rate movements. It is also the risk of reduction in market value of the interest rate risk position. ALM management concepts, reporting, and limits have to reflect this dual view.
- Liquidity Risk – risk of insufficient funds resulting in illiquidity. This risk is managed by keeping liquidity buffers that can be turned into liquidity in the case of stress.
- Liquidity Cost Risk – risk of the reduction of interest income (or mark to market value) through an increase in liquidity cost (funding spread).
- FX Risks – losses from unfavourable movements in the foreign currency exchange rates.
- Credit Spread Risk in the Banking Book (CSRBB) – mark to market losses from spread variations in the bond and derivatives portfolio.

IRRBB, CSRBB, and FX risks in ALM are limited within the Internal Capital Adequacy Assessment Process (ICAAP) by decisions of the Management and Supervisory Board (Risk Strategy); meanwhile, the Liquidity Risk and Funding Cost Risk are covered by the Internal Liquidity Adequacy Assessment (ILAAP). Those risks are managed mostly independently from the customer business.

In the introduction I stated that there are different ways of structuring the ALM unit within the financial institution. These are:

- ALM is a part of the Market Organisation (Financial Markets, Capital Markets, and Treasury). The ALM committee, headed by the respective board members, decides on risk positioning and the ALM department manages the positions within operative limits for daily management on its own. In this set-up, the Treasurer will make a prediction about the future movements of interest rates and will position the banking book in favour of the bank. For example, if the bank is *asset sensitive* on the short end of the interest rate curve (the short end is usually intended to be up to the 1-year time period) and the treasurer will increase the total GAP under

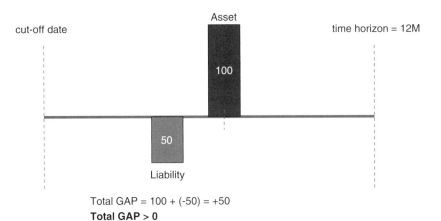

FIGURE 1.2   Directional Gap – asset sensitive position.
Source: own elaboration.

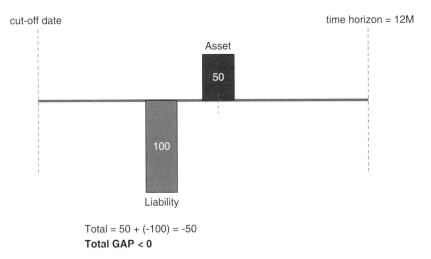

FIGURE 1.3   Directional Gap – liability sensitive position.
Source: own elaboration.

a 1-year time horizon in order to boost the impact on earnings. Similarly, the treasurer won't do so in a case where there is an expectation of a rates decrease. This technique is known as *directional GAP* (Figure 1.2 and Figure 1.3) and has nothing to do with trading (selling or buying positions at short term with the aim of making a profit).

A bank which has this ALM set-up usually hands the execution of deals to the trading unit. In banks without a trading unit, ALM executes the market deals itself. In both cases ALM will have an earnings budget to fulfil; this setting is commonly known as a business unit model.

■ ALM is a part of the Non-Market Organisation (Finance, Risk) and, in this case, ALM is not allowed to enter risk positions by itself. Instead, all actions that are not defined by the ALM committee (e.g. actions between ALM committee meetings) need to be in strict line with the risk policy and risk strategy of the bank. In addition, the ALM department must not have market access; therefore, the deals have to be handed over to some market unit for execution. This set-up is common in cases where the IRRBB strategy of a bank pursues an immunisation strategy.

The FTP process has already been introduced very briefly and will now be looked at in more detail. The FTP process is a sum of policies and methodologies which separates the results of a transaction into the customer contribution and risk contribution and transfers the ALM risks (interest rate risk and liquidity risk) from business units to ALM to be managed. Additionally, FTP is an important balance sheet management tool to deliver a bank's strategy, and a robust FTP framework enables it to achieve the steering and control needed to attain strategic balance sheet goals.

Matched Maturity Funds Transfer Pricing (MMFTP) follows the opportunity cost principle – defining the cost of hedging risk inherent in the transaction at financial market prices and independently of whether the hedging will really take place or not. FTP separates the customer from risk business: the application of Funds Transfer Prices for each single transaction assumes that every deal will be hedged against risk. It can be clearly seen in Figure 1.4.

There is no real hedging between the business unit and ALM department (there is the 'fictitious' hedge instead) as ALM provides to the *Asset centre*; in this example, 5-year funds at the FTP rate. In this way, business does not carry any exposure to interest rate risk (it receives fixed rate funds from ALM and provides fixed rate loans to the external client) or liquidity risk (it receives 5-year term funds from ALM and provides 5-year term loans to the external client). It is said that the exposure of the business unit is 'closed' from the interest rate risk and liquidity risk perspective. The only risk the business has to manage is its relationship with the external client and the magnitude of the commercial spread which is gained through the deal. The commercial spread is the

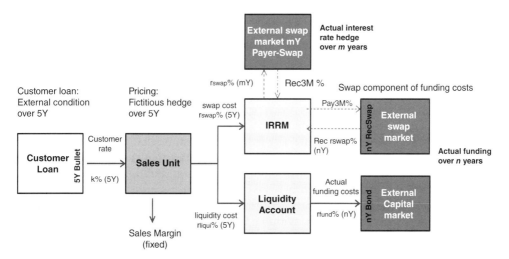

FIGURE 1.4 ALM and FTP process.
Source: own elaboration.

P&L account of the business unit is constant throughout the life of the transaction. ALM has to gather funds either from the external market (in this particular example it is done through bond issuance) or from the *Liability centre*, the unit responsible for collecting funds at the bank level. The financial characteristics of funds do not necessarily mirror the characteristics of those provided to the asset centre; consequently, ALM is left with a mismatch in terms of funds maturity and interest rate. The treasurer manages this inherited mismatching through a split between interest rate risk account (IRRM) and liquidity account. Then, they decide whether to mitigate the open exposure through derivatives (in our example, interest rate swaps) or to leave it 'open', hoping that the market will not turn against it.

In our particular and simplified example, based on one transaction (lending 5-year term loan at fixed rate to the external client), the treasurer has potentially three choices:

a) to keep the exposure to liquidity risk open and to close the exposure to interest rate risk;
b) to keep interest rate risk open and to close the exposure to liquidity risk; or
c) to close all risks (interest rate risk and liquidity risk).

So, let's answer the question of what happens if the treasurer decides to

a) enter the 5-year payer swap (m = 5Y), issue the 5-year coupon bond to fund the asset and enter the 5-year receiver swap (n =5Y);
b) enter the 5-year payer swap (m =5Y), issue the 3-year coupon bond to fund the asset and enter the 3-year receiver swap (n = 3Y); or
c) enter the 3-year payer swap (m =3Y), issue the 5-year coupon bond and enter the 5-year receiver swap (n =5Y).

In the first strategy, all risks are closed, as both maturity of funds (coupon bond) and rate tenor (payer swap) match the characteristics of funds provided to the external client. In the second case, the exposure to interest rate risk is closed (the tenor of the payer swap is the same as that of the originated loan) but liquidity risk remains open (maturity of coupon bond is shorter than originated loan). In the third case, the liquidity risk is closed, and interest rate risk remains not fully hedged.

The above example is meant to show how the FTP split is realised and what happens in the central unit (ALM), which needs to manage both the liquidity and IRRM accounts through different techniques.

As a consequence of the above, it is possible to calculate the customer margin without risk (both funding risk and interest rate risk). Through the application of the FTP process, the customer margin remains constant during the whole product life, independently from interest movements, higher liquidity cost, or changing currency prices. Consequently, the balance sheet management presupposes that customer business and risk business are clearly separated with sound methodology. Building on this separation, ALM can manage risks independently from customer business without mixing risk and customer margins. Also, the separation of risk and customer business is a precondition to the sound target operating model within FTP and being compliant with the regulatory requirements. This will be discussed in detail in Chapter 3.

Figure 1.5 shows the FTP process from the ALM standpoint. It highlights its role as '*a bank within a bank*' as it gathers funds from the liability centre at the FTP rate and lends those funds to the asset centre at the FTP rate. As a result of this process,

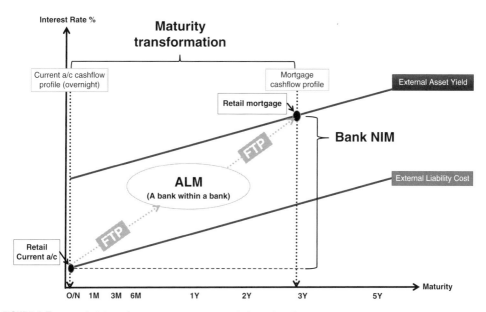

FIGURE 1.5   Funds Transfer Pricing process and the role of ALM.
Source: own elaboration

the maturity transformation run by the bank is managed by ALM and generates profitability for the bank. On the other hand, the profitability of the asset centre and liability centre is assessed through the difference between the external product price and FTP rate, i.e. the concept of external asset yield and external liability cost.

Once we have the FTP split clear, it is possible to calculate the profitability of every single unit as designed in Figure 1.1. The profitability (P&L impact) of the asset centre is equal to 2.69% (the difference between the external asset rate and FTP rate); meanwhile, the profitability of the liability centre and ALM are equal to −0.68% and 0.99% respectively. There is a loss in the liability centre because the external cost of funds is higher than the FTP rate recognised by ALM. Instead, ALM unit runs a positive P&L impact of 0.99% obtained by running the maturity and rate transformation (concepts explained in detail in the next chapter).

OVERVIEW OF FINANCIAL RISKS EXISTING IN THE BANKING BOOK

The importance of the proper management of the financial risks embedded in the banking book has significantly increased from the 1970s and has been driven by high fluctuation of interest rates over time and uncertainty upon the environment, which had a direct impact on the Net Interest Income of banks. In fact, the changes in the external market environment have had a huge impact on banks' performance. One of the most evident examples, these days, is related to the impact of a negative interest rate environment on the banking book. A fundamental concept in finance is that money has a time value that results from different investment opportunities. Thus, a fixed income security bought today for a specified term will return the payoff or future value that is dependent on both the compounding method and interest rate employed. Interest rates paid or charged for money depend, to a great extent, on the length of the term of investments. Therefore, the interest rate represents the price paid to use money for a period of time and is commonly referred to as the time value of money.

In recent years, central banks in Europe have employed negative rates as an unprecedented measure to combat recession and foster recovery. The idea of being charged for lending is counter-intuitive and puts into question the above-described concept of the time value of money. Such a move is viewed as controversial by economists, as there is a clear impact on the economy and the banking system. One of the primary concerns over negative rates is fuelling cash hoarding behaviours as depositors are penalised instead of being compensated. Consequently, they are incentivised to hold cash. There is also a clear impact on banks' profitability. Negative rates increase cost for banks with excess liquidity (known as negative *cost of carry*), thus resulting in a search for ways to offset higher costs through raising accounts fees and charges, and in extreme cases cutting back lending to the real economy.

The negative rates have caused a *margin compression* for banks. This is because of the floating rates (or short-term repricing) assets which are funded by behavioural liabilities. Banks are unable to charge the negative rates on the retail or corporate depositors (this is known as implicit zero floor in the product); meanwhile, they have to reprice their assets according to the market. This impossibility of charging the negative rates on depositors is driven both by the regulatory oversight and the commercial strategy of the bank itself, as it doesn't simply want to lose clients. Interest rate risk management has become more difficult under the negative rates environment. This is because it is not just the net interest income (under a short-term view) that is impacted. The zero floors embedded in the deposits position can be seen as the short automatic option position with the floor at 0%. The negative intrinsic value of this option becomes even lower as the rates go further down (the economic value of the banking book is the sum of the banking book's present value and the economic value of the automatic options embedded in its structure). The banks had to learn to manage this risk, as they had never needed to face it in times when interest rates were in the positive territory.

Thus, the interest rates concept is extremely important because changes in interest rates affect a bank's earnings and its risk situation in different ways. For this reason, it is necessary for the bank to put in place systems and appropriate and precise methods for the measurement of the interest rate risk, which enables it to reveal all its significant sources and to evaluate its impact on the operative profile of the bank.

The objective of the gap management techniques for management of the IRRBB is developed from two different perspectives of interest rate risk valuation; the first one refers to the effects that changes in the rates level have on the Net Interest Income (NII impact), and the second one looks at the changes in the portfolios market value deriving from interest rates movements. The quantification of the impact of profits in the short-term period (as already pointed out, this is usually a 1-year time period) is performed through the maturity gap model; meanwhile, changes in the economic values of assets and liabilities are calculated through the duration gap analysis and/or economic value of equity (EVE) analysis. This is known as a dual view for IRRBB which has to be captured in the management of this risk category. There is a reason why IRRBB has to be measured both under an EVE and an NII perspective. A simple example could be:

Banking Book – bank A
Treasury portfolio – 30   Behavioural liabilities – 70
Mortgages – 60   Wholesale funding – 20
Fixed Assets – 10   Equity – 10

The bank has significant investments in fixed term bonds and long duration mortgages which are funded by behavioural liabilities, i.e. current and savings accounts (CASA). However, some portion of the investment portfolio is due to expire in the coming months and the treasurer has to decide how to deploy those funds. The treasurer's decision is mainly driven by an expectation related to the direction of movement in interest rates; in fact, it is an expectation of the sharp increase in rates within the near future. Therefore, the treasurer decided to wait to reinvest the maturing funds.

The bank chose as its **objective variable** the change in the Net Interest Income (herein ΔNII) and does not have any formal limit on the change in the economic value of equity (ΔEVE). The funds are kept temporarily in the cash accounts.

This structure (behavioural liabilities funding fixed rate assets) exposes the bank to the structural mismatching on the medium long part of the curve (usually measured through ΔEVE or dynamic measures such as *Value at Risk* (VaR). In our example, the rates went down instead, and the treasurer was wrong about the prediction. There is an immediate impact in terms of the ΔNII, as the cash account yields an even lower return. Additionally, there is an impact in terms of the customer's behaviour on the asset side, i.e. increased prepayments. The combination of increased prepayments with maturing (and not reinvested) bonds causes shortening of the total duration of the assets portfolio and opens the structural mismatching. The bank behaves now as the net liability position on the medium long part of the curve and suffers embedded loss in terms of ΔEVE. Summarising, there is a loss in terms of Net Interest Income which is measured by ΔNII metric and the loss is driven by the exposure to structural risk which is not measured by any official metric. The biggest problem here is that the treasurer drives banking book exposure based on only one IRRBB metric which aims to measure changes in NII under the short-term horizon and does not monitor the structural risk which is becoming a problem for the bank. If ΔEVE metrics were in place, the treasurer would probably breach the limit at some point and would be forced to increase the duration of the asset portfolio through deployment of cash.

Exposure to the interest rate risk can manifest in different forms:

1. Direct, identifiable by means of contractual characteristics of assets and liabilities.
2. Related to the behavioural characteristics of items; for example, rate sensitivity of demand deposits or savings accounts.

For example, the interest rate risk coming from rate mismatching falls into the direct category, along with the refixing risk and the structure of respective cash flows. On the other hand, a change in the item's characteristics caused by the behaviour of customers (early termination of loan or its partial prepayment), which is driven by the interest rate movements (financial prepayments phenomena), can cause a change in the balance sheet structure. The most common form of interest rate risk results from the rate mismatching between assets and liabilities (for example, fixed rate assets funded by liabilities at floating rate). This rate mismatching exposes the bank to reinvestment and refinancing risk:

1. Refinancing risk arises when the maturity of liabilities is shorter than the maturity of assets. If, for example, the bank funds its medium long-term assets, which mature within 1 year through 3-month deposits, it exposes itself to the refinancing risk, since the increase in the interest rates will diminish the Net Interest Income of the bank.
2. Reinvestment risk arises when maturity of assets is shorter than liabilities. For example, reinvestment risk arises in cases where a bank funds its 6-month investment portfolio with 1-year funding. This is because there is a risk that after 6 months the interest rates decrease, and it will have to reinvest funds at the lower rate (the problem faced by Treasurer in the example above).

The same principle is valid for assets and liabilities at a floating rate. If the refixing period of assets is shorter than the refixing period of liabilities, the bank is still exposed to the reinvestment risk and consequently to the downward movement of the curve, even if the contractual maturity of this asset is longer than the maturity of liability.

Liquidity risk is the second very important risk inherent in the banking book. There are two types of liquidity risk:

- **Liquidity Risk (Refinancing Risk),** which means the lack of sources for the refinancing of the bank, needed to meet the obligations. In extreme cases, this could lead to a bank's inability to pay. Besides credit quality deteriorations, overall market illiquidity can also lead to refinancing risks.

  Liquidity risk, therefore, occurs when the capital commitment on the assets side is longer than the capital commitment for liabilities – so-called maturity transformation, which represents a fundamental bank function. Banks are usually exposed to refinancing risks, which have to be limited and managed by ALM.
- **Liquidity Cost Risk,** which means an increase in liquidity costs without being exposed to illiquidity, is a market risk comparable to the interest rate risk. Increased liquidity costs reduce a bank's capital (profit) through increased cost of refinancing (Enthofer and Haas 2016).

To be able to manage the cash flows from the tied-up capital of the assets and liabilities, the positions have to be displayed within the capital commitment gap known as the maturity ladder. The cumulative liquidity position can be used for the observation of the liquidity position's development through a specific time span. The bank is thereby provided with an analysis of instruments that allows the managing and observing of the entire liquidity development. Capital redemption of asset positions leads to a positive gap and to an increase in liquidity, whereas the redemption on deposits of the liabilities results in a negative gap, reducing the liquidity position (Enthofer and Haas 2016). Therefore, the liquidity management process must ensure that a firm has access to diversified sources of funding in an appropriate range of tenors. Those responsible for liquidity management must ensure that the governing body is aware of the composition, characteristics, and degree of diversification of assets and liabilities sources. The purpose of the funding diversification is to ensure that firms have in place alternative sources of funding so that they can withstand severe yet plausible institution-specific or market-wide stress. It follows that firms should take into account funding diversification when conducting the business planning process. Firms should regularly test the capacity to raise short, medium, and long-term funding from funding sources (McCarthy 2015).

Another important point in liquidity management is the intraday liquidity position and related risks, as all the obligations the bank faces need to be met on a timely basis, both under normal and stressed conditions. The intraday liquidity process should allow banks to calculate daily gross inflows and outflows and forecast the range of potential net funding shortfalls that may occur during the day. In order to appropriately monitor the intraday liquidity, early indicators should be put in place, indicating the stress conditions of the bank. Such indicators are based on:

- Rapid asset growth, especially when funded with potential volatile liabilities.
- Growing concentrations in assets and liabilities.
- An increase in currency mismatching.
- A decrease of weighted average maturities of liabilities.
- A credit rating downgrade.
- Declining stock prices.
- Widening debt or credit default swaps.
- Increasing retail deposit outflow.
- Increasing redemptions of corporate deposits (CDs) before maturity.
- Counterparties that begin to request additional collateral for credit exposure.
- Correspondent banks that eliminate or decrease their credit lines.
- Difficulty placing short-term liabilities (commercial papers).

Stress and scenario testing is a key tool used to identify, measure, monitor, and control liquidity risk, and hence is a major part of a liquidity management process. Stress testing is used to identify sources of potential liquidity strain to ensure that current exposure continues to conform to their liquidity risk tolerance. Through stress testing, firms will evaluate the resilience to liquidity stress and consider both contractual and non-contractual cash flows (Blair and Akkizidis 2011).

The liquidity cost risk is part of Internal Capital Adequacy Assessment Process (ICAAP). The ICAAP assesses risk arising from the increase of liquidity costs, which impacts the bank's P&L and therefore their own funds. This kind of risk must be measured and limited, ensuring the preservation of the bank's capital. The risk situation here is represented by increased or changed liquidity costs and their influence on capital.

The liquidity cost risk starts with capital commitments in a normal case, and then asking how much the revenue is affected with an increase in the liquidity costs. This is done in three different views that are predetermined by the regulator in pillar 2 of the ICAAP, i.e. normal situation (going concern), liquidation (gone concern), and stress scenario. In all three cases, the effect of change in the refinancing costs (liquidity transfer price) on the liquidity risk results in the profit or loss and, in the end, on the own funds. Generally, to calculate the liquidity cost risk, the negative cumulative gaps are refinanced under the assumption of an increased liquidity spread. As a base for the spread, the credit spread volatility per holding period can be used. Another way of calculating the liquidity risk is the use of the Value at Risk approach (Liquidity VaR) that considers spread volatility and correlations.

The FX risk is, in addition to interest rate risk and liquidity risk, a big risk potential. This is due to the fact that banks, companies, and investors are confronted with a constant currency risk; therefore, the FX risk is one of the classical risks controlled by the ALM.

The FX is usually defined as the risk that bank earnings are reduced due to unfavourable changes in FX rates. For the banks, the FX risk arises in principle if there are mismatches between assets and liabilities positions in foreign currencies on the balance sheet.

Since open FX positions are valued at their market prices, any changes in the market prices will have a direct impact on the P&L result. As a consequence, for the assessment of this risk the negative price change on the bank's result should be measured. When measuring the FX risk, the bank can either use the standardised approach or internal model approach. Under the standard method, the sum of all long positions and short positions will be determined for each currency. Subsequently, the larger of the two results has to be backed by capital. In the case of a standard method this implies an 8% price change. The limitations of this approach are clear, as it assumes the maximum rate of change in all currencies. The basis for the determination of the position is the net position (difference between assets and liabilities) in each currency that results from the net cash positions (including accrued interest in the currency), forward positions, guarantees, and delta weighted net position of all FX options. Structural FX positions which are deliberately entered by a bank in order to hedge against the negative effect of exchange fluctuations on the equity ratio are excluded from the determination of the net foreign exchange position.

The conditions for the use of internal models have been refixed in the EU Directive 2010/76 of 24 November 2010 (CRD III). Banks with significant open FX positions usually enforce the VaR methodology for quantifying FX risks. The most common tool for the management of FX positions and, hence, risk, is the use of FX forwards and FX swaps products.

Another risk category which is managed in ALM is the credit spread risk. The credit spread is the yield difference of a bond compared to a risk-free interest rate. The importance of this risk category is also driven by the fact that the new regulatory requirements (Basel III or CRD IV and CRR I) within the ICAAP framework demand a separate and explicit measurement of the credit spread risk for the adequate calculation of the required own funds for the ICAAP risks. The credit spread risk represents the risk of a value loss which is caused by changes in credit spreads while the counterparty's rating remains the same. For all of a bank's assets which are valued with market prices in the balance sheet, the bank will have the risk of changed credit spreads and this should be calculated additionally. Initially, banks had to measure their spread risk just for their trading books. In recent years, however, the regulator has been demanding the measurement of the spread risk for both trading and banking book (Enthofer and Haas 2016).

The importance of the credit spread risk has grown since the financial crisis, as the spread volatility in the market has significantly increased. From one side, the new regulatory Basel III requirements demanding the stock of liquidity portfolio, mainly composed of the bonds, and from the other side, market volatility and uncertainty have pushed regulatory bodies to demand from the banks credit spread risk evaluation, both for trading and the banking book. Credit spread risk is seen as market risk, and for this reason, the common market risk measurement techniques apply here also. The VaR is the methodological approach followed in quantification of the credit spread risk.

However, from a practical standpoint it is difficult to gather all the information needed for calculating volatilities and correlations of the credit spreads. In such cases, the benchmark approaches are followed, i.e. a group of bonds for each asset class/credit rating. The credit spread history of each group can be defined and the evaluated average can be used for further calculation. Credit spreads can be also derived from credit default swaps (CDS) or indices. Until recently, most banks calculated the risks and results measured for the bond portfolio as one figure with no differentiation of their origin. This situation is currently changing, as the regulator and the transparency principle within ALM results forced banks to split the total bond portfolio result into a separate credit spread and interest risk result. In fact, this trend is reflected in the revised IRRBB principle launched by BCBS and the European Banking Authority (EBA) in 2016 and 2017 respectively.

REGULATORY REQUIREMENTS – BASEL III

Since the financial crisis in 2008, the business of banks has been heavily discussed and regulators have taken serious steps to reduce systemic and economic risks coming from the banking sector. The global standard for capital is a relatively recent innovation. Basel I came into force in 1988 and was related only to credit risk. Before then, there were no standardised rules on capital adequacy for banks. In 1996, market risk rules were added. In December 1998, the BCBS recognised that Basel I needed to be revised to reflect credit risk more effectively and to prevent increasing use of arbitrage by the banks, which were using more and more sophisticated internal models to measure and understand risk. The Committee also decided to recommend a capital charge for operational risk. Basel II was born and took five years to be developed and then a further four years to be implemented. Basel II was in place from January 2007 (or 2008 for those on the advanced approaches under Basel II) to 2013. Basel III was agreed by the members of the Basel Committee on Banking Supervision in 2010–2011, and was scheduled to be introduced from 2013 until 2015; however, changes from 1 April 2013 extended implementation until 31 March 2018 and then again to 31 March 2019. The Basel Committee's remit extends a long way beyond capital adequacy. Its other global standards and consultations include interest rate risk, liquidity risk, stress testing, risk management, and alignment of risk and reward.

The aim of Basel II was to align economic and regulatory capital more closely than was the case under Basel I. Basel II introduced three different approaches that a bank could adopt to achieve this: the standardised approach which applied more risk – weighting categories and using formal credit ratings – and the foundation and advanced internal rating based (IRB) approaches, which were more complex and allowed a bank to use its own risk models and risk exposure data in line with the Basel II framework. The implementation of the Basel II rules resulted in changes in specific areas of bank and ALM activity, with certain products and sectors seeing greater activity and others less, as capital was realigned and banks sought to meet adjusted required target rates of return. Given that the primary objective of Basel II was to better align economic with regulatory capital, it was an obvious conclusion that banking activity exhibiting a low economic risk attracts a low capital charge.

The cornerstone of the Basel II rules was, as already mentioned, the three-pillar approach. These are minimum capital requirements, the supervisory review, and market discipline. The idea under pillar 1 was to create a closer link between economic and regulatory capital through a more tailored regime with more specific targeting of individual credits rather than the broad-brush approach of Basel I which targeted whole asset classes. The clear example of this point was the treatment of corporate loans regardless of their credit quality, which under Basel I all received 100% risk-weighting. Basel II provided the distinction according to their credit quality.

However, it is important to highlight that the Committee conclusions and recommendations do not have legal force – its role is to formulate supervisory standards and guidelines. It recommends best practice that individual authorities are supposed to implement through detailed national arrangements which are best suited to their own national systems. The Committee encourages convergence towards common approaches and standards without attempting detailed harmonisation of member countries. Even in the EU, where Basel III is enshrined in version four of the Capital Requirements Directive (CRD), there are differences in national interpretation and implementation.

Before the crisis there was a period of excess liquidity. As a result, liquidity risk has not been taken too much into consideration. When liquidity became scarce (particularly as wholesale funding dried up) as the crisis developed, banks found that they had insufficient liquidity reserves to meet their obligations.

Basel III's main set of recommendations were issued by the Basel Committee on Banking Supervision (BCBS) in December 2010 (revised June 2011) and titled *Basel III: A Global Regulatory Framework for More Resilient Banks and Banking Systems*. With a view to implementing the agreements of Basel III and harmonising banking solvency regulations across the European Union as a whole, in June 2013 the European Parliament and the Council of the European Union adopted the following legislation:

- Capital Requirements Directive 2013/36/EU (hereinafter CRD IV) on access to the activity of credit institutions and the prudential supervision of credit institutions and investment firms. CRD IV entered into the force in the EU on 1 January 2014.
- Regulation (EU) No 575/2013 of the European Parliament and of the Council of 26 June 2013 on prudential requirements for credit institutions and investment firms (hereinafter CRR).

The capital adequacy framework consists of three pillars, each of which focus on different aspects of capital adequacy:

- Pillar 1, called 'Minimum Capital Requirements', establishes the minimum amount of capital that a bank should have against its credit, market, and operational risks. It provides the guidelines for calculating the risk exposures in the assets of a bank's balance sheet (the 'risk weighted assets' and the components and sets the minimum capital requirements.
- Pillar 2, called 'Supervisory Review and Evaluation Process' involves both banks and regulators taking a view on whether a firm should hold additional capital against risks not covered in Pillar 1. Part of the Pillar 2 process is the 'Internal Capital Adequacy Assessment Process' (ICAAP), which is a bank's self-assessment of risks not captured by Pillar 1.

- Pillar 3, called 'Market Discipline', aims to encourage market discipline by requiring banks to disclose specific, prescribed details of their risks, capital, and risk management.

In January 2013, the BCBS agreed the final form of the Liquidity Coverage Ratio. These requirements aim to improve the transparency of regulatory liquidity requirements and enhance market discipline. Consistent with the Basel III agreement, national authorities gave effect to these disclosure requirements, and banks are required to comply with them, from the date of the first reporting period after 1 January 2015. These standards aim to achieve two separate but complementary objectives. The first objective is to promote short-term resilience of a bank's liquidity risk profile while ensuring that it has sufficient high-quality liquid assets (HQLA) to survive a significant stress scenario lasting for 30 days. To this end, the Committee published Basel III: The Liquidity Coverage Ratio and liquidity risk monitoring tools. The second objective is to reduce funding risk over a longer time horizon by requiring banks to fund their activities with sufficiently stable sources of funding in order to mitigate the risk of future funding stress. To achieve this objective, the Committee published Basel III: The Net Stable Funding Ratio. These standards are an essential component of the set of reforms introduced by Basel III and together will increase banks' resilience to liquidity shocks, promote a more stable funding profile, and enhance overall liquidity risk management (Lekatis 2014).

As stated above, the Liquidity Coverage Ratio aims to ensure that a bank has an adequate stock of unencumbered HQLA to meet its liquidity needs for a 30-calendar day liquidity stress scenario. HQLA consists of cash or assets that can be converted into cash at little or no loss of value in private markets. At a minimum, the stock of unencumbered HQLA should enable the bank to survive until day 30 of the stress scenario, by which time it is assumed that appropriate corrective actions can be taken by management and supervisors or that the bank can be resolved in an orderly way.

$$LCR = \frac{stock\ of\ HQLA}{total\ net\ cash\ outflow\ over\ the\ next\ 30\ calendar\ days} \geq 100\% \qquad (1.1)$$

There are two categories of assets that can be included in the stock. Assets to be included in each category are those that the bank is holding on the first day of the stress period, irrespective of their residual maturity. 'Level 1' assets can be included without limit, while 'Level 2' assets can only comprise up to 40% of the stock (Ahmed 2015).

Level 1 assets are limited to:

- coins and banknotes;
- central bank reserves;
- marketable securities representing claims on or guaranteed by sovereigns, central banks, PSEs, the Bank for International Settlements, the International Monetary Fund, the European Central Bank and European Community, or multilateral development banks which satisfy prescribed by Basel III conditions.

Level 2 assets comprise:

- marketable securities representing claims on or guaranteed by sovereigns, central banks, PSEs, or multilateral development banks which satisfy prescribed by Basel III conditions;

- corporate debt securities (including commercial paper) and covered bonds which satisfy prescribed by Basel III conditions;
- residential mortgage back securities (RMBS) that satisfy prescribed conditions;
- common equity shares that satisfy prescribed conditions.

Certain additional assets may be included in Level 2 at the discretion of national authorities. In addition, the Level 2 assets are subject to a haircut in the market value of those assets.

The term total net cash outflows – in the denominator of the liquidity coverage ratio (LCR) equation – is defined as the total expected cash outflows minus total expected cash inflows in the specified stress scenario for the subsequent 30 calendar days. Total expected cash outflows are calculated by multiplying the outstanding balances of various categories or types of liabilities and off-balance sheet commitments by the rates at which they are expected to run off or be drawn down. Total expected cash inflows are calculated by multiplying the outstanding balances of various categories of contractual receivables by the rates at which they are expected to flow in under the scenario up to an aggregate cap of 75% of total expected cash outflows (BCBS January 2013).

In addition to LCR, there are monitoring tool metrics which provide the cornerstone of information that aids supervisors in assessing the liquidity risk of a bank. These metrics include the following:

- Contractual maturity mismatch – represents contractual cash and security inflows and outflows from all on- and off-balance sheet items, mapped to defined time bands based on their respective maturities,
- Concentration of funding – includes the reporting of funding liabilities sourced from each significant counterparty as a percentage of total liabilities, funding liabilities sourced from each significant product/instrument as a percentage of total liabilities, and the list of asset and liability amounts by significant currency.
- Available unencumbered assets – represents available unencumbered assets that are marketable as collateral in secondary markets and available unencumbered assets that are eligible for central banks' standing facilities.
- LCR by significant currency – calculated as foreign currency LCR which is equal to the stock of HQLA in each significant currency divided by total net cash outflows over a 30-day time period in each significant currency.
- Market-related monitoring tools.

The Net Stable Funding ratio is another initiative of the Basel Committee to promote a more resilient banking sector. It requires banks to maintain a stable funding profile in relation to the composition of their balance sheet. As a consequence, it limits overreliance on the short-term wholesale funding and promotes funding stability. The problems related to the excessive maturity transformation run by financial institutions arose during the financial crisis in 2007 when most banks experienced difficulties coming from improper liquidity management and framework.

The NSFR is defined as amount of available stable funding relative to the amount of required stable funding. The ratio should be equal at least 100% on an ongoing basis. The NSFR is calculated through the following equation:

$$\frac{Available\ amount\ of\ stable\ funding}{Required\ amount\ of\ stable\ funding} \geq 100\% \tag{1.2}$$

The amount of available stable funding (ASF) is measured based on the broad characteristics of the relative stability of the institution's funding resources, including contractual maturity of its liabilities and the difference in the propensity of different types of funding providers to withdraw their funding. When determining the maturity of an equity or liability instrument, investors are assumed to redeem the call option at the earliest possible date. Instead, the amount of required stable funding (RSF) is measured based on the broad characteristics of the liquidity risk profile of an institution's assets and off-balance sheet (OBS) exposures. The amount of required stable funding is calculated through the application of the RSF factor to the carrying value of assets to the categories prescribed by the BCBS. The RSF factors assigned to various types of assets are intended to approximate the amount of assets that would have to be funded, either because it will roll over or because it could not be monetised through sale or used as collateral in a secured borrowed transaction over the course of one year without significant expense (BCBS 2014). It is important to highlight that it consists of internationally agreed calibrations and definitions. Some elements, however, remain subject to national discretion.

The calibration reflects the stability of liabilities across two dimensions:

1. Funding tenor – the NSFR is calibrated so that longer-term liabilities are assumed to be more stable than short-term liabilities.
2. Funding type and counterparty – short-term deposits provided by retail customers and funding provided by small business customers are behaviourally more stable than wholesale funding of the same maturity from other counterparties.

With reference to RSF for various assets, the following criteria have been taken into account:

1. Resilient credit creation – some portion of lending needs to be financed by stable funding to ensure the continuity of intermediation and business.
2. Bank behaviour – the bank may seek to roll over a significant portion of the maturing loans to preserve the customer relationships.
3. Asset tenor – short-term dated assets (maturing in less than 1 year) require a smaller portion of stable funding because banks would be able to allow some portion of those assets to mature instead of rolling them over.
4. Asset quality and liquidity value – the unencumbered, high-quality assets that can be securitised or traded and can be readily used as collateral to secure addition funding or sold in the market do not need to be fully funded with stable funding.

Additionally, a small part of stable funding is required to support at least a small portion of the potential calls on liquidity arising from off-balance sheet commitments and contingent funding obligations (BCBS 2014).

Capital Requirements According to Basel III/CRD IV

At the centre of the Basel III/CRR/CRD IV requirements are strict rules for capital requirements for banks. Those rules are more stringent both in terms of the capital quality and capital quantity than previously existing capital requirements. The objective of the new regulation imposed on banks is to improve the stability of the financial system.

Accordingly, the Common Equity Tier 1 (CET 1) has to make up at least 7% of the total risks of the bank as of 1 January 2019, i.e. after the expiration of the transition period. CET 1 is composed of 4.5% minimum rate and 2.5% capital conservation buffer. The entire Tier 1 capital (Common Equity plus Additional Tier 1) must be at least 8.5% and the total capital (Tier 1 plus Tier 2) must be 10.5%. The minimum rate for regulatory capital, which is calculated as total capital less capital conservation buffer, therefore remains as under Basel II at 8%.

In addition, Basel III introduces the countercyclical buffer which depends on the state of the economy and varies from 0% to 2.5%.

Tier 3 capital will be no longer counted. Also, the systemic risk buffer and the buffer for systemically important institutions are allocated on a case-by-case basis and depend on the bank/country and economic situation. Furthermore, the internal capital requirement prescribed by the regulator under Pillar 2 has to be met (Supervisory Review and Evaluation Process, or SREP). Thus, the total capital requirement can add up to be 20% or more. To ensure the quality of the regulatory capital there are strict rules regarding eligibility of capital instruments which can be included in the regulatory capital. Tier 1 capital is primarily to be used to cover the bank's losses from ongoing operations; meanwhile, Tier 2 capital is intended to be taken as a liability mass in cases of insolvency (gone concern).

Common Equity Tier 1 includes the following items:

- common shares issues by the bank that met the criteria of this category;
- share premium accounts related to CET1 items;
- retained earnings;
- accumulated other comprehensive income;
- common shares which were issued by consolidated subsidiaries held by third parties and meet the requirements for CET 1;
- 'regulatory adjustments' that are applied in determining Common Equity Tier capital.

The Additional Tier 1 capital essentially comprises hybrid capital instruments (contingent convertible bonds, mandatory convertible notes) and consists of the sum of the following components:

- instruments issued by a bank that meet the criteria for inclusion in the category 'Additional Tier 1 capital' (and which are not part of CET 1 capital);
- share premium accounts related to Additional Tier 1 capital;
- instruments which were issued by consolidated subsidiaries, held by third parties, and meet the requirements for Additional Tier 1 capital and are not part of CET 1.

The remaining Tier 2 capital consists of the following components:

- instruments issued by the bank that meet the criteria for Tier 2 capital and which are not already part of Tier 1 capital;
- share premium accounts related to Tier 2 capital;
- instruments which were issued by consolidated subsidiaries, held by third parties, and which meet the requirements for Tier 2 capital and are not part of Tier 1 capital;
- regulatory adjustments that are applied in determining Tier 2 capital.

In addition to the risk-sensitive capital requirements in the area of Pillar 1, a leverage ratio is introduced under Basel III/CRR as a key figure, which restricts the excessive build-up of debts in the banking system and prevents on- and off-balance sheet growth in relation to equity. The leverage ratio determines a maximum debt ratio to avoid deleveraging processes that could harm the whole financial system. The leverage ratio is defined as the ratio of the total eligible Tier 1 capital to the total of both (not weighted) on- and off-balance sheet assets. Basel III/CRR demands it to be a maximum of 3% (Enthofer and Haas 2016).

SELECTIVE REVIEW OF THE LITERATURE RELATED TO ALM AND INTEGRATED MANAGEMENT OF THE INTEREST RATE RISK AND LIQUIDITY RISK IN COMMERCIAL BANKS

There are many definitions of ALM in the banking industry and I have already provided some of them (definitions used mainly by practitioners). However, this brief chapter is meant to be devoted to the contribution brought by scholars to the ALM discipline and focuses on the definitions which are used commonly in the scientific world. It is important to remember that the current shape of techniques used in risk management and ALM has been accomplished through extensive research, published in articles and books.

In its formal definition, Asset Liability Management (ALM) can be defined as a mechanism to address risks faced by a bank due to a mismatch between assets and liabilities, either due to liquidity or changes in interest rates. Although ALM is not a relatively new tool, it has evolved from the simple idea of maturity matching of assets and liabilities across various time horizons into a framework that includes sophisticated concepts, such as duration matching and the use of static and dynamic simulations.

As stated by Ronald J. Ryan in *The Evolution of Asset/Liability Management* (a summary), insurance companies may be considered the birthplace of ALM and constituted the model of ALM discipline. Banks and insurance companies have practised ALM since their inception. Their ALM approach centres on the interest rate risk management of assets versus liabilities such that their risk/ reward behaviour is similar or matched (Ryan 2013).

The interest rate risk for financial intermediaries, defined by Zen as the possibility of fluctuations in the market rate producing significant variations in one direction or the other on the balance of assets (Zen 2008), has been an object of attention for the supervisor since 1997 when the Basel Committee published guidelines on interest rate management (BCBS 1997 and 2004). The literature has amply debated the various types of interest rate risk to which banks are exposed; such a debate is reflected in works of Gualandri (1991) and Lusignani (2004). The various types of interest rate risk are discussed in detail in the next chapter.

The main contributions published over the years focus on analysing the various approaches used to assess exposure to this risk. The first one is based on 'earnings perspective' and comprises the so called 'gap management' models, in which the objective (target) variable is set to be the operating interest margin (Resti and Sironi 2007). The second approach, 'economic value perspective' measures the effects of variations in the interest rate on the market value of a bank's financial assets and liabilities. The analytical models most often used in this context rely on techniques originally developed to measure the interest rate risk in bond portfolios (Brigo and Mercurio 2007; Staikouras 2006; Grundke 2004). The progress in risk management techniques has extended this concept to all banking book items and currently is adopted as a best practice by the European regulator (EBA).

The interest rate term structure and its relationship with the interest rate risk exposure of banks and, consequently, the level of profitability achieved has been investigated by Memmel in 2011 through the sampling of 1562 German banks during the period between September 2005 and December 2009. The results showed that the exposure to the interest rate risk moves in accordance with the possible earnings from term transformation, but it is very much determined by the bank's size and particularities. Thus, small and medium-sized banks showed significant exposure while the large banks seemed to have much less risk on their banking book. This trend can be still observed in banks. The challenger banks are willing to accept higher exposure in terms of 'riding the yield curve strategy' while larger and international banks keep their exposure limited.

Given the importance of IRRBB, in terms of the impact on capital base and earnings stability, the management of this risk has received increasing attention from the regulator and from the banking industry in recent years. As such, it has become a hot topic for national and European regulators. In May 2015, the EBA issued 'Guidelines on the management of the interest rate risk arising from non-trading activities' which was addressed to institutions in Europe and replaced the CEBS guidelines as of January 2016. In April 2016, the Basel Committee on Banking Supervision (BCBS) issued Standards on IRRBB that replaced the 2004 Principles. The new standards set out the Committee's expectations on the management of IRRBB in terms of identification, measurement, monitoring, control, and supervision. The updated IRRBB Principles reflect recent changes in market and supervisory practices due to a low and negative interest rate environment and provide methods and models to be used by banks in a wider and enhanced risk management framework.

Finally, on 19 July 2018 the EBA published a final version on the update of its 'Guidelines on the management of the interest rate risk arising from non-trading book activities'. The long-awaited update for the management of IRRBB builds on the original guidelines published in May 2015. It is effectively the translation to European law of the IRRBB Standards published by the BCBS in April 2016. The guidelines will apply from 30 June 2019. As this book is being written, the EBA is still working on a number of technical standards as part of the ongoing CRD and CRR revisions in which they will prescribe disclosure requirements and the standardised approach for IRRBB. These technical standards will be published separately at a later stage. Compared to the 2015 version, the guidelines have increased in size significantly. It contains over 40% of new articles, which originate partly from BCBS Standards but also contain some new guidelines. The EBA guidelines, among other things, impose the inclusion of credit spread risk in the banking book (CSRBB) into the IRRBB framework. It is an important step towards standardisation of risk management across the banking industry and attempts to integrate the IRRBB with another kind of financial risk. Another main addition to the guidelines is the requirement to include market value changes in earnings metrics. This change will require banks to start modelling a true IFRS Profit and Loss at Risk and take into account the increase and reduction in total earnings and capital. Traditionally, earnings metrics just focus on NII and ignore any interest rate sensitivity in other areas of the P&L account. It will have a significant impact on the modelling of earnings measures, as the accounting treatment of instruments will start to determine how the measure will be impacted. Although this seems a logical extension of earnings metrics, it presents challenges, especially in the areas of derivatives used for hedge accounting and instruments in an Available for Sale (AFS) portfolio, for which only the coupon payment was included until now. The updated EBA guidelines indicate an important trend that seems to be emerging on the banking horizon, i.e. the necessity to revise the current *silo basis* approach towards the management of different kind of risks and to implement a more holistic view on risk management practices.

The first clear attempt to integrate interest rate risk and another type of risk (credit risk) was proposed in 2010 by Drehmann et al. The work performed by Drehmann et al. constructs the general framework for measuring the riskiness of banks, which are subject to correlated interest rate and credit shocks. The results show a strong interaction between credit risk and interest rate risk, sufficient to influence the net profitability and capital adequacy. In particular, the magnitude of each risk component and the speed with which the profits return back to equilibrium after the hypothesised shocks depend, among other things, on the re-pricing characteristics of the positions in the banking book and the cost of funding (Baldan, Zen and Rebonato 2012).

In January 2018, EBA launched its EU-wide stress test based on a number of macroeconomic scenarios which simultaneously have an impact on the credit risk, market risk, and liquidity risk of financial institutions. This is a clear attempt, from the regulator side, to see the overall picture, in terms of the exposure to financial and credit risks. The integrated stress testing is also promoted in the updated 'Guidelines on institutions' stress testing' published by the EBA in July 2018. These guidelines aim to achieve convergence of the practices followed by institutions for stress testing across the EU. They provide detailed guidance to be complied with by institutions when designing and conducting a stress testing programme/framework. The consideration of links and correlations between different risk types while performing the stress testing is emphasised by the Regulator. In fact, institutions should cover all material risk categories (and sub-categories) that the institutions are exposed to with regard to both on- and off-balance-sheet assets and liabilities in relation to all material portfolios.

In fact, the topic of liquidity risk attracted the interest of scholars well before the financial crisis in 2007, as the first papers date from the nineteenth century when Knies (1876) underlined the need for a liquidity buffer to compensate for negative gaps between inflows and outflows. In 1942, Saraceno claimed that 'the search for the most fruitful combination of lending and borrowing operations among all the operations that ensure the bank has the necessary balance between income and expenditure is the core problem of banks management. A bank's liquidity can be defined as its capacity to achieve this balance economically and at all times.' The most recent contributions provided the definition of liquidity and consequently the bank's liquidity risk (Gualandri 2009). In 2011, Cornett et al. analysed the financial crisis of 2007–2009. They pointed out the correlation of the liquidity risk exposure to loan growth during the crisis and also the growth in liquid assets which displaced funding to support new lending. The new international rules on liquidity risk management, standards, and monitoring were introduced by the Basel Committee on Banking Supervision in 2010. This new framework established standards for funding liquidity: *Liquidity Coverage Ratio* (LCR) and

Net Stable Funding Ratio (NSFR). Resti (2011) makes the point that the introduction of the mandatory LCR and NSFR will have significant impact on a bank's activity in terms of a decrease of their profitability. The necessity to extend funding maturities and to build a high-quality liquid assets buffer will give rise to reduction in a bank's interest margin and opportunity costs.

The link between financial risks can be seen in one of the main functions of credit institution, i.e. maturity transformation. Banks finance their investments by issuing liabilities with a shorter maturity than that of their investments; the resulting imbalance between the terms for the assets and liabilities means that they take on the interest rate risk and liquidity risk. Baldan, Zen, and Rebonato launched the hypothesis that there is a direct relationship, so that reducing the exposure to the liquidity risk induces a reduction in the interest rate risk as well. Their study analysed a small Italian bank during the years 2009 and 2010 which had to modify its liquidity profile in order to become compliant with the Basel III requirements. As a result, it generated a simultaneous reduction in its exposure to the interest rate risk exposure. The authors conclude that in order to achieve integrated risk management, the control of each of these risks is placed in relation to the bank's different functions and influences its strategic decisions.

After the regulatory updates, the *silo basis* approach is being slowly replaced by more integrated management of ALM risks. This is because profitability remains a key concern for the EU banking sector. The low profitability and widespread dispersion for some countries, along with high operating costs, continues to dampen the profitability prospects for the European banking sector as a whole. Thus, there is a need to come up with new approaches which could address shrinking profitability, a heavily regulated landscape, and exposure to financial risks. This necessity has been highlighted by Choudhry 2018 in 'Strategic ALM and integrated balance sheet management: the future of bank risk management'. In this article, Choudhry suggests that the discipline of ALM, as practised by banks worldwide for over 40 years, needs to be updated to meet the challenges presented by globalisation and Basel III regulatory requirements. In order to maintain viability and a sustainable balance sheet, banks need to move from the traditional 'reactive' ALM approach to a more proactive, integrated balance sheet management framework. This will enable them to solve the multidimensional optimisation problem they are faced with at present. In his book *Anthology – Past, Present and Future Principles of Banking and Finance* the author describes a 'vision of the future' with respect to a sustainable bank business model. This vision of the future contains the concepts of strategic, integrated, and optimised ALM. The need for integration is becoming recognised by treasurers, risk managers, and regulators. It has also started to be considered among the ALM systems providers. They attempt to build ALM solutions which focus on the integration between IRRBB, liquidity, and FTP, supporting the view that, today, more holistic balance sheet risk management is required. Interest rate risk, both in the banking and the trading book, cannot be viewed in isolation from liquidity risk, funds transfer pricing, or capital management. Balance sheets have become more volatile – a result of changing term structures, optionality, better informed customers, and the use of derivatives. This book represents an attempt to further develop the integrated ALM concept and contributes to the work of Professor Moorad Choudhry, advisory firms, and others who acknowledge the need for change. It attempts, at least partially, to address the regulatory requirements and proposes potential solutions to arising challenges in the banking industry.

CHAPTER 2

Methods of Measurement and Management of the Interest Rate Risk and Liquidity Risk

Chapter 1 described the concept of asset and liability management (ALM) in a financial institution. The ALM role and the importance of achieving trade-off between profitability of the ALM unit and its exposure to financial risks, which such a position creates, has been discussed based on the analysis of the strict interrelation between interest rates risk and liquidity risk. Moreover, the chapter introduced the process of transferring interest and liquidity risk from business units to ALM, known as the funds transfer pricing (FTP) process, and founds the basis of the balance sheet management. The FTP process is further developed in Chapter 2, along with a detailed description of the interest rate risk in the banking book (IRRBB) and liquidity measurement techniques and key metrics. Building on the concepts of IRRBB and liquidity risk already discussed, this chapter will expand upon the main risks managed by ALM. Consequently, it provides an overview of the main measurement techniques adopted by banks in order to measure the IRRBB and liquidity risk and focuses on the key metrics which provide senior management with knowledge of the extent of the exposure to those risks. It concludes with an analysis of the FTP process components of the FTP rate and balance sheet shaping tools used under the FTP practice. Additionally, this chapter touches on the concept of *behaviouralisation* and proposes methods for the calculation of the FTP rate for items without deterministic maturity.

It is important to highlight the main difference between IRRBB and liquidity risk. Interest rate risk is measured from two different perspectives: the earnings approach and the economic value approach. The first approach concentrates on the effects of interest rates movements on the bank's net interest income (NII) over short time horizons that could span from 1 to 2 years. However, the earnings perspective fails to indicate the long-term impacts of interest rate movements, as mismatches might be hidden beyond the horizon of the analysis (as already shown in the example in the previous chapter). In order to have a comprehensive view of the long-term effects of changes in rates, banks must adopt the economic value approach, which is based on the change in the present value of all cash flows under prescribed interest rate shocks.

Liquidity risk cannot be discussed, measured, or managed outside the context of scenario analysis. Stress and scenario testing is accepted as a key tool to identify, measure, monitor, and control liquidity risk. Stress testing is used to identify sources of potential liquidity strain, to ensure that current exposures continue to conform to the liquidity risk tolerance. Through stress testing, banks evaluate the resilience to liquidity stress and consider contractual and behavioural cash flows. The purpose of liquidity analysis is to identify future periods where the inflows can be lower than the outflows. The main point for the liquidity analysis is the determination of the size of liquidity asset buffer (LAB). In order to determine its size, the stress test tool is employed to reflect the expected requirements under stress. A detailed analysis of these two risks follows, based on the practices employed by a number of banks across Europe. It must be emphasised that there are many techniques to measure these risks and there is no one-size-fits-all approach. This chapter is intended to walk the reader through some of techniques employed by banks.

INTEREST RATE RISK IN THE BANKING BOOK – MEASUREMENT AND MANAGEMENT

Exposure to Short-Term Interest Rate Risk – Maturity Gap Analysis

Current financial regulation requires banks to have interest rate risk methods in place which are commensurate with the size and complexity of the bank. This is known as a proportionality approach. The bigger the bank in terms of size of risk sensitive assets (RSA), the more sophisticated the methods should be for the measurement of IRRBB. This chapter is focused mainly on the static methods, and contains an interpretation of results obtained through the application of those methods based on practical examples.

According to the regulator, the maturity gap is the simplest technique for measuring a bank's interest rate risk exposure. It distributes interest-sensitive assets, liabilities, and off-balance sheet positions into a certain number of predefined time bands according to their maturity (if fixed rate) or time remaining to their next repricing (if floating rate). Those assets and liabilities lacking definitive repricing intervals (e.g. sight deposits or savings accounts) or actual maturities that could vary from contractual maturities (a mortgage with an option for early repayment) are assigned to repricing time bands according to the judgement and past experience of the bank. There are statistical methods to support the allocation decision for behavioural items and some of these are described in Chapter 3.

To evaluate earnings exposure, interest rate sensitive liabilities in each time band are subtracted from the corresponding interest rate sensitive assets to produce a repricing gap for that time band. This gap can be multiplied by an assumed change in interest rates to yield an approximation of the change in net interest income that would result from such an interest rate movement. The size of the interest rate movement used in the analysis can be based on a variety of factors, including the historical experience of the bank, a simulation of the potential future interest rate movements, and the judgement of the bank's management (Basel Committee on Banking Supervision 2016). Current regulatory guidelines require banks apply +/− 200 bps parallel shock for this analysis.

The application of this method is very simple and can be easily extended to the measurement of the exchange rate risk.

The static maturity gap method presents, however, significant limitations. For example:

- It considers only transactions existing in the banking book at the date of analysis (there is no new business assumption).
- It disregards different maturities of the transaction within the same time buckets (all transactions falling into the same time bucket have the same risk profile).
- It allows for estimation only of the uniform movements of the interest rates.
- It assumes that asset and liabilities in maturity will be reinvested/refinanced within the gapping period (without altering the balance sheet structure) – there is no new business strategy applied here.

However, some of these limitations can be quite easily overcome by application of a simulation module for net interest income in order to get a more precise picture of the risks run by the bank on the short end of the curve.

The impact on the net interest income (ΔNII) resulting from the movements of the interest rates is calculated as a product between the changes in the interest rates and the difference between an interest rate risk sensitive asset and liabilities known as GAP:

$$\Delta NII = \Delta i \times GAP = \Delta i \times (RSA - RSL) \qquad (2.1)$$

where:

RSA   represents assets sensitive to interest rates movements (for example, fixed or floating rate loans);

RSL   represents liabilities sensitive to interest rate movements (for example, wholesale funding or sight deposits);

GAP   is the difference between outstanding of RSA and RSL over the given time horizon;

Δi represents magnitude of the interest rate shock.

The concept of the gapping period (GP) is now introduced, which represents the time horizon chosen for this type of analysis, for example 1 year.

Thus, the delta of net interest income is the function of two elements:

- interest rates movements Δi;
- difference between RSA and RSL (GAP).

Using the maturity gap method, the bank can manage its position to the interest rate risk through:

- The immunisation of interest rate risk keeping the GAP close to zero.
- Directional GAP keeping the voluntary mismatching according to the expectation of the future movements of the interest rate curve and an analytical understanding of the maturity profile of the balance sheet.

If GAP > 0, then the bank is exposed to reinvestment risk, meaning that in cases of interest rate increases it is going to show a profit. Conversely, in cases of interest rate decreases it is going to show a loss.

If GAP < 0, then the bank is exposed to refinancing risk meaning that in cases of interest rate increases it is going to show a loss. On the other hand, it realises profits if the interest rates decrease.

In consequence, if GAP = 0, the bank is immune to interest rate risk and movements of the curve. Of course, in this sense the directional GAP strategy consists of the adjustment of the sign of the GAP (increasing it when there are upward expectations for the interest rates and reducing it when there are downward pressures from the market).

Example

Imagine the following structure of the banking book:

Cash 100	Time depo 200
Corporate loans at floating rate 1000	Behavioural liabilities 900
Other assets 200	Wholesale funding 100
Fixed assets 50	Equity 150

Figure 2.1 shows the maturity gap for this structure.

The repricing gap shows that under a short-term time horizon the bank is *asset sensitive* as the total GAP is equal to 500MM, which means that, under a 12-month time horizon, the NII will increase if the rates go up. Conversely, the opposite will happen if the rates go down. On the other side, on the medium-long part of the curve, the bank behaves as a net liability position, as an increase in rates will have a positive

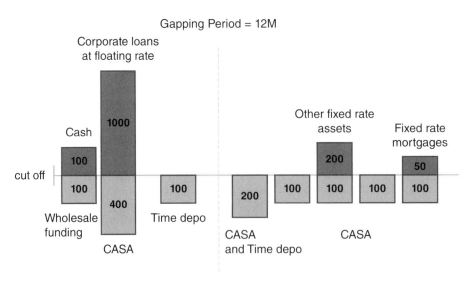

FIGURE 2.1 Repricing gap – IRRBB.
Source: own elaboration

impact on the economic value of equity (EVE), while a decrease will have a negative one. The difference between those two metrics is the time horizon. The first metric looks at the short time period and immediate impact on NII; the latter measures the change in the present value of the banking book for all items in the banking book while they exist.

A maturity gap analysis, as described by the regulator, can be easily performed in an Excel spreadsheet; however, the significant limitations deriving from this approach cannot be underestimated (Lubinska 2014). This basic method has been enriched through the introduction of the incremental gap method where the incremental gap is obtained by the summation of the subsequent gaps weighted for the time factor (Lusignani 1996). This time factor represents the time between the central value of the bucket and the end of the gapping period:

$$\Delta NII = \sum GAP \, x(T - t) \times \Delta i, \tag{2.2}$$

where:

T represents the length of the gapping period;
t maturity related to the time bucket;
Δi shock in the interest rates curve.

Example

Calculation of ΔNII under the Gapping period of 12M for the -200-bps scenario for the EUR currency.
  Assumption: short-term rate in the negative territory.
  Asset at floating rate repricing (with zero floor) in 1 month's time – 100MM.
  Liability at floating rate repricing within 3 months' time (no floor) – 300MM.

$$\Delta NII = 100 * \frac{11}{12} * 0 - 300 * 9/12 * -2\% = 4.5MM$$

Maturity Gap Analysis According to the Advanced Approach As already mentioned, the simple GAP technique presented above is static, as it is not taking into account the evolution of the interest rate curve and changes in the composition of the balance sheet. However, static methods have evolved over time and have been enriched through the introduction of the advanced deviations of the basic methodologies proposed by the regulator. This methodological progress aims to provide the bank with the clear picture of the underlying forms of IRRBB.

Before entering into details of the methods for measuring IRRBB, it is necessary to introduce briefly the subtypes of this risk category and define it properly.

Interest rate risk in the banking book (IRRBB) refers to the current or prospective risk to the bank's net economic value (EV), capital, and earnings arising from adverse movements in interest rates that affect the bank's banking book positions. The exposure to the interest rate risk derives both from the variation of the interest rate to which the transaction is linked at the fixing date and consequently having an impact on the interest flow and the interest margin, and from the positions in maturity which are going to be reinvested or refinanced at the new rate. The first type of risk exists only in the case of floating rate transactions and only for the component in refixing (as opposed to the component in maturity). The second one refers to transactions at fixed rate.

There are the following subtypes of IRRBB:

- Gap risk, which arises from the term structure of banking book instruments, and describes the risk arising from the timing of instrument rate changes. The risk to the bank arises when the rate of interest paid on liabilities increases before the rate of interest received on assets or reduces on assets before liabilities. The extent of gap risk depends on whether changes to term structure of interest rates occur consistently across the whole yield curve (parallel risk) or differently by period (non-parallel risk). Banks measure and control the gap risk through the repricing gap and analysis of the net mismatch for every time band and by material currency.
- Basis risk describes the impact of relative changes in interest rates for financial instruments that have similar tenors, but are priced using different interest rate indices (bases). It arises from the imperfect correlation in the adjustment of the rates earned and paid on different instruments with otherwise similar rate change characteristics. Banks measure basis risk by monitoring different benchmarks of assets and liabilities by every time bucket and shocking them by 1 bp to see the potential impact on the P&L. Certain banks, by default, adopt the strategy in terms of the minimisation of the exposure to the basis risk, which consists of an attempt to match the risk factors on the asset and liability side as much as possible.
- Option risk arises from option derivative positions explicitly or implicitly embedded within the banking book positions. Those automatic options aim to protect a bank from the decrease/increase in the interest rates and their impact needs to be assessed on the potential change in the EVE (the impact of automatic options on EVE is presented in Chapter 3). There is also an optional element embedded in banks' customer deposits providing them with a contractual right to withdraw their balance. This phenomenon is known as behavioural optionality embedded in the banking book and is thoroughly examined in Chapter 3.
- Yield risk – the risk arising from unanticipated non-parallel shifts of the yield curve such as steepening, flattening, inverted curve, and parallel shifts on the medium-long part of the curve.

IRRBB has received increasing regulatory attention and has become one of the hot topics for national and European regulators in recent years. There are clear prescriptions on how this kind of risk needs to be measured, monitored, and mitigated. The IRRBB guidelines known as the Final Report were issued on 19 July 2018. As a result, adequate IRRBB management needs to consider several dimensions, not only in terms of integrated software solutions, but also revision of metrics and introduction of a model validation framework. The simple maturity gap analysis performed in an Excel spreadsheet is no longer fit for purpose. The technical implementation of an NII simulation, clearly needed for the strategic positioning and definition of a steering approach, is a major challenge for banks. This is because the results of expected NII are required for different purposes and under various views. For example, an NII simulation required for European Banking Authority (EBA) stress testing implied certain assumptions related to pricing, time horizon, and changes in the banking book structure over time, while the internal measure is usually focused on the pure impact of interest rates on NII under a short time horizon and does not include any changes in the composition of the banking book. It is said that the banking book is constant for the purposes of this kind of analysis, i.e. without a new business assumption. Expiring items are replaced on a like for like basis, i.e. based on the same financial characteristics. Consequently, in order to capture all the above aspects, an integrated and flexible approach is needed, and it requires software solutions that serve the various purposes of NII simulation (not just a static approach). The advanced approach to the measurement of the impact on NII needs to include additional essential features; for example, to provide an indication of which risk factors banking book positions are indexed to in every single time bucket, and if this is the simple (one risk factor) or average indexation (a number of risk factors). Secondly, there has to be clear separation through FTP between the interest rate risk component, liquidity component, and commercial spread in order to allocate the interest income to sales and Treasury.

Brief Comparison of Two Approaches (Basic Maturity Gap and Advanced Repricing Gap) Both methods take into consideration the flows related to the underlying transactions and position them at the date at which they become sensitive to the interest rates. Meanwhile, the simple maturity gap classifies them in the function of the time bucket into which they are expected to fall and, as such, the position is weighted by the mid-point of the time bucket; under the advanced repricing gap approach it is expected to position transactions at the exact date of risk. In both cases these flows are used to determine the expected change in the interest margin for a predetermined gapping period, given a parallel shock of 200 bps (obviously it is possible to assign any other magnitude of shock) to the rate curve associated with the transaction. One of the most important limits of the maturity gap analysis consists of the impossibility of the identification of the parameters (risk factors) to which the transaction is linked. This means that the transaction at floating rate is distributed to the appropriate time bucket according to the time left until its repricing. Therefore, if the transaction falls into the time bucket of 3–6 months, it is not clear to which market parameter it is linked. Instead, the advanced repricing gap approach allows for estimating the impact of each parameter in terms of its contribution to the interest margin for each time bucket. Additionally, using the simple maturity gap approach it is not possible to know if the estimated sensitivity of the expected margin is derived from maturity flows (the transactions which amortise or mature and have to be reinvested or refinanced at the 'new' interest rate) or from the flows in refixing. This is an important disadvantage with respect to the advanced repricing gap approach, which calculates the NII sensitivity caused by the component in maturity reinvesting (refinancing) it at the forward rate until the end of the gapping period. Finally, the most important thing which gives such a big advantage to the repricing gap, locating it at the top of the static methods family, is that it captures the sensitivity deriving from the non-perfect indexation of the transaction. In particular, if the transaction is the floating rate perfectly indexed, the repricing flow is positioned at the first rate reset date for the transaction as a whole. If not, the sensitivity captured from the non-perfect indexation is calculated and shown also for the subsequent refixing dates. Imperfect indexation arises in the following situations:

- the rate fixing period is different to the interest payment period;
- in the presence of financial spreads;
- the weight of the indexation parameter is not equal to 1;
- average indexation.

Two Different Views of the Maturity Gap　Besides the differentiation between the simple and advanced repricing gap, there are also two different views of the maturity gap. These views are applied on a daily basis but serve different purposes.

The first view is known as the *flow approach* as shown in Figure 2.2, and designs the maturity gap in terms of cash flows (for the fixed rate items) and outstanding at repricing (items at floating rate). This approach is commonly used for the calculation of the ΔNII for a certain gapping period and shock magnitude.

The second view is known as *stock analysis*, shown in Figure 2.3, and designs the maturity gap in terms of outstanding for every item. The residual gap creates NII sensitivity and indicates the extent of the exposure to interest rate risk. This approach is usually used for calculation of the bucket exposure and hedging.

Repricing Gap Analysis and Refixing Gap Analysis　The repricing gap here refers to the advanced derivation of the maturity gap which was described above. In this stage, the purpose is to focus on its application and the difference with respect to the refixing gap which shows all flows in refixing (not only the first refixing date but also the subsequent dates). The repricing gap usually shows a picture of the exposure to the interest rate risk within a short time period (12 months). It captures the positions both at the fixed rate, which matures and needs to be reinvested (if assets) or refinanced (if liabilities), and the floating rate, which will reset its rate, generating in this way the interest rate risk exposure. The gapping period (usually 12 months) is split into monthly time buckets, giving in this way more precise information about the time when the risk is present. The more precise information about the timing related to the presence of risk, the more

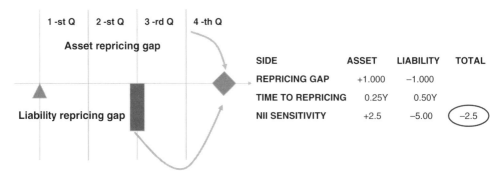

FIGURE 2.2　Repricing gap analysis – flow approach.
Source: own elaboration

REPRICING STOCKS
NII sensitivity calculated as differential change in funding costs for unmatched position

SIDE	ASSET	LIABILITY	TOTAL
AVERAGE UNBALANCE (3^{rd}Q)	-	−1.000	
HEDGING EXPOSURE (3^{rd}Q)	-	−250	
NII SENSITIVITY	-	−250	−2.5

FIGURE 2.3 Repricing gap – stock approach.
Source: own elaboration

accurate the measure of the exposure to the interest rate risk. It is worth highlighting at this point that even if it delivers a fast overview from the interest rate risk perspective, it does not consider the structure and the positions of the subsequent repricing gaps related to the given position. Instead, it 'sees' only the first risk date of the position in the fixation. For example, imagine that a bank has an amount of liabilities which reprice in January 2019, April 2019, July 2019, and October 2019 (it is indexed to EURIBOR 3 M). Under the repricing gap approach, we will see only the repricing in January 2019 if analysed in December 2018 (the cut-off date). Under this approach, the positions in maturity and in refixing are separated, which greatly facilitates interpretation of the results. The bank is aware of when the risk derives from the expiration of the position and when it is caused by refixing. In order to calculate the sensitivity of the interest income, flows in refixing and in maturity are summed up. Again, the sensitivity of the interest income driven by the amount in refixing is separated from the sensitivity caused by the flows in maturity. This helps a lot in the analysis of the results. The repricing gap of the bank is now analysed, as shown in Figure 2.4.

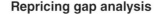

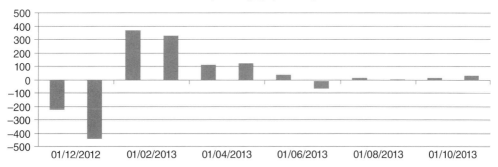

FIGURE 2.4 Repricing gap analysis (numbers are in euro/millions).
Source: own elaboration

   The figure shows a significant negative gap in January, which refers to the liabilities in refixing. From the IRR perspective, this net amount of liabilities will reset its rate and consequently expose the bank to the upward movement of the curve. Furthermore, positive gaps in refixing can be noticed in successive months. Conversely, they expose the bank to the downward movement of the curve. The subsequent presence of both negative and positive gaps in refixing partially offsets the exposure to the fluctuations of interest rates. The refixing gap analysis enriches the details provided by the repricing gap. It gives information about the existing mismatching between assets and liabilities at the floating rate indexed to the different risk factors (EURIBOR 3 M, LIBOR1 M, etc.) grouped in monthly or bi-weekly time buckets (or even daily) within the predetermined time horizon (for example, 12 months). The simplest form of the refixing gap approach does not incorporate the projection of the new volumes which the bank is going to disburse under the examination period. Instead, the positions are inertial (in a run-off). Unlike the repricing gap, the refixing analysis takes into consideration all the refixing dates of accounts related to the assets and liabilities under the gapping period. This is important information for the bank in order to contain the risk of mismatching and the high sensitivity driven by interest rate fluctuations. It is a fundamental tool for setting the hedging strategy and containing the negative impact on the interest income of a bank. Let us consider Figure 2.5 representing the refixing gap of a bank:

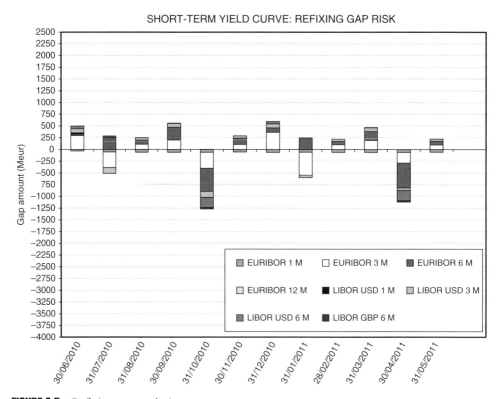

FIGURE 2.5 Refixing gap analysis.
Source: own elaboration

The figure shows negative mismatching, in the analysed example, in October 2010 and April 2011, caused by the EUR1bn net position in liabilities. This position is linked to EURIBOR 6 M. Instead, from the asset side, the numerous net positions in assets are distributed steadily over time (in this case 12 months) linked mainly to EURIBOR 6 M and 3 M. The bank is significantly exposed to upward movements in the level of the EURIBOR 6 M while approaching the refixing date in October. Furthermore, this risk is concentrated in a 1-month time period. Suppose that in October 2010, following some important sudden event, the market responds through a hike in interest rate level. This bank incurs losses due to the negative gap in refixing. Subsequently, the market adjusts interest rates to pre-October levels. The bank has positive mismatching in November and again incurs losses. As can be seen, not only is the magnitude of the single gap important, but also its distribution over time. The hedging strategy consists of entering into the Forward Rate Agreement (FRA). The bank, in this case, buys an FRA, locking the rate on the negative mismatched position in October.

The method presented above is a static one. That is, with the evolution of the balance sheet from the perspective of new business production, customers' behaviour with reference to the items with embedded options and the future evolution of the interest rates are not taken into consideration. Instead, the positions of the balance sheet are in a run-off, and the impact on NII is calculated under a forward curve scenario.

Maturity Gap Analysis from the Economic Value Perspective

Economic value of equity (EVE) measures the theoretical change in the net present value of the balance sheet excluding equity, i.e. risk sensitive assets – risk sensitive liabilities. The measure therefore depicts the change in equity value resulting from an interest rate shock. Under this method, the value of equity under alternative stress scenarios is compared with the value under a base scenario. This base interest rate scenario is the present value of assets less liabilities under the current interest rate environment. All cash flows from on-balance sheet and off-balance sheet interest rate-sensitive items in the banking book may be included in the computation. The market value of equity is computed as the present value of assets cash flows, less the present value of liabilities cash flows, without including assumptions on the interest rate sensitivity of equity (the equity position is excluded from this approach). The balance sheet is then revalued under the alternative interest rate scenarios and the difference between the value of equity under the base scenario and the alternative scenario is calculated. The accuracy of the valuation of the balance sheet positions is extremely dependent upon the cash flows calculated and the discount rate used. The discounting rates used should match the duration and risk of the cash flows (the category of the instrument which is discounted). In the BCBS Standards, there is an assumption that the cash flows in certain time buckets are discounted with the rates at the mid-point of the time bucket with the risk-free rate (internal view), or adjusted rates if the cash flows include the commercial margins (external view). Bank have the choice of whether to deduct the commercial margin and other spread components from the notional repricing cash flows through the FTP methodology. Consequently, the discounting factor must be consistent with the view chosen for the EVE cash flows calculation (see Figure 2.6).

Under the static approach (unconditional cash flows) there is an additional assumption related to the fact that the timing of the cash flows and their size do not differ under

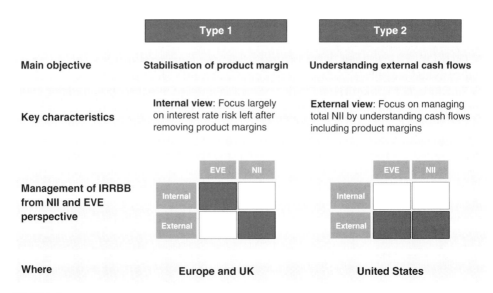

	Type 1	Type 2
Main objective	Stabilisation of product margin	Understanding external cash flows
Key characteristics	**Internal view**: Focus largely on interest rate risk left after removing product margins	**External view**: Focus on managing total NII by understanding cash flows including product margins
Management of IRRBB from NII and EVE perspective		
Where	Europe and UK	United States

FIGURE 2.6 Management of the EVE under internal and external view.
Source: own elaboration

the various scenarios as a result of customer behaviour. In reality, there is a specific relationship between the interest rate scenario and the extent of prepayment and growth of deposits. For example, if the rates go down the prepayment rate tends to go up, as the clients are shopping for cheaper borrowing opportunities. However, on the liability side, savers tend to search for the new investment opportunities and the volatility of this product could increase. The cash flows which are adjusted by the potential changes in behaviour of the clients are known as conditional cash flows and represent the best practice of the EVE calculation.

The new regulatory framework (the EBA Final Report on IRRBB issued on 19 July 2018) in Europe represents a clear attempt to standardise the IRRBB methodologies across countries and financial institutions demanding the application of the standardised approach (prescribed by the regulator) along with the internal methodology banks may have already adopted (for example *value at risk*). The EBA Final Report does not claim to replace the existing methodologies. Instead, it is the additional analysis that banks must perform in order to comply. For smaller institutions, the standardised framework could be used as a platform on which to set up the whole IRRBB framework of the bank.

Under the standardised approach, for the calculation of impact on EVE, institutions are expected to apply six regulatory shocks with prescribed movements in interest rates. These are as follows:

- parallel up (the shift of the whole curve up);
- parallel down (the shift of the whole curve down);
- short up;
- short down;
- steepener (short rates go down and long rates go up);
- flattener (short rates go up and long rates go down).

The above shocks are calibrated by material currency, i.e. the magnitude of the shock differs for EUR, GBP, USD, etc.

Even though this approach is simple and easy to interpret, it has its own pros and cons. The main benefits of the EVE model are the ability to capture the convexity embedded in the banking book, i.e. the extent of the difference between the linear approximation and the full valuation under certain interest rate shock scenarios. Additionally, the objective variable in this approach is the economic value of the banking book and, as such, the risk is measured in terms of economic value.

Under the static view, the ΔEVE approach shows a snapshot in time of the risk based upon the current portfolio or balance sheet composition; however, it is possible to 'simulate' the potential impact of the future business based on the assumption coming from forecast growth or cannibalisation of certain products. The impact of such a simulated position is made at the wide time interval, for example on an annual basis, and reflects the situation at that specific point of time taking into account the new composition of the banking book. Thus, it is still a static approach but the assumption about growth is taken into account. On the other hand, the dynamic approach simulates the position of the banking book based on a number of external and internal factors and the simulated curve at a certain point of time.

Case Study Imagine that the change in EVE metric under six regulatory shocks of a financial institution looks as in the table below:

Economic value analysis – behavioural

	Δ'EVE	Δ'Options	Δ' EVE + Options
2010 scenario	31.724	(6.692)	25.032
Parallel up	39.615	(6.787)	32.828
Parallel down	(42.065)	131.558	89.493
Short up	24.539	(6.238)	18.301
Short down	(25.349)	38.499	13.150
Flattener	13.571	(180)	13.391
Steepener	(6.866)	9.074	2.208
Worse	(42.065)	(6.787)	2.208

We want to analyse how the bank is positioned from an IRRBB perspective under the economic view.

It clearly appears that there is no loss under any of the interest rate shock scenarios. This is because the loss in the banking book value is compensated by the change in the economic value of the automatic options under all downward scenarios (parallel down, short down, and steepener). Instead, under all upward scenarios (parallel up, short up, and flattener) the bank shows a gain embedded in the banking book but the automatic options become *out of the money* (under upwards interest rate shocks the difference in the economic value of automatic options under the shocked scenario and base scenario is negative). This picture indicates that this illustrative financial institution has medium long-term liabilities (for example behaviouralised liabilities) which fund the short-term repricing assets. This is because under upward scenarios, the bank takes the net liability position and the increase in rates results in an increase in the economic value of its banking book. Overall, it is clear that this bank is not assuming any IRRBB risk on the medium-long part of the curve. Neither is it riding the yield curve at this particular point in time.

The importance of automatic options is highlighted in the BCBS Standards and, consequently, reflected in the EBA Final Report on IRRBB. Below is an extract from the BCBS Standards published in 2016 and related to the calculation of the EVE measure:

Calculation of the EVE Measure

The gain or loss in economic value of equity $\Delta EVE_{i,c}$ under scenario i and currency c is calculated as follows:

1. Under each scenario i, all notional repricing cash flows are slotted to the respective time bucket $k \in \{1, 2, \ldots, K\}$. Within a given time bucket k, all positive and negative notional repricing cash flows are netted to form a single long or short position, with the cancelled parts removed from the calculation. Following this process across all time buckets leads to a set of notional repricing cash flows $CF_{i,(k)}, k \in \{1, 2, \ldots, K\}$.
2. Net notional repricing cash flows in each time bucket k are weighted by a continuously compounded discount factor: $DF_{i,c(tk)} = \exp(-R_{i,c}(t_k) \cdot t_k)$ that reflects the interest rate shock scenario i in currency c and where t_k is the midpoint of time bucket k. This results in a weighted net position, which may be positive or negative for each time bucket. The discount factors represent the risk-free rate.
3. These risk-weighted net positions are summed to determine the EVE in currency c under scenario i (excluding automatic interest rate option positions which the bank might have):

$$EVE_{i,c} = \sum\nolimits_{k=1}^{K} CF_{i,c}(k) \, {}^* DF_{i,c}(t_k) \tag{2.3}$$

The EVE in currency c under base scenario is calculated as:

$$EVE_{0,c} - \sum\nolimits_{k=1}^{K} CF_{0,c}(k) \, {}^* DF_{0,c}(t_k) \tag{2.4}$$

Finally, the full change in EVE in currency c associated with scenario i is obtained by subtracting $EVE_{0,c}$ from the EVE under shocked interest rate term structure $EVE_{i,c}$ and by adding the total measure for automatic interest rate option risk $KAO_{i,c}$ as follows:

$$\Delta EVE_{i,c} = \sum\nolimits_{k=1}^{K} CF_{i,c}(k) \, {}^* DF_{i,c}(t_k) - \sum\nolimits_{k=1}^{K} CF_{0,c}(k) \, {}^* DF_{0,c}(t_k) + KAO_{i,c} \tag{2.5}$$

In this regard, if $\Delta EVE_{i,c} > 0$ then the economic value of the banking book is going to increase, while in the case where $\Delta EVE_{i,c} < 0$ the bank faces a reduction in its economic value. $KAO_{i,c}$ is an add-on for the calculation of the change in the value of the automatic interest rate options, whether explicit or embedded.

An example of a risk-free curve, as specified in the BCBS Standards or ECB IRRBB stress test performed in 2017, could be a secured interest rate swap or Overnight Index Swap (OIS) curve.

Time Bucket Sensitivity Analysis – *PV01* While dealing with IRRBB, the usage of the term of *IRRBB sensitivity* or *PV01* is essential.

Sensitivity analysis is a method for calculating the change in the present values of items due to a 1 bp shift in the interest rates curve for a given currency. The sensitivity (*PV01*) of the transaction is calculated as the difference between its Present Value (*PV*) determined with the current market rates and its Present Value under the curve shocked with 1 bp (*PV**):

$$PV01 = PV^* - PV \tag{2.6}$$

The traditional approach consists of positioning cash flows at the date (time bucket) at which the flow is expected to occur (according to its contractual or modelled maturity) with calculation of its Present Value with the discount factor corresponding to the mid-point of time bucket (in case of the simplified approach) or to the exact risk date of the transaction (in the ALM system). This representation has a crucial importance in hedging or monitoring of the IRRBB structural exposure (usually related to the items at fixed rate), as it allows for the identification of the tenors of the term structure of interest rates, which are excessively sensitive to the movements of interest rates, and 'closing' them with hedging or natural hedging. The total time bucket sensitivity is a sum of sensitivities by time bucket.

Figure 2.7 shows the *PV01* sensitivity by time bucket of a financial institution.

It can be clearly seen that the sensitivity of this bank falls into the time buckets between 1 and 5 years and this is due to the liability position. An increase in rates by 1 bp, in those time buckets, results in a gain for the institution. On an overall basis, the increase in rates will lead to the positive impact.

Duration Gap Analysis Duration is a measure of the average life of the security. It represents the speed of payment of a security, and consequently the price risk relative to other securities with the same maturity. Duration is calculated as the weighted average time until the receipt of all cash flows from the security, where the weights are the present values of the cash flows to the total present value of the security:

$$D = \sum_{t=1}^{n}(t \times PVCF_t)/ \sum_{t=1}^{n} PVCF_t \tag{2.7}$$

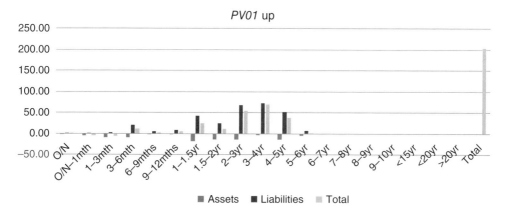

FIGURE 2.7 Time bucket sensitivity in the banking book.
Source: own elaboration.

where D is the duration of the security, t is the length (number of months, years, etc.) to the date of payment, and $PVCF$ is the present value of the payment CF made at t, calculated as $CF_t/(1 + r)^t$, where the summation Σ is taken from the first to the last payment n and r is yield to maturity. Duration can be measured in two forms.

The primary application of this metric is to measure the interest rate risk in the market and is known by the term *Modified Duration* (MD). This interpretation of duration represents the price volatility of the security and, consequently, its interest rate risk. Mathematically, duration is an approximation acceptable only for very small interest rate movements and it becomes imprecise in cases of significant shifts in the term structure.

As mentioned earlier, duration relates changes in interest rates and percentage changes in security prices linearly as follows:

$$\frac{\Delta S}{S} = -MD \times \frac{\Delta r}{1 + r} \approx -MD \times \Delta r \qquad (2.8)$$

where MD is the Modified Duration of the security, S is price of the security, r is the yield to maturity, and Δ is the change from the previous value (shock).

The second form of duration is measured in units of time, e.g. months or years, and is referred to as Macaulay's duration. The two forms are strictly related and can be transformed through the relation:

$$MD = \frac{Macaulay's\ Duration}{\left(1 + \dfrac{YTM}{n}\right)}$$

where:

YTM yield to maturity;
  n number of coupon periods per year.

Meanwhile, the first form is commonly used to reflect the riskiness of the single transaction.

Duration is very often used to monitor the value of capital of the financial institution in case of fluctuations of the curve. The assumption of a particular degree of risk exposure is a function of the bank's senior management risk appetite ('risk appetite' of the institution is usually formalised in the Asset/Liability Committee – ALCO – policy). The choice of selecting the capital value as a target position is dictated by the fact that this is a primary concern to the shareholders of the bank. While the interest rate sensitivity or risk of individual position is related to its modified duration, the interest rate risk of the target position is related to the difference, or gap, between the average duration of the assets of the institution and the average duration of the liabilities. The duration gap ($DGAP$) is:

$$DGAP = D_A - w \times D_L, \qquad (2.9)$$

where D_A and D_L are the average duration of assets and liabilities, respectively, and w is the weight defined as L/A (market value of liabilities to the market value of assets).

Let us imagine that the $DGAP$ of the banking book items of the financial institution is positive. In this case the bank behaves as a net asset position. Consequently, when the interest rates increase, the value of capital will diminish accordingly. Conversely, in the case of an interest rate decrease the capital value will increase as a function of the magnitude of the $DGAP$, the shock in the interest rate movement, and the dimension of the assets of the financial institution. Exactly the opposite will happen in the case of the $DGAP < 0$. The institution can change its degree of interest rate exposure by any extent it wishes by changing the composition of the balance sheet in such a way as to obtain the desired duration gap for its target position. The greater the duration gap, the greater is the institution's risk exposure for a particular target position and, conversely, the smaller the gap, the smaller its exposure. The elimination of this risk consists of putting into place the immunisation strategy and setting the Duration Gap to zero. The financial institution, however, attempts to maximise its profits, but profit maximisation presumes a desired level of risk exposure. The desired risk-return tradeoff for a financial institution is determined by its ALCO policy and may be different from bank to bank. Managing the interest rate risk consists of determination of both the direction and size of its gap on the basis of its predicted interest rates. A bank may pursue two interest rate risk strategies: a passive (immunisation) strategy or an active strategy. The example below shows the immunisation strategy of a bank. It should be underlined that where a bank has gained income through correct interest rate management, it may it reduced or even lost as a consequence of the immunisation strategy. On the other hand, by immunising, the bank also decreases its chances of suffering losses if the risk is mismanaged. Let us consider that the initial value of capital is equal to 100 euro. The average duration of assets is equal to 4.17 years, meanwhile the average duration of liabilities (deposits P for example) is equal to 1 year and $P/A = 0.9$. This yields a duration gap: $4.17 - 0.9 \times 1 = 3.27$ years. The immunisation condition is not maintained. The bank can reduce the gap to zero through:

- Shortening the duration of its assets by 3.27 years to 0.9 years.
- Lengthening the duration of its deposits to 4.63 years so that $0.9 \times 4.63 = 4.17$.

Let us suppose that the bank prefers to go through with the second possibility (lengthening the duration of deposits). It can do so by reducing the volume of the liabilities with shorter duration and increasing the volume of the liabilities with a longer duration. Consequently, the immunisation condition is satisfied. An interest rate increase, by say 200 bps, will decrease the value of assets in exactly the same way as before, changing the composition of the balance sheet (the assets side has not been changed). Instead, the composition of liabilities has been changed by reducing the proportion of shorter-term deposits. Through the immunisation strategy, the bank protects its capital level as the change in the asset market value is offset by the change in the market value of deposits (Kaufman 1984).

Managing the Interest Rate Risk through the Duration Gap Approach   Let us suppose that the bank predicts a decline in the level of interest rates in the next period and, in accordance with its ALCO policy, accepts the risk in terms of duration gap of one year so that:

$$D_A - w \times D_L = 1 \qquad (2.10)$$

Imagine also that the average duration of assets is equal to 4.17 years, meanwhile the average duration of liabilities (deposits P for example) is equal to one year and P/A = 0.9. The market value of total assets is equal to 1000 euro. Again, as in the previous example, the bank can go through a strategy of shortening the duration of assets from 4.17 to 0.9 years or lengthening the duration of liabilities from 1 to 4.63 years. The bank will gain an increase in the value of capital if the interest rates decrease as predicted by the Treasurer of the bank. Now, contrary to the bank's expectations, let interest rates increase by 200 bps rather than decrease. The bank is worse off. The market value of capital has declined by 20 euro (1000 x 2%). The bank has deteriorated the market value of capital. However, it is worth remembering that in order to undertake the active strategy for the interest rate risk management, the bank has to be able to predict the interest rate movements and be right (Kaufman 1984).

Limits of Duration Gap Analysis   This is theoretically appealing, but requires the complete information of a data set related to items on the balance sheet (such as the maturity and the repricing frequency of every single position). Moreover, the early redemption of loans or other options included in the transactions are not taken into account. From a mathematical standpoint, a duration gap analysis works well only for small interest rate changes and it assumes that when the level of the interest rates changes, interest rates on all maturities change by exactly the same amount (parallel shift). However, despite all the above-mentioned limits, it is still commonly used in banking practice (Lubinska 2014).

ICAAP − Assessment of the Internal Capital to Cover IRRBB Risks   Before the BCBS Standard was published, banks had quite a lot of discretion regarding the amount of internal capital to cover IRRBB risks. Many banks based their approach to ICAAP on the *value at risk* metric at a certain point of time. The maximum loss meant the need for potential capital coverage against risks.

The revised final guidelines published on 19 July 2018 on the management of interest rate risk arising from non-trading book activities revised the methodological approach to ICAAP and set up new rules to be followed. In particular, it proclaims that institutions should base the contribution of IRRBB to the overall internal capital assessment, taking into account both the impact on the ΔEVE and ΔNII. The ΔEVE must be assessed under a number of interest rate scenarios at a certain point in time. The overall level of capital should be commensurate with both the institution's actual level of risk and its risk appetite, i.e. it represents the highest negative impact which the institution can face in terms of the ΔEVE. There is a need for a buffer, in terms of ΔNII impact to cover the immediate loss in case of adverse movement in the interest rates. This and additional requirements are clearly formulated by the regulator.

Institutions must consider:

- internal capital held for risks to economic value that could arise from adverse movements in interest rates and internal capital needs arising from the impact of rate changes on future earnings capacity and the resultant implications for the internal capital buffer levels;
- the size and tenor of internal limits on IRRBB exposure, and whether these limits are reached at the point of capital calculations;

- the effectiveness and effective cost of hedging open positions that are intended to take advantage of internal expectations of the future level of interest rates;
- the sensitivity of the internal measures of IRRBB to key or imperfect modelling assumptions;
- the impact of shocks and stress scenarios on positions priced with different interest rate indices (basis risk); and
- the drivers of the underlying risks.

Furthermore, the Final Report states:

to calibrate the amount of the internal capital requirement for IRRBB, institutions should use measurement system and a range of interest rate shocks and stress scenarios that are adapted to the risk profile of the institution in order to quantify the potential scale of any effects under adverse conditions. In considering whether an allocation of internal capital should be made in respect of IRRBB, the institution should take into account the following:

- The potential for actual losses to be incurred under stressed conditions, or because of secular changes in the market environment, e.g. where it might become necessary to liquidate positions that are intended as a long-term investment to stabilise earnings.
- The fluctuation of net interest income, the strength and stability of the earnings stream and the level of income needed to generate and maintain normal business operations. Institutions with a high level of IRRBB that could, under a plausible range of market scenarios, result in losses, in the revision of the dividend policy, or decrease in business operations should ensure that they have sufficient capital to withstand the adverse impact of these scenarios.
- Institutions should consider internal capital buffer adjustments where the results of their stress testing highlight the potential for reduced earnings (and therefore reduced capital generation capacity) under stress scenarios.
- The actual levels of net interest income achievable under different scenarios (i.e. the extent to which margins are wide enough to absorb volatility arising from interest rate positions, changes in the cost of liabilities).

The author perceives this revised approach as an attempt towards the overall standardisation of the methodological approach to IRRBB. This is also big opportunity as outcomes achieved by different banks are easily comparable and introduce a standardised methodological approach toward risk management in general.

LIQUIDITY RISK IN THE BANKING BOOK – MEASUREMENT AND MANAGEMENT

This section addresses the liquidity measurement and management practices in a commercial bank. It focuses on the quantification methods which are undertaken in order to estimate the appropriate amount of liquidity buffer (LAB) through the stress testing methodology and appropriate liquidity framework. This section will also present approaches to funding risk, funding profile, and funding plan.

In addition, it discusses briefly the funding plan, the forward-looking process to assess the key sources and uses of funds based on the business forecast. Furthermore, it walks the reader through the contingency funding plan (CFP), the document which defines the metrics, processes, and procedures put in place in case of extreme external or internal driven conditions which impact in an adverse manner the funding ability of the bank.

Liquidity risk is defined as the risk that the financial institution either does not have enough financial resources available to meet its obligations as they fall due, or can only access these financial resources at excessive cost. A bank should distinguish between short-term and structural liquidity risk which is aligned with the definition of liquidity risk and funding risk respectively.

- Short-term liquidity risk is defined as the risk that a financial institution does not have sufficient financial resources in the short term to meet its obligations as they fall due, or can access these financial resources only at excessive cost.
- Structural liquidity risk is defined as the risk for actual or potential loss because the bank cannot pursue its desired business strategy or growth objectives due to a sub-optimal balance sheet structure, including excessive reliance on particular sources of funding.

The liquidity risk is raised when the payment obligations are failed and may be caused by:

- **Funding liquidity risk:** the inability to raise funds or to regulate payment obligations at market costs but only using a higher cost of borrowing.
- **Market liquidity risk:** the presence of difficulty in asset selling or capital losses due to a disinvestment of these assets.

It is important to underline that liquidity risk has the following components:

- **Funding risk:** the risk that potential changes in the cost of funding (deterioration in creditworthiness or 'illiquidity' in the market spreads) could impact the profitability of the bank. The funding risk is idiosyncratic, which means it is caused by events that are internal to the financial institution and can generate fast reactions from the market counterparties, causing unavailability of funding for the usual transactions and higher remuneration.
- **Market liquidity risk:** the risk that the bank is not able to liquidate its assets without generating a loss due to the illiquidity conditions in the market.
- **Liquidity mismatch risk:** the risk of mismatching between amounts and/or maturities of inflows and outflows in the specific time buckets (this will be discussed in the section on liquidity measurement techniques). Consequently, the medium-term funding plan should guarantee consistent matching with asset duration according to the appetite of a bank for the extent of maturity transformation (discussed later on).
- **Liquidity contingency risk:** the risk that unexpected future events may require an amount of liquidity greater than the amount currently forecast by the bank. This risk could be generated by events such as the non-repayment of loans, the need to finance new assets, or difficulty in selling assets or obtaining new funds during a liquidity crisis period.
- **Operational liquidity risk:** a bank's inability to respect current obligations due to errors, violations, or damages, even if remaining in financial solvency conditions.

■ **Margin calls liquidity risk:** the risk that a bank is exposed to negative changes in relation to financial instruments and is contractually required to renew margins through collaterals/cash.

The robust liquidity risk management framework (RMF) provides the architecture for the overall management and control of all risks. It sets out a bank's risk principles and standards, and defines the risk tolerance statement. The liquidity risk framework articulates the maximum level of risk that a bank is willing to take in pursuit of its strategy.

In order to discuss the RMF, each risk type (mentioned above) is required to set a risk appetite and risk tolerance. Risk appetite is the amount of risk which a bank regards as optimal in order to generate returns, taking account of current and forecasted market conditions. Risk appetite cannot exceed risk tolerance. Risk tolerance is the boundary defined by a bank that determines the maximum level of risk it is willing to take in pursuit of its strategy and in accordance with its risk principles. Finally, the term risk capacity defines the maximum level of risk a bank can assume, given its current capabilities and resources, before breaching constraints determined by regulatory capital and liquidity requirements.

RMF has the following objectives:

■ Ensuring a bank's solvency under normal business conditions and also in crisis periods.
■ Ensuring a liquidity level that respects the contractual obligations of the bank, at any time, by optimising the cost of funding in relation to both current and future market conditions and performance of the bank.
■ Managing the liquidity risk position to comply with the regulatory framework defined by the local regulator and, at the same time, the bank's specific operational features.
■ Defining a policy and metrics for measuring and monitoring liquidity risks to ensure the achievement of previous objectives under the normal conditions (ongoing concern) and stress scenarios.

The aforementioned objectives are implemented through the liquidity policy document which must contain the following topics:

■ Separation of roles and responsibilities between the treasury/ALM function and the liquidity risk monitoring department.
■ Definition of liquidity risk tolerance and risk appetite by the board of directors in terms of survival period and adequacy of the size of the liquidity portfolio.
■ Measurement of the liquidity risk exposure.

Before going into details of the liquidity measurement techniques, the Liquidity Risk Tolerance Statement of a bank will be analysed.

The bank intends to meet its payment and collateral obligations under extreme but plausible liquidity stress scenarios without recourse to extraordinary central bank support.

Such a statement needs to be extended in order quantify both the length of the period under which such a statement is fulfilled and the definition of stress scenarios.

For example, it can say that it intends to meet its payment and collateral obligations for at least 60 days in a combined name-specific and market-wide liquidity stress, without recourse to extraordinary central bank support. These are two fundamental dimensions which characterise liquidity risk: determination of a certain period of time and a number of stress test scenarios. The common stress tests used in liquidity practice are market, idiosyncratic, and combined stress test. Under the market stress test there is an assumption about the adverse conditions in the external market. Under the idiosyncratic one, internal factors play a crucial role. A combined stress test includes both internal and external factors.

It is important to highlight that the robust liquidity framework addresses the long-term liquidity as well. It introduces the concept of maturity transformation, i.e. funding long-term assets with short-term liabilities or, in other words, different maturities of asset base and liability base.

A common technique for measurement of the liquidity risk exposure is based on the *liquidity risk mismatch model*, which includes metrics differentiation for the liquidity risk monitoring and measurement on both the short-term (cash flow from operations) and medium long-term (structural liquidity) horizon.

In this context, short-term liquidity refers to the liquidity management in a 1-year period and is characterised by the following aspects:

- Calculation of liquidity mismatches considering liquid assets, coming from the liquidity portfolio which comprises eligible and marketable securities and any additional cash reserves.
- Net flows related to assets and liabilities which expire in different time buckets are determined within a predefined threshold expressed as a cumulative percentage value, considering the application of *run-off* factors related to the different balance sheet items. These thresholds reflect prudent management of cash flows and the ability of a bank to fund itself in the money market, capital market and deposits.

Medium long-term liquidity refers to the liquidity beyond one year (which is known also under the term of *structural liquidity*) and is characterised by the following aspects:

- Calculation of the liquidity mismatch that results in the gap ratios between assets and liabilities, usually grouped in different time buckets beyond 1 year, 3 years, and 5 years.
- Use of statistical/quantitative behavioural models for items without deterministic maturity and with embedded options.
- Definition of liquidity risk factors related to the specific business model, to strategic direction, to operational complexity, and both current and prospective capacity of funding.
- Identification and definition of liquidity portfolio.
- Definition of stressed scenarios and their measurement on a monthly basis, which, based on both endogenous and exogenous shock scenarios, can generate simulations regarding the liquidity risk exposure and, consequently, can allow one to verify the survival capability of a bank and potential increase in liquidity buffer.
- Definition of the contingency funding plan (CFP) in order to define endogenous and exogenous early warnings indicators, and the action plan to be implemented to protect the solvency of the bank.

Short-Term Liquidity Management Principles

Short-term liquidity management aims to ensure the ability to meet expected or unexpected cash payment obligations within a 1-year time horizon, as it is typically considered to represent the short-term liquidity time frame, i.e. up to 1 year.

The maintenance of a sustainable imbalance (mismatching) between cash-in and out is an essential condition for the normal banking activity.

The risk indicators for short-term liquidity risk monitoring can be summarised into the following categories:

1. Limits between the cash inflows plus the *liquidity portfolio* (*counterbalancing capacity*) and the cash outflows for time buckets up to very short time periods (for example 45 days).
2. Common practice consists of putting in place warnings for the longer time buckets, for example 3- and 6-month buckets.

The liquidity management limits and warnings are set up in order to monitor the limit's utilisation and are based on the specific bank's characteristics, i.e. they are tailored to the business model of the financial institution.

Cumulative Short-Term Limits   As already mentioned, the liquidity risk measurement system is based on the *maturity mismatch approach*. One of the examples for the liquidity risk limits is to set them up in terms of gap ratios. Each time bucket is limited by the maximum amount of mismatching allowed. Liquidity limits are defined and calculated on a cumulative basis and expressed in terms of the incoming cash flows (including the liquidity asset buffer), and the outgoing cash flows for each time bucket. Therefore, the gap ratio is defined as follows:

$$\frac{Cash\ in + CBC}{Cash\ out} \geq a\% \tag{2.11}$$

where:

- *Cash in* represents the sum of actual daily operation cash inflows put in place with parties outside the bank over a short-term time horizon (for example, 45 days).
- *Cash out* represents the sum of actual daily operation cash outflows put in place with parties outside the bank over a short-term time horizon (for example, 45 days).
- *Counterbalancing capacity (CBC)* is the sum of highly liquid items used by the bank to meet its liquidity needs during the stress situation.
- *a* is a threshold related to the short-term liquidity ratio. For the short-term time buckets it is usually set up at 100% or above.

In addition to the threshold *a*, the bank limits its exposure to the short-term liquidity risk through the setting up of warning thresholds for the successive time buckets.

Table 2.1 shows an illustrative example of limits and warnings breakdown for single time buckets:

The exposure to short-term liquidity risk needs to be performed for all material currencies. The *gap ratio* lower than the corresponding bucket trigger means that the limit has been breached. In case of breach of limits the authorisation and communication procedures are activated as defined in the *liquidity policy* document of the bank and/or *contingency funding plan*.

TABLE 2.1 Illustrative short-term liquidity thresholds.

Time Buckets	Limits (Gap Ratio)
45 days	110%
Warnings	
3 months	80%
6 months	60%

Source: own elaboration.

Also, the definitions of cash inflows/outflows have to be consistent in the whole liquidity management framework. In particular:

- **Outflows** are defined as disbursements arising from maturing liabilities, from the use of irrevocable lines of credit and from negative income components.
- **Inflows** are defined as the inflows arising from the maturity of asset, the use of irrevocable credit lines (liabilities), from the sale of marketable activities and positive components of income.
- **Estimated cash flows** are defined as the cash flows related to random events, regular or occasional, such as dividends, tax and benefit repayments, early repayments of bonds, or extraordinary operations.
- **Actual cash flows** are defined as the cash flows with a contractual maturity. For the assets and liabilities callable cash flows, the most conservative criteria, should be used (last maturity for callable assets, closest maturity for callable liabilities).
- **Cash flows with no contractual maturity date** are defined as assets and liabilities with a due date that cannot be established on a contractual basis. For these items, the bank needs to use statistical/quantitative models for their appropriate estimation. The models must first be validated by the ALCO and Risk Committee as well as revised by the internal independent audit function.

Medium Long-Term Liquidity – The Principles of Structural Liquidity Management

The structural liquidity management of a bank aims to guarantee the healthy structural balance between assets and liabilities with residual maturities beyond 1 year.

The maintenance of an adequate dynamic relationship between medium long-term assets and liabilities is intended to avoid pressures on short-term sources of funding. This is a valid point given that in the past banks used to 'abuse' the process of income generation through the maturity transformation, i.e. funding long-term assets with short-term liabilities, and as a response to this global practice the regulator put in place the mandatory metric for the structural liquidity, which is the net stable funding ratio (NSFR).

Typical actions in order to avoid excessive maturity transformation run by a bank include:

- Extending the maturity profile of liabilities to reduce less stable sources of funding, optimising at the same time its costs (integrated strategic and tactical approach).

- Financing growth through strategic funding activities by defining the appropriate duration.
- Reconciling the medium long-term wholesale funding needs with the necessity of cost minimisation, sources, currencies, and instruments diversification.
- Defining and assessing, on an annual basis, the impact of stress test scenarios in order to prepare the robust and fit-for-purpose *funding plan*.

It is the author's belief that the application of optimisation techniques to achieve the trade-off between maturity transformation and the robust stable funding position of a bank will become increasingly important in the near future. This is not only because it helps to reduce the overall funding costs, but also because it ensures the regulatory compliance and target utilisation across all liquidity metrics.

Structural Liquidity Risk Measurement and Management   In order to monitor the structural liquidity risk a *maturity ladder* is produced by allocating assets and liabilities to the respective time buckets. The cash projection for different time buckets will be a function of maturity or, alternatively, for items without contractual maturity, it is necessary to model their corresponding cash flow profile through quantitative/behavioural models validated on the regular basis (for example, corresponding to the internal controls structure). The structural liquidity analysis should include all balance sheet items (See Table 2.2) that generate cash flows at the cut-off date under a number of agreed internally assumptions (for example, a balance sheet in *run-off*, under *growth* assumption, or *constant* balance sheet).

The monitored time buckets for structural liquidity are as follows:

IY   2Y   3Y   4Y   5Y   7Y   10Y   15Y   20Y   30Y   Unspecified   Unredeemable

From a practical standpoint, the structural limits can be defined using the following formulas.

Structural Limit   *Gap ratio* between cash inflows and outflows beyond 12 months must be higher than the **threshold level** established by the board of directors (usually 100%).

$$\frac{\Sigma \, Cash \, Out \, T > 1Y + Equity}{\left(\Sigma \, Cash \, In \, T > 1Y\right)} \geq b\% \tag{2.12}$$

where $b\%$ is the threshold of structural ratio established by the board of directors. Taking into consideration the Basel III requirements related to the maintenance of the healthy balance between stable funding and medium long-term assets, this threshold is supposed to be above 100%.

Structural Warning 1   Gap ratio between cash inflows and outflows beyond 3 years must be higher than the **threshold level** (usually lower than 100%).

$$\frac{\Sigma \, Cash \, Out \, T > 3Y + Equity}{\left(\Sigma \, Cash \, In \, T > 3Y\right)} \geq c\% \tag{2.13}$$

where $c\%$ is the warning threshold level for the time buckets beyond 3 years. It is suggested, under a prudent approach, to keep it at or above 70%.

Structural Warning 2 Some banks set up additional warnings for time buckets beyond 5 years. For commercial banks it is common to see it at or above 60%.

$$\frac{\Sigma \, Cash \, Out \, T > 5Y + Equity}{(\Sigma \, Cash \, In \, T > 5Y)} \geq d\% \tag{2.14}$$

where $d\%$ is the warning threshold level for time buckets beyond 5 years. It is suggested, under a prudent approach, to keep it at or above 60%.

The gap indicators presented above are intended to maintain the consistency between the strategy set up to fund medium long-term assets and liabilities with the same maturity. A gap ratio value lower than those defined indicates that the amount of medium long-term assets funded by short-term liabilities is bigger than that established by the policy of the bank.

The profile of a *maturity ladder* depends on assumptions related to the future cash flows associated with both on- and off-balance sheet items. These assumptions are validated in line with the internal process and include:

- Amount of maturing liabilities that the bank may renegotiate or renew (known as *rollover* assumption).
- Behaviour of liabilities without deterministic maturity (for example, balance volatility of CASA).
- Possibility of early repayment of certain instruments (for example, loans with a prepayment option).
- Marketability of assets (investment portfolio) and the amount of liquidity presumably generated from their sale (haircuts).
- Off-balance sheet potential cash flows including the use of undrawn commitments to customers.

These specific assumptions are based on internal econometric and statistical models. In particular, for the current accounts and savings deposits modelling, a behavioural model is used to estimate the maturity profile of these items.

Table 2.2 shows the illustrative breakdown of items included in the detection of structural limits specifying the mapping rules provided for each compartment.

Maintaining a sustainable ratio between assets and liabilities for medium long-term obligations aims to avoid short-term funding pressure for current and future periods. This means that the management of the structural liquidity is closely related to:

- **Funds planning process** – aimed at defining the structural funding needs in the medium long term and integrated with the planning process of a bank.
- **Process of cash flows management** – strategic and short-term views simultaneously allow highlighting the interactions between the funding plan process and cash management and having a complete oversight of the liquidity risk exposure.

TABLE 2.2 Example for mapping of assumptions for the calibration of limits related to the structural liquidity.

		Categories		Model assumptions
Financial Statement items	Items with and without a contractual expiry date	Asset	Cash	Liquid and considered into *Counterbalancing Capacity*
		Asset	Liquidity portfolio	Liquid and considered into *Counterbalancing Capacity*
		Asset/Liability	Credits/Debts vs. banks: ■ mutual C/C, Central Bank reserve	Liquid and considered into *Counterbalancing Capacity*
		Asset/Liability	Credits/Debts vs. demand deposit customers	Defined on the result of statistical model – allocation is based on the behavioural assumptions
		Asset	Equity Investment/tangible assets/intangible assets and equity securities AFS	Irredeemable
		Asset	Tax assets (DTA)	Unspecified
		Asset	Other assets	Unspecified
		Liability	Tax liabilities	Unspecified
		Liability	Other liabilities	According to the residual maturity
		Liability	Equity	Irredeemable
		Asset	Haircuts on eligible instruments	Irredeemable
		Asset/Liability	Derivatives (Hedging + Trading without options)	According to the residual maturity
		Asset	Receivables from banks: deposits and other assets	According to the residual maturity
		Liability	Banks debts: deposits and other liabilities	According to the residual maturity
		Asset	Receivables from customers: other than demand assets	According to the residual maturity
		Liability	Payables to customers: deposits and other liabilities	According to the residual maturity
		Asset	NPLs	According to the expected repayment schedule. If an estimate is not available, then allocated to unredeemable time bucket
		Liability	Bonds debts	According to the residual maturity
	Off balance	Guaranteed lines, letter of credit, undrawn commitments, etc.		Basel III run off factor could be applied

Source: own elaboration.

THE ROLE OF FUNDS TRANSFER PRICING IN BANKS

The funds transfer pricing (FTP) process is the sum of polices and methodologies that banks apply to charge or credit products for the liquidity consumed or gathered during a bank's activity (see Figure 2.8).

Active balance sheet management through FTP should be a key priority for all banks that want to optimise resources such as capital and funding. There are several reasons why active and conscious balance sheet structure management has increased in importance, including scarcity of resources and the new regulatory landscape which sets minimum levels for funding structure and liquidity buffers. Therefore, the FTP framework is used as a tool to incentivise behaviour that helps to achieve a bank's goals and the fair pricing of interest rate and liquidity costs.

Banks must have a true and fair value and the FTP scheme has to be aligned to their strategic objectives through incentivising or subsidising businesses and activities which are aligned with the overall strategy. For this reason, the set up of the FTP framework needs to be an integrated part of the overall optimisation process.

This section introduces the main concepts of the FTP process and explains how it can be used in the optimisation process. Consequently, it walks the reader through the main balance sheet shaping techniques.

The basic concept behind FTP is that assets are charged their cost of funds which is credited to the bank's funding units. This is the foundation of matched maturity

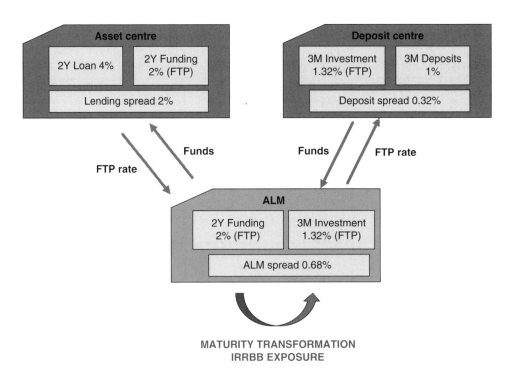

FIGURE 2.8 Maturity matched funds transfer pricing process.
Source: own elaboration.

funds transfer pricing (MMFTP). In this process, ALM (treasury) plays the role of 'a bank within a bank', which means it provides funds to the asset centre and charges the FTP rate for it. At the same time, it 'buys' funds from the liability centre and pays the FTP rate. As a result of this intermediation, ALM is left with all the mismatches from the interest rate risk and liquidity risk perspective and its main mandate consists of managing those mismatches. For this activity, it gets the spread differential between the FTP rate it charges to the Asset centre and the FTP rate it pays to the Liability centre. Additionally, ALM manages the *liquid asset buffer* (LAB) and, as such, it is supposed to boost the bank's profitability through the appropriate investment strategies.

In some banks, ALM has its own P&L account. This is the case when it acts as a business unit with a clear budget objective. The achievement of those objectives represents the key performance metric for the treasurer (or head of ALM department). The ALM account is split between the IRR book, the liquidity book, and the liquid asset portfolio management book. The ALM system will split those accounts to provide an overview of the performance in terms of effectiveness of strategies applied. Figure 2.9 provides an example.

Having the picture of ALM working as a bank within a bank in mind, it is simple to see why FTP can be easily used as a tool to shape the banking book. If there is a need to gather more funds from, for example, the retail current accounts then ALM can potentially increase the FTP rate paid for this particular product. This additional mark up on the FTP rate will boost the product profitability and encourage the business line to increase its share in the total funding structure. Conversely, charging more for a certain asset class will act as a disincentive for the business unit, decreasing the product's share in the total asset base. This simple mechanism forms a strategic tool for a bank to get rid of unprofitable products and to retain only the profitability boosters. However, lack of transparency in the framework could turn to be value detrimental to the institution; therefore, a proper target operating model around FTP is an imperative.

			Jan 14	Feb 14	Mar 14	Apr 14	May 14	June 14	July 14	Aug 14
VOLUMES	ASSETS	Liquidity run-off	100	100	100	100	100	100	100	100
		Repricing run-off	100	100	100	100	100	100	100	100
	LIABILITIES	Liquidity run-off	−100	−100	−100	−100	−100	−100	0	0
		Repricing run-off	−100	−100	−100	0	0	0	0	0
					INTEREST RATE RISK EXPOSURE ←			LIQUIDITY RISK EXPOSURE		
Interest Rate Risk		Open Interest Risk Position	0	0	0	−100	−100	−100	−100	−100
		Bucket exposure	0	0	0	−8.2	−8.4	−8.2	−8.4	−8.4
Liquidity Risk		Open Liquidity Risk Position	0	0	0	0	0	0	−100	−100
		Bucket exposure	0	0	0	0	0	0	−8.4	−8.4
Sensitivities		Shock on risk free parameter 0.20%	0	0	0	0.016	0.017	0.016	0.017	0.017
		Shock on liquidity spread 0.60%	0	0	0	0	0	0	0.017	0.017

FIGURE 2.9 Illustrative example of split between ALM accounts and NII sensitivity resulting from open positions.
Source: own elaboration

Thus, any incentives and subsidies need to be made very transparent and come on top of a 'true and fair view' of the bank's liquidity costs. Highlighting the importance of FTP as a strategic tool for balance sheet shaping purposes it is necessary to touch base also on other FTP objectives.

In fact, FTP is the means by which a bank's overall net interest income can be split into originating units and subunits, thus enabling the bank's management to perform an effective planning, monitoring, and control cycle (Widowitz et al. 2014). The FTP rate is composed of several components, which basically represent the transference of the interest rate and liquidity risk from the business units to the treasury/ALM, to be managed centrally and keep the business units immune to financial risks. This risk transference can be clearly seen in Figure 2.8 (ALM is left with IRRBB and liquidity mismatches). As a result, it separates the net interest income components arising from the client business margins, interest rate positioning, and liquidity maturity transformation. It is an extremely powerful tool which is deeply rooted in any divisional P&L or profit centre calculation See Figure 2.10).

The FTP framework should cover the following aspects:

- The default FTP and internal transfer pricing (ITP) curves to use and the discretion around the adoption of the default methodology.
- The interest rate risk profiling for contractual maturity and non-defined maturity products/items:
    a) fixed rate products;
    b) floating rate products;
    c) fixed or floating rate loans against committed facilities;
    d) core, non-core, and price sensitivity;

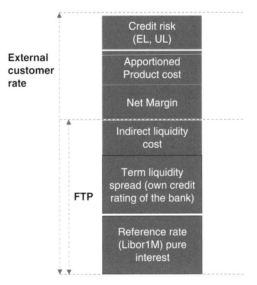

FTP building blocks approach

FIGURE 2.10 Funds transfer pricing components.
Source: own elaboration.

e) index-linked asset hedges;

f) products with early redemption optionality;

g) investment term of equity deployed.

- The liquidity risk profiling for all products.
- The cost of liquidity (COL) to transfer regulatory indirect liquidity costs, for example LCR and NSFR.

There are at least four elements that need to be included in the integrated FTP framework. The first element consists of the definition of the framework for all products which represent the sources of liquidity cost, both based on the deterministic cash flows (known as term liquidity) and for contingent liquidity arising from the stochastic cash flows. It should include all relevant balance sheet and off-balance sheet positions that need to be considered from a liquidity and interest rate risk perspective. The FTP landscape should include all products which represent sources of liquidity cost, both based on the deterministic cash flows (known as term liquidity) and contingent liquidity arising from the stochastic cash flows. The FTP rate should be allocated to these products based on their financial characteristics; for example, both floating and fixed rate loans get charged the liquidity premium which depends on the length of time for those funds to be consumed. The same point is valid for liabilities which have recognised liquidity value based on their liquidity tenor.

The second one – and the most important one in the author's view – is the FTP curve set up. This is driven by the underlying principle that assets get charged by their cost of funds, which is credited to the bank's funding units, and the base of this calculation is the FTP curve. The FTP methodology is based on a gross marginal cost approach, which reflects the opportunity cost to fund one unit of new asset volume in the market; however, this approach should be adjusted in order to reflect the funding characteristics of the balance sheet. Where a liquid interbank yield curve is available (at which ALM is able to deal at the margin) then the choice of that FTP yield curve is clear. The default treatment is to use the benchmark rate identified by a bank. The FTP rate should be applied both to assets and liabilities, i.e. there is no internal spread on a matched position basis in ALM since this is FTP methodology which is based on the matched maturity transfer pricing (MMFTP) methodology. In a case where there is no practical interbank yield curve, then transactability should drive how the curve is set. In most instances, this will mean the use of government paper/CD yields, with interpolation.

Table 2.3 shows a number of curve construction methodologies as a function of different scenarios.

The shape of the medium long FTP curve could be determined by referencing to a bank's senior debt issuance levels by tenor. However, in some cases, in order to steer the growth of the balance sheet, the FTP curve is dampened, i.e. the medium long-term curve set up is lowered by a factor so that only a certain portion of the bank's funding spread paid in the wholesale market is charged to assets.

For example, the medium-term curve rates could be set in such a way that rates are limited to some extent by, for example, the 12-month FTP levels. Thus, the medium-term curve rates should not be set lower than the lower of 12-month FTP levels and the senior debt issuance level at the respective tenor. The proportion of senior debt cost included in the medium long-term FTP benchmark curve is determined by a factor set by ALCOs.

TABLE 2.3 FTP curve construction methodologies.

	Curve scenario	Examples of the curve choice
1	Deep, liquid interbank yield curve is available	This curve should be used
2	Interbank yield curves are available, but liquidity may not be consistently available at all required points	This curve should be used with a process of interpolation
3	Only curve available is derived from government securities	The government securities curve should be used with a process of interpolation
4	Where there is no effective curve at all	In the extreme case that no external reference rates are available, ALCO may apply a simplified methodology of averaging the weighted average customer loan and deposit rates for use as the FTP rate

Source: own elaboration

On some occasions a bank's senior management may decide to introduce an incentive premium (IP) on specific assets or liabilities with an offsetting charge on specific assets or liabilities to achieve precisely defined, short-term balance sheet objectives. There are very precise rules that need to be followed when introducing the IP scheme. In particular, it should be recognised/charged out to businesses, it should only represent a temporary tool for steering, it should not seek to compensate for regulatory liquidity value, and it should not replace the role of the curve in establishing marginal funding costs. This is because the objective of the IP scheme is to achieve a specific short-term balance sheet objective, i.e. subsidise a specific product to protect the bank's liquidity, or to manage a regulatory ratio. The IP application must be compliant with the FTP policy in terms of the duration and transparency of the funding cost with a strong governance process around it.

There are different solutions for the dynamic FTP curve construction, and, in the view of the author, there is no best practice with reference to it. Setting the right curve is a very bank-specific and individual task. However, the importance of this element in the FTP framework needs to be stressed, as the curve construct should be aligned with the strategic objectives (decided on by the senior management) and support the business model of the institution. The first rule, to achieve this goal, is transparency in the curve setting and a deep understanding of the specifics of the balance sheet (target funding base and the extent of maturity transformation run by the bank). Defining the FTP methodology is a very broad topic (see Figure 2.11).

Pricing of Different Products in the Banking Book

One of the central tenets of the FTP framework is to transfer liquidity risk from the business to ALM to manage. Furthermore, FTP should cover all material business activities, incorporating all relevant liquidity costs, benefits, and risks, and allowing management to give appropriate incentives for managing liquidity risk. As such, pricing of products should follow the following rules:

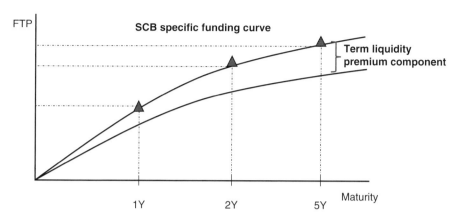

FIGURE 2.11 Example of the specific FTP curve.
Source: own elaboration.

1. FTP should attribute liquidity and funding cost or benefits to the businesses and products to enable appropriate business decisions and to allow ALM to manage the liquidity and funding risks in an effective and consistent manner.
2. Liquidity transfer pricing should consider both business-as-usual and stressed costs. Hence the liquidity profiling for FTP purposes should consider the liquidity cash flow under normal business conditions and under liquidity stress conditions.
3. Cost of maintaining a liquidity reserve (or LAB) should be allocated to the source of liquidity risk. The liquidity reserve or liquid asset requirement can be driven by internal or regulatory stress parameters including LCR or internal stress testing (e.g. survival horizon).
4. Regular review to ensure the liquidity transfer pricing is appropriately calibrated.

The differences between behavioural liquidity tenor and the behavioural interest rate tenor should be captured under the FTP framework. The recent Basel III requirements for liquidity pose significant challenges on banks, as it is still an open issue how to integrate the cost to comply with Basel III into the FTP framework. There are clear additional costs resulting from the implementation of the new regulatory requirements which need to be recognised and charged back to businesses in the revised FTP process. Furthermore, there is a need to enhance the FTP framework in order to effectively transfer interest rate risk and liquidity costs to the central unit. Inefficient FTP processes can lead to margin compression and loss in competitiveness of a bank. This book proposes FTP profiling as a possible solution to overcome both issues. It provides a methodological overview on how to calculate the FTP rate to reflect both interest rate risk and full liquidity costs. In addition, it shows how the liquidity profiling can be structured to include both the contingency costs and liquidity value the product is generating or consuming. This is particularly important for products which do not have deterministic cash flows, such as current accounts. The FTP rate, in this case, needs to reflect the behaviour of the product cohort both from the interest rate risk and liquidity perspective.

For example, the transfer price for the revolving credit facility is calculated according to two approaches. The simplified approach consists of the allocation of the FTP rate to the drawn part of the product, in line with its drawn amount and its tenor. For the undrawn portion, the contingency liquidity costs are allocated. Although simple, this approach presents some limitations, such as the necessity of generating a large number of funding tickets that have to be adjusted upon each change of the drawn amount. Furthermore, the treasury/ALM neglects the fact that many short-term draws are rolled over and are actually drawn until the final maturity of the facility.

In order to overcome limitations coming from the simplified approach, an alternative is to carry out the behavioural analysis of portfolios of the revolving facility and identify the core and volatile part of the product. The core part, which is supposed to be drawn until the final maturity, is charged by the term liquidity cost equal to the final maturity of the facility. Meanwhile, the volatile part is short term with a short-term fluctuating usage. For the uncertainty of the volatile part, the contingent liquidity, for which the costs should be allocated to the product, needs to be held. Behavioural analysis is also performed for other items, such as current or savings accounts.

One of the main objectives of the target operating model for the FTP is to ensure that transparency is the main principle in the FTP framework. To achieve this transparency, interest rate risk and liquidity risk need to be separated into different portfolios within Treasury/ALM. As a basic rule, the banking book results can be split into the following components:

- Result of interest rate positioning and interest rate maturity transformation.
- Result from liquidity maturity transformation.
- Result from the investment book management (credit spread risk management).

Transparency and simplicity in the FTP framework should be an unquestionable driver in the definition of the target operating model, as only clear methodology rules shared by every single participant in the FTP process can lead to the achievement of the strategic objectives of a bank and the correct shaping of the balance sheet. Another important aspect in the FTP governance and framework is the oversight of the incentive premium scheme and of the management overlays. A Prudential Regulation Authority (PRA) cross-firm review of the FTP practices at major UK banks revealed important issues in banks' internal transfer pricing policies and framework. One of the major issues, underlined in the PRA's review, was that banks were not separating the management overlays from their funding curve. Some banks were found to be applying different cost of funding curves to new loans and deposits to incentivise loan origination and deposit-gathering simultaneously. The PRA view is that this is a vulnerability in the FTP framework of the bank, as dampening practice skews business incentives and makes it less clear what the performance is for individual products before and after any management overlay. An important point was made that strategic decisions need to be made acknowledging the true economics of business, and not unwittingly as a result of the inappropriate internal pricing methodologies (Cadamagnani et al. 2015). Given that the internal FTP methodologies play a key part in profit allocation within a bank and influence business lines' activities, a robust FTP regime is a must. If funding costs are underestimated, business lines offer customers cheaper loans and increase funding volumes in the mistaken belief that they are profitable. If funding costs are overestimated, business lines may mistakenly require higher customer rates to be perceived as profitable.

As already mentioned, those tools are powerful and for this reason their implementation and inclusion in the FTP framework should be well governed, documented, and transparent.

This is why the product pricing (asset *all in* rate and deposit customer rate) is not a random activity. It is based on predetermined principles aligned with the strategic objectives of a financial institution and according to transparent rules and methodologies. The product pricing is always based on the FTP curve, which acts as an internal product price benchmark.

Behaviouralisation Concept in FTP

The introduction of Basel III liquidity metrics, namely the liquidity coverage ratio (LCR) and the net stable funding ratio (NSFR), surely has introduced complexity into the FTP framework, as the methodology as to how to embed those costs into it still remains still an open issue for many banks. There are no regulatory guidelines in this respect, nor is there a best practice in the market. Consequently, banks need to do their homework and revamp the FTP methodology. From the other side, this clear challenge creates an opportunity for banks to enhance their FTP framework to incorporate regulatory cost as part of an integrated approach and to grow the right balance sheet in an increasingly regulated external environment.

The overall objective of such an exercise is to construct a framework that is better defined, simple to understand, makes internal drivers of the bank's net interest margin (NIM) more transparent and less volatile, and appropriately considers regulatory liquidity costs. The main challenge of the inclusion of LCR and NSFR requirements into the FTP framework consists, in the author's view, in the fact that banks already have the stress test metrics and scenarios for liquidity which, in many cases, are already included in FTP. Consequently, there will be a necessity to align those metrics with LCR in the first place. There are three main enhancements which need to be made on the existing FTP framework in order to align the FTP model with Basel III:

1. Introduce a precise and integrated regulatory and internal stress view, for example LCR and short-term liquidity metrics.
2. Embed the NSFR cost into the FTP framework.
3. Establish an internal price that combines the transference of liquidity and interest rate risk as well as an allocation of cost arising from liquidity regulation.

With these enhancements, the new FTP framework will provide transparency on how internal rates are applied and allow the bank to see its all-in cost of funding and provide greater visibility over its NIM. One of the solutions to achieve this is an approach to liquidity profiling which aims to capture the stress liquidity assumptions and liquidity behavioural assumption for various products and client segments.

Stress liquidity assumption (either internal stress liquidity risk view or regulatory view) reflects the customer behaviour or product characteristic under the stress scenario(s). The net stress outflow will determine how many liquid assets (or high-quality liquid assets HQLA) a bank is required to hold in order to survive under stress conditions. Therefore, holding liquid assets can be costly (for example, in case of a big difference between cost of funding and opportunity cost). ALM bears this cost for the bank; consequently, in principle, FTP will have to allocate this cost back to business in order to reflect the full and true liquidity cost of doing business.

The stress liquidity portion will profile at the short-term stress tenor, for example Overnight, 1-Month or 2-Month, or 30-Day LCR stress outflow horizon (or 30-Day in the name-specific stress) and 60-Day in the market-wise stress horizon. Profiling the stress portion at shorter tenor will reflect a lower liquidity valuation for liability (net) outflow.

Stress liquidity assumption will be adopted from either the internal stress liquidity risk view or regulatory view. Internal stress liquidity risk view is based on a bank's internal stress testing survival horizon, which models combine (name specific and market wide) stress scenarios for a period of, for example, 2 months. The regulatory view will refer to Basel III LCR assumption or local regulatory requirement for 30-day stress. The guiding principle, in this approach, is to use the more binding metric between the internal stress liquidity risk view and regulatory view. It applies at country level, product level, or client/segment level and depends on the availability of sufficiently granular data.

The stable liquidity assumption (not in the stress scenario), on the other hand, reflects the customer behaviour or product characteristic on a medium-term time horizon. It is looking at the liquidity behaviouralisation aspect which can be linked to the bank's structural liquidity risk appetite, stable funding profile, medium-term assets composition, maturity transformation, and funding resource allocation. There is an internal view and a regulatory view as well. The internal view comes from the internal balance sheet modelling, such as the core model of non-maturing products, actuarial study for loans (like mortgages), or the bank's assets recovery assumption. The regulatory view is referring to NSFR assumptions – available stable factor (ASF) for liabilities and required stable factor for assets (RSF).

Corporate Current Account	Stress Portion	Residual Portion	Stable Portion
Portion	25%	5%	70%
Tenor	1M	3M	3Y

The stable liquidity portion, under this approach, is profiled to medium-term tenor which is equal or higher than 1 year.

For liabilities, a 1-year point is considered to best represent the stable balance modelling for structural liquidity risk measures (like NSFR).

The extension beyond 1 year for non-maturing liabilities is considered, in this approach, as an incentive reward for balance sheet needs.

Illustration

A. NMD liabilities

The liability is recognised with the liquidity value equal to 2-year tenor on the FTP curve (behaviouralised tenor for the product). This value also includes the regulatory cost that the product is bearing due to the liquidity buffer which needs to be held against the outflow under a stress scenario (seen as the stress portion). Given that the NSFR provides the instruction related to the stability factor over 1 year, the 3-year tenor can be considered as the additional liquidity value the ALM is going to recognise for the high-quality source of funding this product represents (see Table 2.4).

The total liquidity value of this product is equal to the blended rate:

25%@1M FTP rate + 5%@3M FTP rate + 70%@3Y FTP rate.

TABLE 2.4 Example of FTP liquidity profiling for a liability.

LCR outflow assumption = 25%
NSFR ASF Factor   = 50%
Internal Core Model %   = 70%

Source: own elaboration.

TABLE 2.5 FTP liquidity profiling for an asset.

LCR inflow assumption		=	0% (assume residual tenor >1M)
NSFR RSF Factor		=	65%
Behavioural maturity (including prepayments)		=	3-year
Mortgage	Stress portion	Residual portion	Stable portion
Portion	0%	35%	65%
Tenor	-	1Y	3Y (Average life)

Source: own elaboration.

The same illustration for an asset, for example mortgages, is shown in the Table 2.5.

B. Assets: Residential Mortgages

This product is charged with the liquidity costs which correspond to a 2-year tenor of the FTP curve (35%@1Y + 65%@3Y). Under the assumption that it is not going to expire over the next 30 days' time horizon, its behaviouralisation consists of the split between the non-liquid part with 3-year tenor (RSF) and the residual part with the liquidity tenor equal to 1 year.

As already mentioned, liquidity profiling is meant to reflect the liquidity cost (if assets) or liquidity value (if liability). However, the FTP rate needs to also reflect the financial characteristics of the product from the interest rate risk perspective. For example, if the product reprices in line with EURIBOR 3 M, then the interest rate risk profiling needs to be the same, i.e. EURIBOR 3 M. For bullet fixed rate products, the interest rate risk profiling will be based on the tenor of the risk-free curve which corresponds to the maturity of the product.

The FTP profiling becomes more complex when behavioural products are concerned, for example, current accounts/savings account (CASA). The FTP profiling has to include both the interest rate part and adjustment by the product's liquidity value. CASA interest rate profiling is always composed of two parts, i.e. the volatile portion of the balance, which won't stay within the bank for the long term, thus it is modelled as a portion which reprices on the O/N basis (in line with the BCBS 368 requirements), and the stable portion. The stable portion is considered to be either risk sensitive, i.e. reprices in line with the market rate, or a core part, which is non-sensitive to the interest rate movements and therefore could be seen as a long-term funding with rate at 0%. This split has to be reflected in the FTP profiling. The complexity appears when the interest rate profiling is overlaid with the liquidity profiling as the total FTP rate includes internal/regulatory stressed test view (contingent liquidity cost), term liquidity value of this product (the product's stability from the liquidity perspective), and IRR behavioural model (product's rate sensitivity and its balance stability).

The FTP behaviouralisation is a methodology that attempts to capture the full (and behavioural) interest rate risk and liquidity cost/value of the product. The correct transference of interest rate risk and liquidity risk from ALM to business units is especially important in profit allocation within the bank, as it directly influences business line activities. If funding costs are underestimated, business lines offer customers cheaper loans and increase funding volumes in mistaken belief that they are profitable. If funding costs are overestimated, business lines may mistakenly require higher customer rates to be perceived as profitable (Lubinska 2017).

Additionally, the liquidity profiling should encompass the contingent liquidity costs, i.e. those which are driven by uncertainty and stress situation. Under stress, customers behaviour can change radically; therefore, banks needs to hold a liquidity buffer which protects them against unexpected cash outflows.

However, as already mentioned, holding a liquidity buffer is expensive as the cost of funding them usually exceeds generated return. This contingent liquidity cost has to be allocated back to business.

Prior to Basel III liquidity requirements, the indirect liquidity cost was allocated on a separate basis, for example, once a month through a separate process. FTP profiling allows this cost to be included into the FTP rate and to be charged back to the business upon origination of the transaction.

Finally, it is important to keep in mind challenges faced by ALM/treasury in light of the LCR and NSFR requirements, as the recognition of these additional costs, resulting from the implementation of the new regulatory expectations, is an imperative for the more sophisticated FTP framework. For many banks, the question of how to integrate the cost to comply with LCR and NSFR ratios into FTP still remains an open issue. The liquidity FTP behaviouralisation represents one of the possible solutions which can be adopted to solve the problem.

The objective of the Chapter 2 has been to provide an overview of common market practice related to the measuring and managing of the main risks in the banking book, i.e. interest rate risk and liquidity risk. It describes techniques, which are still commonly used in commercial banks, to understand the extent in advance of a bank's exposure to changes in the factors, such as interest rates in the market, funding costs, and availability of liquidity in the market. The detailed analysis of those metrics is driven by the intent to inform the reader about the methodological approach adopted in the construction of the constraints functions used in the optimisation model.

The section on FTP highlights the importance of this process in banks and the evolution it is undergoing in a modern banking. Only recently, the possibility of balance sheet shaping through FTP techniques, such as application of FTP curve dampening, the incentive scheme, and management overlays has been examined in detail and is now receiving due recognition from the regulator and from the market practitioners.

CHAPTER 3

Customer Behaviour and Its Impact on Interest Rate and Liquidity Risk

SIGNIFICANCE AND IMPACT OF BEHAVIOURAL ISSUES IN THE BANKING BOOK

To analyse behaviour, banks combine statistical information with some assumptions. An interesting characteristic of behaviour assumption is that it does not always follow market conditions. In some cases, clients or counterparties behave contrary to their own interest but in ways that are aligned with their psychological demands. In other cases, behaviour is driven by rumours or loss of confidence in the financial institutions. The impact of behavioural issues can be seen in terms of both interest rate and liquidity risk exposure.

One of the biggest challenges of ALM is the management of the interest rate risk associated with customer products with an undefined interest rate commitment. Even the regulator demands a documented and validated approach to how the interest rate commitments are derived and managed in the bank (Enthofer and Haas 2016). In products with undetermined maturity, interest rate risk that is not fully transferred to ALM/ Treasury causes significant residual risk left within the business, and therefore earnings and equity volatility, which has to be monitored and managed by ALCO.

Balance sheet items require behavioural assumptions in order to manage the interest rate risk correctly, as raising interest rates may reduce the net interest margin given the banks' limited ability to raise client rates in line with the market rates, especially when market rates rise to very high levels. Early redemption of assets, if not accounted for in the hedging strategies of the bank, cause overhedging because the number of swap payers is higher than the actual amount of fixed rate assets. Consequently, the bank has to adjust hedging positions and, in the meantime, is left open to time bucket sensitivity and negative impact in terms of the $PV01$ metric. The prepayment pattern will change as a function of the interest rate movements. In the case of a low interest rate environment, i.e. higher differential between the committed interest rate paid by the client and external market rates, the prepayment events tend to increase as clients want to refinance their loans in order to pay lower rates. The early redemption of mortgages (prepayments) and withdrawal of deposits have an important impact on both the repricing gap analysis and refixing gap analysis.

Another important source of the interest rate risk driven by behavioural assumptions is pipeline risk. It is driven by the time difference between agreement of the mortgage product rate and drawdown of balance and the consequent risk that repricing in interest rates move, compressing the margin of the product. To reduce the impact of this risk the pipeline is typically pre-hedged on the basis of expected volumes. Expected volumes are modelled using observed experience with management judgement overlay-based factors, such as where the product is priced relative to the market. There is the model risk that expected volumes differ due to incorrect assumptions. There is also the option risk that customer behaviour changes due to changes in interest rate, e.g. take up is higher if rates have risen or less if rates have fallen.

There are four main types of behaviour directly linked to liquidity:

1) Drawings.

   This is related to the items of the banking book that are without deterministic maturity, for example current and savings accounts. The behavioural aspects consist of the contractual possibility given to the customer to withdraw the entire balance of their accounts at short notice or with no prior notice at all. Under normal risk conditions, the behaviour of 'cash in' and 'cash out' is defined based on statistical analysis. Numbers identified through this analysis are considered the expected behaviours of the clients and applied in the liquidity models of the bank. It is well known that under stressed conditions the counterparties tend to withdraw more money than during normal times – consequently additional scenarios must be made for mapping unexpected behaviour of clients (Blair and Akkizidis 2011).

2) Prepayments.

   This phenomenon represents the right of the counterparty to prepay a remaining obligation before the contractual maturity date. In terms of liquidity, such behaviour will cancel out all expected cash flows just after the prepayment option is exercised. Financial institutions use historical data on past behaviour to model prepayment behaviour under normal and stress conditions respectively; i.e., when counterparties are suffering from liquidity shortfall they tend to prepay less and to defer the payments they do make as long as possible. Another example of behavioural phenomenon is the existence of the option where the borrower draws down the loan facility gradually in accordance with liquidity needs. The sum of total payouts is agreed but not the exact payment dates. Under normal conditions, institutions estimate the payouts based on project plans and statistical observations. However, in drawdown cases, interest payments are not always defined in advance. Consequently, the expected pattern of 'cash ins' depends on future market conditions. Under stress conditions, construction projects may slow down or even be postponed and thus the expected drawdowns may be delayed. Hence there is a clear impact on the bank's future liquidity (Blair and Akkizidis 2011).

The behavioural assumptions for balance sheet items are key drivers for the interest rate risk profile in the banking book and hence ultimately drive management actions. The behavioural assumptions can be based on historical observations, expert judgement, and industry standards. An ALM department has to strike a fine balance between risk measures that lose effectiveness if the *behaviouralisation* process, which consists of the allocation of the average life to the product without contractual maturity and analysis of its stability, is too simplistic, and those that lose effectiveness as the process has been over-engineered.

MODELLING OF CUSTOMERS' DEPOSITS – LIABILITIES SIDE

Many banks worldwide are funded with non-maturing deposits, and the way the product is modelled has significant implications in terms of the exposure to the interest rate risk, liquidity risk, and Funds Transfer Pricing (FTP). The whole picture of risks a bank is running can change, driven by changes in customer behaviour. For this reason, an understanding of the main underlying factors is of crucial importance. Usually, balance fluctuations are a function of multiple factors, including the macroeconomic environment as well as the product pricing structure. Presumably, by increasing the rate paid to the consumer, inflows of deposits will in turn increase. The analysis of the customer–financial institution relationship indicates that there is certainly positive correlation, which may exhibit a linear or even exponential relationship over a particular interest rate interval. Consequently, it is the main objective of the bank deposit pricing committees to understand the rate–balance elasticity equation (Soulellis 2014). The purpose of this chapter is to present two different methods which have been used in international banks to determine the structure of liabilities with undetermined maturity – current and saving accounts. The first, common approach, is based on the application of the regression model that predicts the likelihood of the event happening. The regression model yields a set of parameter variables (and their associated estimates) that would feature the relationship to the dependent variables.

Regardless of the methodology used, the first step in current account modelling is to apply the correct segmentation scheme. The main goal of product segmentation is to preserve the underlying balance and rate characteristics of products/product subdivisions for the full deposit modelling, while also ensuring a minimum threshold of materiality and simplicity. The segmentation process seeks to reach a balance between three ideals:

- Homogeneity: The balances within each segment should behave in a similar manner with respect to balance volatility, average life, and rate administration.
- Simplicity: The number of segments should be kept as small as possible, while capturing differences in behaviour.
- Materiality: Each segment should represent a significant portion of the portfolio.

It should be noted that, all else equal, the first criterion calls for more segments while the second and third criteria call for fewer segments. The 'sweet spot' is to divide the portfolio into the fewest number of classes while capturing major differences in behaviour.

In a majority of cases the portfolio can be optimally segmented along three main dimensions:

- Geography: Products from different geographies should not be examined together since the economic and regulatory conditions tend to differ between countries.
- Product type: Only products of the same type should be examined together, i.e. savings products should not be examined together with checking accounts.
- Currency: Products with different currencies should not be examined together.

The segmentation process requires information about a product's characteristics, contractual specifications, history, information on whether it is a new product or whether it is a run-off product, etc. Along with this information, joint historical evolution of the balance and interest rate paid data should be considered to come up with the segmentation of the products. Once an intuitive and appropriate segmentation scheme has been defined and established, the modelling process may begin. The overall goal is to forecast the future trajectory of the liabilities so that the volatility of balances may be estimated. One simplistic way to estimate balance volatility is to model it singularly as a function of time. Balance volatility analysis splits the balances as core balances, which stay with the bank under almost all economic conditions, and non-core balances, which tend to leave the bank either idiosyncratically or with the movements of macroeconomic factors.

The balance volatility model determines what level of balances will remain with the bank in the long term, given a level of confidence. As an output, the balance volatility model divides the balances into two portions: core balances which remain with the bank under almost all market conditions, and non-core balances which fluctuate over time due to market and idiosyncratic reasons and are typically characterised as short term. There are multiple approaches to modelling the non-maturity deposits and each bank follows its own approach. Some banks underline the importance of the simplicity of the model; others prefer sophisticated approaches using stochastic interest rates and credit spreads. The complexity of the methodological approach is often commensurate with the size of the financial institutions and its business model.

This section presents two simple methodological approaches followed by sample banks in Europe.

One method of performing the analysis of core vs. non-core balances consists in application of a growth-based regression model. In this approach, the model fits the product balances to find both a trend line (exponential, linear, or logarithmic) and the variation of actual balances around the trend line. It then sets the trend line at a certain confidence level. The confidence level should be set by the management depending on the risk appetite of the bank.

The following section describes the exponential model. Under this model the product balances are modelled to fit balances to an exponential curve of the form:

$$Balance = B_0 e^{rt} \tag{3.1}$$

where

B_0 represents the initial balance and r denotes the fixed growth rate. Obviously, this simplified approach ignores the fact that, in practice, the growth rate of balances is not constant over time but depends on the different, both internal and external, factors (for example interest rate and product pricing).

The exponential model can be converted to a linear relation through the log function:

$$ln(Balance) = ln(B_0) + rt \tag{3.2}$$

A regression model is utilised to compute the growth rate of the natural logarithm of the balances, and the standard error of the estimate, σ_{Fit}.

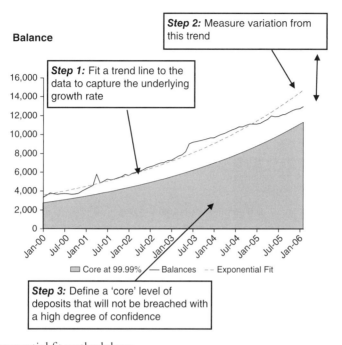

FIGURE 3.1 Exponential fit methodology.
Source: own elaboration based on the methodology applied by a number of banks based in Europe and the US.

To ensure that the probability of core balances dropping below the actual balances is minimal, the fitted equation is lowered with some multiple of standard deviation (see Figure 3.1). Approximately 99.9% corresponds to a 3.1 standard deviation shift in balances for a normal distribution. The growth rate is decreased by $n * \sigma$, or 3.1 times the standard deviation, to decrease the chance of the total balance level falling below the core level to 0.1% of the time, or approximately one month in every 83 years. The resulting core balance equation is:

$$Balance_{Core} = B_0 e^{rt - n\sigma_{Fit}} \tag{3.3}$$

In cases where the exponential fit function results in a very small R^2, implying that the fit is very poor or the fit for the last 12 months is poor, the usage of a different model should be taken into consideration.

The core percentage for a given fit equation is calculated as the average of the last 12 months:

$$Balance_{Core} / Balance_{Fit} \ ratio$$

By the virtue of the exponential fit, this core percentage is fixed for every month. The core percentage number is converted to a core amount by considering the balance behaviour of the last 12 months. The core amount is calculated with the following equation:

$$Core = Core\% \ x \ min \ (Balance_{last \ month}, Balance_{average \ from \ last \ 12 \ months}) \tag{3.4}$$

This equation introduces a level of conservatism to the core amount. If the balances are declining, the core percentage is multiplied by the balance of the last month; if the balances are increasing, core percentage is multiplied by the average of the balances of the last 12 months. The remaining balances not identified as core are defined as non-core, which are then tested for further decomposition as volatile and sensitive through sensitivity analysis:

$$Balance_{NONCORE} = Balance_{ACTUAL} - Balance_{CORE} \qquad (3.5)$$

Another approach consists of the calculation of the monthly relative returns for each business day as an equation:

$$M_i = ((X_i - X_{i-30})/X_{i-30}) * 100 \qquad (3.6)$$

where:

M is the computed relative change between months (expressed in percentage terms);
X is the product balance for the given reporting date (expressed in absolute terms).

Subsequently, *monthly volatility* (MV) is computed. This is done through ordering all monthly returns from the highest percentage balance increase through the highest percentage balance decrease. The 95th percentile worst decline in balance is taken and represents the volume which the bank considers to flow out of the portfolio over 1 month at a 95% confidence level. Obviously, the confidence level is decided by the management team and represents the risk appetite of the bank.

The non-core portion is calculated by annualising the monthly volatility. This is done by multiplying MV by the square root of time (as MV is annualised then a 12-month time interval is used). The core % is the difference between 100% of the portfolio and the computed non-core %.

$$Non\text{-}Core\ \% = 95^{th}\ percentile\ of\ monthly\ returns * sqrt\ (12) \qquad (3.7)$$

$$Core\ \% = 100\ \% - Non\text{-}Core\ \% \qquad (3.8)$$

In order to obtain the *core* amount the core % is multiplied by the lower of the last one month average or last three month average balance (in absolute terms) in the historical data series of the relevant cohort.

$$Core\ Amount = Core\ \% * min\ (1\text{-}month\ average\ balance\ of\ the\ cohort,$$
$$3\text{-}month\ average\ balance\ of\ the\ cohort) \qquad (3.9)$$

Rate sensitivity analysis captures the repricing behaviour of the product; it explains the changes in the product rate with the changes in the market rates. Characterisation of administered rates for deposit products ascertains the significance of market rate changes on the rates paid by the bank. By modelling the behaviour of interest rates paid relative to market rates, a better understanding of repricing behaviour and the sensitivity of interest expenses to market rates can be gained, i.e. how rates paid to customers vary with market conditions. This determines the effective duration and value of deposits. Rate sensitivity modelling is a key aspect of FTP in determining which assets the bank can match with minimal risk.

The interest rate paid to indeterminate maturity products' depositors is generally a combination of one or more market rates, and an idiosyncratic 'fixed' component. The repricing frequency for the market-driven component is simply the maturity associated with that rate. The fixed component is assumed to have a repricing frequency equal to the duration, i.e. in line with the observed core/volatile split. For example, if the core part of the balances has the duration of 5 years it is assumed to reprice after 5 years. On the other hand, the volatile part, which is assumed to outflow after day 1, is assumed to reprice O/N.

The interest expenses are regressed with key market rates to determine the repricing sensitivity of balances (pass-through rate). Rate sensitivity analysis requires regression of the changes in the administered rates on the changes in the various market rates. It is also possible that administered rates are driven by the market rates with a lag, e.g. changes in the 3-month rate in June 2019 might have an effect on the changes in the administered rates in August 2019 (2 months' lag). In order to determine which of the market rates explain the changes in the rates paid by the bank, a multiple regression is employed. Regression analysis forms an equation with multiple explanatory variables which jointly explain the changes in the administered rates. In addition, it forces all the independent variables to contribute to this explanatory power beyond some threshold. This threshold is determined by the significance level which can be set to be 95% in the calculations. The mechanics of the regression equation is explained in Figure 3.2.

It is very likely that more than one significant regression equation can be formed that explains the changes in administered rates with the changes in the market rates. For most of the products, the most significant equation is the one that captures the repricing behaviour.

Coefficients of this regression equation tell us what percentage of the portfolio reprices with the associated market rate.

For example, given the following regression equation,

$$\Delta \ Product \ rate = 14\% \ of \ \Delta \ EURIBOR \ 3 \ M + 25\% \ of \ \Delta \ EURIBOR \ 1 \ M \quad (3.10)$$

the repricing behaviour tells us that 14% of the portfolio reprices with the 3 M rate, 25% of the portfolio reprices with 1M rate, and the remaining 61% of the portfolio is not rate sensitive.

In order to estimate the economic life of non-maturing deposit (NMD) products, banks perform an analysis of the decay profile of the portfolio over a certain time horizon (for the sake of the statistical significance minimum, 2 years of data is required). The average life modelling assigns a life to the product by tracking the closing behaviour of the customers' accounts. This can be done through tracking the decay in the number of accounts or through decay of balances. When data is available, tracking the decay of balances is preferred and that which is calculated by tracking the decaying number of accounts is usually used for sanity checking purposes.

The analysis of the decay profile can be done through the following approach:

1. **Collect the account level data and form the 'triangle':** 'Triangle' is a form of representing the account level data such that the continued presence of the number of

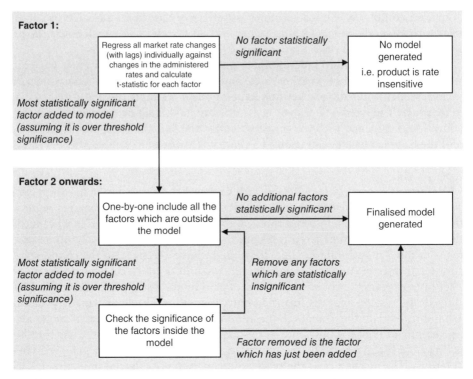

FIGURE 3.2   Assessment of the regression analysis outcome used in the deposit characterisation model.
Source: own elaboration based on the main concepts of the regression technique.

    accounts (sum of average balances) opened in 1 month can be tracked through different age buckets. It gives the remaining number of accounts (sum of average balances) for a given age bucket for a given opening month. It has the triangle form (an example is given for decaying number of accounts).

2. **Calculate the mortality ratio for each age bucket:** The mortality ratio is defined as the number of accounts closed at that age to the number of accounts that were alive at the beginning of that age (or in balance terms, the ratio of balances that left the bank at that age to the total balances that were available at the beginning of that age). All the mortality rates for each age bucket together tell how fast (or slow) the accounts close.

3. **Compute the average life of accounts:** Once the mortality rates are determined, one can track what percentage of all the accounts remain at each age.

Balance Sensitivity Modelling

The goal of balance sensitivity analysis is to further decompose the non-core component into two categories: a rate-sensitive component and purely volatile component. Rate sensitive balances are those for which the volatility in the balances can be explained by changes in macroeconomic factors.

Balance	Definition
Core	Balances that are stable under all market conditions as long as pricing behaviour remains as it is.
Rate sensitive	Balances that fluctuate when interest rates or macroeconomic conditions change.
Volatile	Balances that fluctuate randomly and independently of time or interest rates.

The first step in the process is to carry out single factor regression analysis between the product balances and each of the macroeconomic variables of interest. This is performed through comparison of the changes in the residual component of the balance (non-core) against changes in the variable of interest. Similarly, the change in spreads from rates paid to the market rates is analysed. The market variables examined are:

- stock market index;
- stock market volatility index;
- inflation – Consumer Price Index (CPI);
- 1-month interbank offer rates;
- 1-year interbank offer rates;
- 10-year swap rate;
- spread between 10-year and 3-month rate;
- Gross Domestic Product (GDP).

Similarly, the spreads between the rates paid and the market rates are analysed:

- product's spread to 1-month market rate;
- product's spread to 1-year market rate;
- product's spread to 10-year market rate.

Moreover, lags between the changes in the macroeconomic factors (and also the changes in spread of rates paid to the market rates) and the changes in the non-core balances should be considered.

Balance sensitivity analysis seeks a strong, structural relationship between the non-core portion and the macroeconomic variables; hence a high R^2 value is set as a threshold. A high threshold for R^2 also prevents spurious correlation to govern the results. For this purpose, threshold R^2 value of 50% is set.

Rate sensitivity analysis captures the repricing behaviour of the product; it explains the changes in the product rate with the changes in the market rates. Average life analysis finds out the average life of the product by making use of account level data and their mortality characteristics. Balance sensitivity tests whether the non-core portion can be explained with the changes in the macroeconomic factors. In addition to the analyses, benchmarks are incorporated into the decision process. The output of the deposit characterisation is crucial in matched funds transfer pricing, interest rate risk measurement and management, pricing of new deposit products, funding management, cash flows and liquidity needs, valuation of deposit, hedging, ALM risk, and economic capital.

MODELLING OF LOANS WITH EARLY REDEMPTION OPTIONALITY – ASSETS SIDE

The prepayment phenomenon has a significant impact on ALM and consequently can alter the structure of the exposure of the banking book to the interest rate risk and liquidity risk. This impact should not be underestimated and modelling of the prepayment rate on the asset side is one of the main activities of the ALM manager.

The prepayment event represents the possibility for the client to reimburse or prepay the credit outstanding fully or partially during the credit contractual life. Prepayments therefore decrease outstanding principal so that the interest and cash flow the investor expected to receive in the future decreases.

There are two types of prepayments:

- Financial prepayments – these prepayments are potentially cyclical and have rational reasons, such as interest rate levels or other macroeconomic conditions. This phenomenon displays significant dependence on the loan seniority, as there is less unwillingness to prepay at the very early stages of the life of the loan. The prepayment likelihood increases with the maturity of the loan to some point of time (around 30 months from the loan origination) and then stabilises, i.e. can be considered constant. An important task in financial prepayments modelling consists of good understanding of the underlying factors driving the model and behaviour of the customers.
- Structural prepayments – these prepayments are partially irrational from an economic point of view as statistically there is always a minimum prepayment rate. The driver of structural prepayment is mainly related to the personal events occurring to mortgagors. Financial prepayments will not explain those prepayments.

Statistical prepayments need to be added to financial prepayments in order to come up with the total prepayment rate.

Statistical Prepayments

As already anticipated, statistical prepayments are driven by sociological reasons and are not related to the level of the interest rates in the market. For example, divorce, inheritance, salary increases (change of the financial status of the client), or geographic mobility affect the financial situation of the client and consequently his willingness to prepay the mortgage. Given the underlying driver of the structural prepayments, it can be modelled through the analysis of the historical data in quite a simple database.

The below describes one possible method to build a simple database based on observation of the client's behaviour over the past period of several years to obtain the structural prepayment rate.

Such a database contains the monthly outstanding of mortgages extended to clients over several years of the observation period, for example, 4 years. These loans should be grouped according to the year in which they were disbursed, for example, loans extended to clients in 2016, 2017, 2018, and 2019. Having the total amount of disbursements, residual outstanding at the observation date, and the total prepayment amount up to the observation date (client default and credit restructuring have to be excluded), it is possible to calculate the hypothetical outstanding amount, i.e. the outstanding amount determined by the contractual schedule of the loans. It is important to split loans according to certain criteria, such as currency in which they are denominated, contract type (mortgages, personal loans), and month of production.

Such a constructed database is sufficient to come up with the prepayment turnover, i.e. the prepayment amount which has occurred between 1 month of the observation period and another (effectively it represents the difference between the residual amount at the observation dates, for example between January 2017 and February 2017).

The prepayment rate is calculated for every loan seniority bucket as a ratio of observed statistical prepayments to the hypothetical (scheduled) outstanding amounts multiplied by 12 (in order to obtain the annual prepayment rate). The average prepayment rate is calculated as a ratio between the summations of the prepayment amount over all seniority buckets to the sum of hypothetical outstanding amount multiplied by 12.

At the beginning of the life of the loan the prepayment rate is low. This is likely to be explained by the unwillingness of the client to prepay (and remortgage) having already gone through the process of applying for one mortgage. At some point in its life the prepayment event becomes more likely as different sociological factors come into effect. Finally, over time the prepayment rate seems to decelerate again. A practical case study can be found in Chapter 5 ('Bank 2).

Financial Prepayments

Financial prepayments are strictly linked to the market rate level. It is rational behaviour fully explained by external factors which impact the mortgagors' decision. The relation between the market rate level and customer rates explains the greater part of these prepayments. This is driven by the fact that a significant rate decrease will encourage customers either to shop for the new loan with a lower interest rate and to prepay the existing loan or to renegotiate the existing loan. In contrast, an increase in interest rates will inhibit the prepayment willingness, as it is unfavourable for the client. Consequently, it can be expected that in the raising rates environment, the prepayment rate will decrease in comparison to the base prepayment rate. The opposite will happen in the case where rates are going down.

Prepayments are very important for the bank and the correct understanding of underlying factors driving the customers' behaviour is ALM imperative. Otherwise, the hedging strategies put in place will be inefficient or impossible to be determined. Macroeconomic variables affect the financial prepayments as follows:

- Unemployment level, which reflects the general 'health' of the economy.
- Growth of the GDP, which indicates the state of the economy.
- House price inflation, which leads towards higher prepayment frequency.

There are three most important variables in modelling of the prepayment rate: interest rate spread, seniority/residual maturity, and burnout.

The interest rate spread is the difference between the loan initial interest rate and re-employment rate. The higher the spread, the higher the customer interest to prepay. Conversely, when the interest rate spread is negative, the customer interest is to keep his initial loan. The interest rate spread is either the absolute spread or relative spread (Adam 2007).

The burnout phenomenon measures the customers' likelihood to react to the interest rate decrease. It turns out that there are different activating levels for the prepayment options among clients. The burnout variable tries to capture the difference in readiness of customers to prepay their mortgage.

It appears that there is strong heterogeneity between customers: their reactivity varies. For example, a 'rational' customer prepays as soon as the prepayment is profitable for them, while other customers will wait. The customer's likelihood to react to the interest rate decrease is known 'burnout phenomenon'. For example, if there is an interest rate decrease followed by an interest rate rise and then another decrease, it will produce less prepayment than two interest rate decreases followed by a rise. This is driven by the fact that a client needs time to assess the prepayment decision, and in the first case there is more time to consider whether the decision is worthwhile.

Theoretically, residual maturity explains both financial prepayment and statistical prepayment. The statistical prepayments are driven by two fundamental circumstances:

1. At the beginning of the loan life, the customer has no real reason to prepay.
2. By the end of the loan life, the customer's wealth has increased, and the customer has more chances to be cash-rich so he will statistically prepay more (Adam 2007).

It turns out that modelling prepayments on conventional parametric models often have bad out-of-sample predictive ability. A likely explanation is the highly non-linear nature of prepayment functions. Non-parametric techniques are much better at detecting non-linearity and multivariate interaction.

CHAPTER **4**

Formulation of the Optimisation Process and Articulation of the Decision Model

Optimisation methods are used widely in engineering, physics, and medicine, and recently found their common application also in the banking industry.

The problem is now presented here in detail.

Put simply, a banking book of a bank is composed of a portfolio of assets with different repricing characteristics and different maturities (short-term and medium long-term assets). The liquidity portfolio is also part of the assets, which, according to Basel III requirements, has to act as a buffer in case of unexpected liquidity outflows. Its minimum amount is assessed through the liquidity stress test analysis.

The profitability of assets is always the result of the bank's willingness to take on a certain amount of risk, subject to constraints such as capital absorption and expected losses generated by this asset portfolio. Thus, the optimisation exercise here will consist of building the objective function which maximises asset profitability along with the appropriate constraint functions. The constraint functions will limit the exposure to the interest rate risk in terms of net interest income (NII) volatility and maturity transformation through keeping the liquidity ratio below the threshold level.

From the liability side, the purpose of the optimisation exercise consists of the determination of the funding structure that is cheapest for the bank. In this case, we will be looking for the values of our variables which cause the objective function to be at its minimal level. Again, certain constraints, related to the *run-off* factor of items without deterministic maturity, or *rollover* factor in the case of part being funded through time deposits, have to be defined. It is important to include the funding concentration constraint as it will help to avoid reliance on one particular source of funding (for example, to avoid the excessive reliance on current accounts).

The output of such a constructed optimisation problem will lead to the achievement of the target profile of the bank in terms of the composition of assets and liabilities of the banking book, taking into account its exposure to the ALM risks, i.e. interest rate risk and liquidity risk.

THE OPTIMISATION METHOD APPLIED TO THE BANKING BOOK

The optimisation methodologies universe is very wide, and it is important to apply the most appropriate method to our problem. The main driver in that choice is to understand the nature of our objective and constraint functions and whether this exercise needs to be dynamic (repeating the optimisation exercise with the predefined time intervals) or otherwise.

If the objective and constraint functions are linear, we can apply the common method (and the easiest one in its application) known as the linear programming problem (LPP).

The application of the LPP requires that the objective and constraint functions are linear and there is the condition of a non-negative variable to be respected. Algorithm simplex is a commonly used algorithm for solving the problems of linear programming. In its geometrical interpretation, this method tests adjacent vertices of a feasible set in sequence so that in each new vertex the objective function improves or is unchanged. The simplex method is very efficient in practice and the problem can be easily solved using this method with MATLAB or Solver in an Excel spreadsheet.

When the objective and constraints functions are more complicated (non-linear) other techniques should be used. In particular, economists make use of the method of *Lagrange multipliers*. Putting it simply, this method consists of finding out the Lagrange function and its multiplier. Subsequently, the function needs to be differentiated with respect to variables and the partials equated to zero (see below for details). Such a constructed sequence of equations (objective function and constraints) must be solved for unknowns and the multiplier giving all pairs of numbers *(x,y)* that can possibly solve the problem.

As already mentioned, the optimisation exercise for the banking book of a bank involves almost always inequality constraints. For example, the limit related to NII volatility is expressed as an inequality, indicating the range for an acceptable level of NII volatility. The same is valid for liquidity ratios, both short term and medium long-term. In such cases, where the constraints are expressed as inequalities, the optimisation problem can be solved by applying the Kuhn–Tucker theorem. The 'cookbook' procedure for using the Kuhn–Tucker theorem to solve an inequality-constrained optimisation problem involves essentially the same steps as those in using the Lagrange theorem in solving equality constraints problems. There are, however, some important differences in the calculation details (for example between min and max problems).

The dynamic programming method and Bellman equations which can be used to solve the optimisation problem should also be mentioned. The main characteristic of this method is the separation of the objective function in time. Thus, it breaks a multi-period planning problem into simpler steps at different points in time and the objective function is a sum of contributions deriving from the previous periods (the previous period's decision and state). The benefit for the financial institution deriving from the optimisation exercise is mainly economical (in terms of decreasing the cost of funding and increasing the profitability of assets) but there is also the point related to the overall awareness of the senior management (treasurer or CFO) as to the direction which has to be taken in order to achieve the target profile of the balance sheet. The optimisation output will support the bank with strategic decision-making, like a funding plan or a new product policy. In addition, it can be constructed under a desirable time horizon and repeated frequently upon request. The regulatory and internal policies requirements are built into the constraint functions; thus, it is ensured that the limits are respected over time. Finally, once the appropriate method has been identified the optimisation code can be written in MATLAB.

This chapter introduces the optimisation concept in terms of the mathematical form (functions) and explains the necessary conditions which need to be met in order that the minimum or maximum point of the function exists and can be found. In addition, the chapter highlights the main differences between the analytical optimisation which involves finding the maximum and minimum of the function by searching for a point at which the function derivatives are zero, and numerical optimisation which is used when the optimised function does not lend itself to the analytical techniques or when the function is not explicitly defined. Finally, the construction process of the objective and constraints functions in the decision model is described in detail.

INTRODUCTION OF THE OPTIMISATION CONCEPT

The optimisation problem has to be described in the form of mathematical functions and the solution is obtained by applying optimisation techniques. The functions are built for the objective variables which need to be optimised (for example, return on assets and cost of funding) and constraints which need to be considered in the optimisation exercise (for example the extent of the exposure to the interest rate risk and liquidity risk).

Optimisation modelling is always performed within a certain time horizon and its general structure is as follows:

$$maximise\ f(x)\ subject\ to\ x \in D\ \text{or} \tag{4.1a}$$

$$minimise\ f(x)\ subject\ to\ x \in D \tag{4.1b}$$

where

f is called the *objective function* and D is known as the *constraints set*.

Problems of the first sort are termed *maximisation problems* and those of the second sort are called *minimisation problems*. From the mathematical standpoint, optimisation is the process of finding the minimum and maximum value of a function. Given that differential calculus estimates the rate of change of the function and whether the rate is accelerating, slowing down, or stationary, it is used to find the 'optimum' points of a function. The first derivative identifies those points and the second derivative looks at their nature. The local maximum and/or minimum are all points where the first derivative is equal to zero, i.e. $\frac{dy}{dx} = 0$. They are all known as *stationary points*. If at a stationary point the second derivative is negative, then $\frac{dy}{dx} = 0$ and $\frac{dy}{dx}$ is falling. Therefore, moving from left to right there is a positive gradient followed by a zero gradient, followed by a negative gradient. This characteristic points towards the local maximum. A similar argument shows that if there is a point at which the second derivatives are positive and moving from left to right, the gradient changes from negative to zero and subsequently to positive, then the point represents the local minimum. In the case of the function of more than one variable, a stationary point of a function is a point where all partial derivatives are zero. To discover the type of stationary point, the Hessian matrix of second partial derivatives is examined. Mirroring the situation with one variable, if at the stationary point the Hessian matrix of second derivatives is positive definite, then there is a local minimum. If it is negative definite, then there is a local maximum. If it is neither, then it is necessary to examine the change in gradient to see which point it is.

In finance, it is common that the function to be optimised is subject to certain constraints; for example, the required expected return or cost of funding. In constrained optimisation, the Lagrange multiplier is used.

Let's construct the Lagrangian for the function $f(x, y)$.

The Lagrangian is constructed as follows:

$$L(x, y, \lambda) = f(x, y) - \lambda g(x, y) \tag{4.2}$$

where: $L(x, y, \lambda)$ is the Lagrangian function of three variables, $f(x, y)$ is the objective function of two variables, λ is the Lagrange multiplier and $g(x, y)$ is the constraint function.

In this case, the Lagrangian is a function of three variables: x, y and λ, where λ is constant. The result for the calculation of partial derivatives of the Lagrangian is as follows:

$$\frac{\partial L}{\partial x} = \frac{\partial f}{\partial x} - \lambda \frac{\partial g}{\partial x}; \tag{4.3a}$$

$$\frac{\partial L}{\partial y} = \frac{\partial f}{\partial y} - \lambda \frac{\partial g}{\partial y}; \tag{4.3b}$$

$$\frac{\partial L}{\partial \lambda} = g. \tag{4.3c}$$

Setting the first two partial derivatives to zero (4.3a and 4.3b) gives the condition that the gradients are in the same direction, i.e. that:

$$\frac{\partial f}{\partial y} / \frac{\partial f}{\partial x} = \frac{\partial g}{\partial y} / \frac{\partial g}{\partial x} \tag{4.4}$$

Setting the third partial derivative (4.3c) to zero gives the constraints $g(x, y) = 0$. Hence, to solve the constrained optimisation problem it is necessary to look for a stationary point of Lagrangian, i.e. a point where all partial derivatives are equal to zero. The value of λ is known as the marginal value of relaxing of the constraint. So, if the constraint were to be changed by small amount h, the constrained maximum would change by λh. As already pointed out, the solution to the constrained optimisation problem is given by finding the stationary point of the Lagrangian, and we require that all partial derivatives are equal to zero. By setting all derivatives (for variables and λ) to zero, the sequence of simultaneous linear equations is obtained. These equations can be written out in the matrix form by extracting the matrix of coefficients, the vector of variables, and the vector of right-hand sides. The system can be solved using the matrix inverse (Parramore and Watsham 2015).

A different approach has to be followed in order to solve the inequality-constrained optimisation problem. For such a problem, the Kuhn–Tucker theorem is applied. The cookbook procedure for using the Kuhn–Tucker theorem to solve an inequality constrained optimisation problem involves essentially the same steps as those in using the Lagrange theorem for equality constrained problems. However, there are differences regarding the solving of maximisation and minimisation problems.

Nevertheless, it is important to keep in mind that in a given optimisation problem, a solution may fail to exist (that is, the problem may have no solution at all) and second, that even if a solution does exist, it does not need necessarily to be unique (that is, there could exist more than one solution). For this reason, it is very important to identify a set of conditions on f and D under which the existence of solutions to the optimisation problem is guaranteed.

Summarising the section related to the solution of analytical optimisation problems, the *Lagrange multipliers* method consists of finding out the Lagrange function and the multiplier. Subsequently, the function needs to be differentiated with respect to variables and the partial derivatives have to be equated to zero. Such a constructed sequence of equations (including the constraints) has to be solved for unknowns and multipliers giving all pairs of numbers *(x, y)* that can possibly solve the problem.

The optimisation exercise for the banking book of the bank involves almost always inequality constraints. For example, the limit related to the NII volatility is expressed as an inequality, indicating the range for the acceptable level of the NII volatility. The same point is valid for the liquidity ratios, both short term and medium long term. In such cases, where the constraints are expressed as inequalities, the optimisation problem can be solved applying the Kuhn–Tucker theorem.

The problem becomes more complex when it comes to the numerical optimisation problems which are formulated frequently, especially in finance. In this case, solving the optimisation problem involves the application of numerical methods which are required to optimise the value of something when it depends on multiple inputs. As opposed to analytical optimisation, which involves finding the maximum and minimum of a function by finding the point at which the function derivatives are zero, numerical optimisation is used when the explicitly defined function to be optimised does not lend itself to analytical techniques, or when the function is not explicitly defined (Parramore and Watsham 2015). This section addresses the optimisation method known as the *interior-point method* which gets its name from the fact that the optimal solution is approached from the strict interior of the feasible region. This method is used in the MATLAB optimisation toolbox known as *fmincon* to find a minimum of a constrained nonlinear multivariable function. Interior-point (or barrier) methods have proved to be successful for non-linear optimisation and they are currently considered the most powerful algorithm for large-scale non-linear programming. Barrier methods for non-linear optimisation were developed in the 1960s but fell out of favour for almost two decades. The success of interior-point methods for linear programming stimulated renewed interest in them for non-linear cases and, by the late 1990s, a new generation of methods and software for non-linear programming had emerged. The terms 'interior-point methods' and 'barrier methods' are now used interchangeably (Nocedal and Wright 2006). The problem under consideration here can be described as follows:

$$\min_{x \in R^n} f(x)$$

subject to: $c_i(x) = 0, i \in \varepsilon$

$$c_i(x) \geq 0, i \in I \tag{4.5}$$

where $c(x)$ is a m - dimensional vector of non-linear constraint functions with i-th component $c_i(x)$, $i = 1, \ldots, m$ and ε and I are non-intersecting index sets. It is assumed that f and c are twice-continuously differentiable. Any point x satisfying the constraints above is called a feasible point, and the set of all such points is the feasible region. In order to solve the optimisation problem, the gradient of objective function f (x) denoted by $\nabla f(x)$ or $g(x)$, has to be determined along with the Hessian matrix of second partial derivatives of $\nabla^2 f(x)$. The gradient and Hessian of *constrained functions* $c_i(x)$ are denoted by $\nabla c_i(x)$ and $\nabla^2 c_i(x)$ (Forsgren, Gill, and Wright 2002).

The logarithmic barrier function associated with Eq. (4.5) is defined as follows:

$$B(x, \mu) = f(x) - \mu \sum_{i=1}^{m} \log c_i(x) \qquad (4.6)$$

here μ is a small positive scalar, often called the barrier parameter. As μ converges to zero the minimum of $B(x, \mu)$ should converge to a solution of Eq. (4.6).

The barrier function gradient is:

$$g_b = g - \mu \sum_{i=1}^{m} \frac{1}{c_i(x)} \nabla c_i(x) \qquad (4.7)$$

where g is the gradient of the objective function $f(x)$ and ∇c_i is the gradient of c_i.

In addition to the original, known as 'primal' variable x, the Lagrange multiplier inspired dual variable λ is introduced:

$$\lambda \in R^m \text{ and } c_i(x)\lambda_i = \mu, \forall i = 1, \ldots, m \qquad (4.8)$$

In order to find the solution to the optimisation problem it is necessary to satisfy the Karush–Kuhn–Tucker (KKT) optimality condition. KKT are first-order necessary conditions for a solution in non-linear programming to be optimal, provided that some regularity conditions are satisfied. Allowing inequality constraints, the KKT approach to non-linear programming generalises the method of Lagrange multipliers, which allows only equality constraints. The system of equations and inequalities corresponding to the KKT conditions is usually not solved directly, except in the few special cases where a closed-form solution can be derived analytically. In general, many optimisation algorithms can be interpreted as methods for numerically solving the KKT system of equations and inequalities.

In this book, the optimisation problem is presented through the application of the optimisation method called interior-point algorithm based on the Lagrange multipliers method which is embedded in the MATLAB solver, *fmincon*.

The optimisation problem herein is defined through the construction of two separate optimisation functions, i.e. the maximisation of the assets income and minimisation of the funding costs of the bank subject to constraints. The analysis needs to be performed over a certain time horizon and predetermined maturity profile for the banking book items; for example, under a constant balance sheet scenario where there is a renewal of assets and liabilities falling under maturity/repricing with items with the same financial features (*like for like* assumption). The objective function for assets is a multivariable equality function, which describes the total income achieved by the asset base with variables representing the proportions of different asset classes in the total asset structure. The objective function for liabilities is a multivariable equality function, which describes the total cost of funding with variables representing the proportions of different sources of funding in the total liabilities structure. The model searches for the maximum for assets and minimum for liabilities value of objective function subject to the certain constraints.

DEFINITION OF THE INITIAL BANKING BOOK PROFILE

The first step in the optimisation process is to identify the initial structure of the banking book which will act as a 'starting point' at the time t_0 of the exercise. It defines the position, in terms of the asset and liability structure, which is given at the analysis date. In addition, certain assumptions related to the liquidity profile of the balance sheet items, in terms of the rollover of term deposits, volatility of current and savings accounts (CASA), and rate sensitivity, amortisation profile, and prepayment rate of assets have been defined as the initial conditions of the analysis and are built into the model.

It is worth highlighting that the analysis of the initial structure of banks based on different geographical locations shows that there are clear differences in the asset base and funding structure adopted by banks. This is why the optimisation model will work differently for different banks, i.e. by providing a different magnitude of benefit.

For example, it appears that commercial banks based in Italy have preferences towards floating rate assets. Personal and commercial loans products are usually indexed to an interbank market benchmark such as EURIBOR. The reset frequency differs between 1 M, 3 M, and 6 M. From the funding perspective, there is significant reliance on current accounts provided by retail and commercial clients and the banks are mostly funded by transactional current accounts.[1]

The commercial banks also fund an important part of their assets through senior debt issuance and short-term wholesale funding. Banks based in the UK, however, tend towards administered rate products (mortgages) which show high correlation to the Bank of England base rate (more than 80%). Floating rate products are predominantly linked to GBP LIBOR 3 M. The retail banks are funded by retail current accounts and retail time deposits. The residual part of their funding structure consists of senior debt issuance. The short-term funding is mostly used for funding of LAB and collateral funding. Some banks assume the 6-month tenor of funding for the liquidity buffer. There is a clear trend in Europe with regards to the majority of funding invested in assets at floating rate and high-quality liquid assets (HQLA). The preference for assets at fixed rate can be seen in the US market. This is a particularly valid point in the field of ALM risks, where the global tendency pushes towards standardisation. For example, the 2018 EBA Final Report relating to the interest rate risk in the banking book (IRRBB) imposes on all European banks the application of the same techniques in the measurement and management of IRRBB. Also, interest rate shocks are standardised. The updated EBA requirements introduce new guidelines on the risk management framework, risk appetite, and model governance applicable to all European banks.

---

[1]Transactional current accounts are those which are not sensitive to the changes in the interest rates fluctuations.

Following the introduction of the liquidity coverage ratio (LCR) and net stable funding ratio (NSFR) in the suite of liquidity metrics, the same convergence can be seen in the liquidity space. All European banks have to calculate those regulatory metrics both under a short-term (LCR) and medium long-term horizon (NSFR).

As already mentioned, there are always some differences among European banks which are located in different countries, especially in terms of the initial structure of the banking book. However, there are many more similarities. A typical example is the common approach towards modelling of items without deterministic maturities (such as CASA). This is not only driven by the heavily regulated environment in which banks operate, but also the prescribed rules imposed on financial institutions regarding the treatment of NMDs. NMDs have the same financial features as a product since banks use the same (or similar) methods to model their behaviour.

The optimisation model applies the output from the deposit characterisation model, which is based on the analysis of the stability of balances over the past period of a number of years and rate sensitivity estimated through the multiple regression. In addition to the behavioural approach to NMDs, the Basel Committee on Banking Supervision in the Standards (BCBS 2016) requires behavioural modelling for the treatment of fixed rate assets through the calculation of the baseline prepayment rate and prescribes parameters for the definition of the prepayment rate under a number of interest rate shock scenarios. The same point is valid for the ratio of the early redemption of time deposits which differs according to the interest rate shock scenario. An overview of the modelling techniques for items without deterministic maturity is provided in Chapter 3.

The model assumes a certain baseline prepayment rate for fixed rate assets and examines the impact of the change in the CPR on the model outcome.

In addition, financial institutions usually apply a number of rollover assumption for liabilities which are usually defined based on the past behaviour of the client and expert judgement. This is driven by the fact that every financial institution defines its internal metric to the short-term liquidity risk and, consequently, the risk appetite under a stress scenario is based on its own observation and history. However, there is a clear trend within the banking industry to align the internal metrics with the regulatory ones; in this case, LCR and NSFR.

Another assumption, made by the model, refers to the pricing policy adopted by a bank. In particular, the determination of the target profile for asset and funding is strongly influenced by firstly, the competitiveness of a bank, i.e. the magnitude of the commercial spread on the commercial asset side and the ability to gather the cheapest funding sources in the market (to attract depositors through the more or less aggressive marketing, commercial offer, etc.); and secondly, by the market perception of a bank's own creditworthiness – its term liquidity premium, which it has to pay in order to fund itself in the market.

The risk appetite towards certain kinds of financial risk also represents an individual characteristic of the financial institution, which sets up a range of assumptions feeding into the optimisation analysis. This book provides the reader with an analysis of the banking book target structure both under *business as usual* and under a number of different scenarios (both internal and external) which aim in this chapter to assess the model's sensitivity to a number of predefined external and internal factors.

Herein, a bank's capital is considered as a bank's 'own funds'. A bank's own funds are items such as its ordinary share capital and retained earnings – in other words, not money lent to the bank that has to be repaid. Taken together, these own funds are equivalent to the difference between the value of total assets and liabilities.

BUILDING THE OBJECTIVE AND CONSTRAINT FUNCTIONS IN THE OPTIMISATION PROCESS

The second step in the optimisation process is to define the objective and constraint functions in the optimisation model. The constraint functions are constructed in such a way as to reflect the risk appetite of banks in different jurisdictions in terms of liquidity, interest rate risk, and capital absorption by asset classes. On the liability side, in addition, there are constraints imposed on the funding concentration to avoid overreliance on one particular funding source.

The liquidity risk is defined as the risk that a firm, although solvent, does not have available sufficient financial resources to meet its obligations as they fall due. This kind of risk is measured through liquidity metrics. There is a distinction between short-term liquidity risk and medium or long-term liquidity risk known as funding risk. The short-term liquidity risk is defined as the potential that a bank does not have sufficient financial resources in the short term to meet its obligations as they fall due or can access these financial resources only at excessive cost. It refers to the short-term horizon (30–90 days).

Liquidity metrics are built for the short-term (30 and 60 days) liquidity risk exposure under stress scenario and medium long-term liquidity exposure, usually known as the exposure to structural liquidity under the business as usual scenario. The inflow/outflow assumptions for the short-term liquidity ratio under stress scenarios are commonly determined based on the internal analysis performed by the financial institution and, as previously highlighted, differs significantly according to the geographical location of a bank. There is a general trend, however, as banks always set up more restrictive assumptions than those prescribed by the regulator.

The objective of the short-term liquidity risk analysis is to assess the adequate amount of liquidity buffer and, at the same time, the counterbalancing capacity (CBC) of a bank. The amount of liquidity buffer must be equal, at least, to the net outflows calculated under stress assumptions. The worst result of the liquidity stress analysis (the highest requirement for HQLA) drives the size of the liquidity buffer which is held by a bank. It has to be highlighted that this book illustrates simplified cases of the application of the optimisation model, and it is important that the decision regarding the metrics to be included into the model is the decision of the bank itself. In the examples provided in Chapter 5, only the internal short-term liquidity metrics have been set up as a constraint function. The 'pure' regulatory short-term liquidity metric, LCR, has not been included into the model (however, it could be easily added into the model in the form of another constraint). This is driven by the fact that the intention of this book is, in addition to the optimisation exercise, to show the variety of internal liquidity metrics applied by banks and their corresponding run-off factors. The LCR metric standardises the liquidity approach across all European countries.

In order to assess the funding equilibrium between the medium long-term funding and medium long-term assets and, consequently, the extent of the maturity transformation a bank is running, the liquidity structural ratio has been set up as another constraint function in the model. The liquidity structural ratio is an important metric, calculated under *business as usual* scenario and can be assessed both on a contractual basis (without *behaviouralisation*[2] of the balance sheet items) and on a behavioural basis (with *behaviouralisation*). The extent of the maturity transformation is set up as an internal limit in order to ensure there is a sufficient amount of stable funding and to keep the frequency of funding rollover limited.

It is proposed to determine a bank's appetite for liquidity and funding risk through the following metrics:

- Cumulative short-term liquidity ratio (often known as *survival horizon*), which covers time horizons of 30, 60, or 90 days and determines the adequacy of the liquidity buffer of a bank.
- Structural liquidity ratio, which measures the extent of the maturity transformation run by a bank.

The short-term liquidity risk is quantified through the survival horizon (SH) metric that defines for how long, during an extreme but plausible liquidity stress, a bank can survive before management actions are deployed. The goal of this metric is to ensure that a financial institution would have sufficient time to react and make decisions in stress which mobilise further liquidity creating actions to offset a significant stress. The survival horizon analysis assesses the liquidity position under stress conditions lasting 30, 60, or even 90 days, constructed through the definition of different assumptions of inflows and outflows for items on the balance sheet. The amount of liquidity buffer has to be at least equal to the net outflows calculated under stress scenarios. The worst result of the stress scenario (the highest requirement for the HQLA) is the driver of the liquidity buffer size which is held by a bank. The inflows and outflows are determined through the application of run-off factors which represent particularities of the client base of a bank, i.e. how sensitive depositors are to the market or idiosyncratic stress and to what extent the incoming flows are exposed to the impact of the increased default rate caused by the market stress.

The below presents an illustrative example of inflow and outflow run-off factors applied to items maturing within the survival horizon period of 2 months:

Inflows
- Trade finance loans:
  1. Trade loans with maturity < 6 months to non-bank financial institutions (NBFI) – 65% over the first month, 35% over the second month.
  2. Trade loans with maturity ≥ 6 month to NBFI – 50% over the first month, 30% over the second month.
  3. Trade loans to banks – 100% over the first month and 60% over the second month (irrespective of maturity),
- Floating rate mortgage: first month 50%, second month 50%.
- Corporate lending: first month 50%, second month 50%.

---

[2]The behaviouralisation exercise consists of the recognition of the behavioural characteristics of items (for example NMDs) which are based on statistical analysis and expert judgement.

Outflows:
- Retail current accounts (CASA):
  1. Stable – 5%.
  2. Less stable – 15%.
- TB current accounts (TB CASA):
  1. Operational current account:
     a) Corporate – first month 25%, second month 0%.
     b) Non -Bank Financial Institutions (NBFI) – first month 25%, second month 0%.
  2. Non-operational current accounts:
     a) Corporate – first month 40%, second month 20%.
     b) Financial institutions – first month 100%, second month 0%.
- Senior debt issuance: 100% outflow in the first month and 100% outflow in the second month.
- Corporate time deposits: 40% in the first month and 20% in the second month.
- Structured deposits: 100% in the first month and 100% in the second month.
- Commercial papers and certificate of deposits: 100% in the first month and 100% in the second month.

The survival (SH) ratio is calculated as follows:

$$SH = \frac{LAB}{TO - TI} \qquad (4.9)$$

where:

LAB liquid asset buffer;
TO total net outflows over a predefined time period;
TI total net inflows over a predefined time period.

$$SH \geq 100\% \qquad (4.10)$$

This kind of liquidity analysis is performed through the behavioural maturity ladder and consists of the allocation of expected inflows and outflows to the time buckets according to their behavioural maturity.

A bank determines the inflow/outflow factors based on either qualitative analysis of the past behaviour of the client base (statistical approach) or the pure qualitative approach which is driven by expert judgement. Recently, banks have started to align their internal metrics with the regulatory ones. For example, the run-off factors for internal liquidity analysis purposes are based on the LCR reporting principles.

Thus, the liquidity stress tests measure and monitor the risk of tenor mismatch by modelling a conservative behavioural profile for non-dated deposits, amongst various other conservative outflow assumptions, and the amount of liquidity buffer is calibrated accordingly.

While the SH metric indicates the exposure to the short-term liquidity risk under a stress scenario, some banks use the cumulative short-term liquidity ratio for tactical liquidity management purposes. Tactical liquidity is related to the liquidity forecast, which the treasury needs to plan in order to incorporate the volumes of the new disbursements and funding under the short- and medium-term horizon.

The calculation of the cumulative short-term ratio is based on the maturity mismatch approach which assesses the size of the liquidity gap by time bucket. As opposed to the stress testing metrics which looks at the liquidity projection under a maximum 90 day stress scenario, the tactical liquidity aims to measure liquidity needs on a slightly longer horizon, i.e. up to 12 months.

The liquidity gap ratio is defined as follows:

$$(TI + LAB)/TO >= m\% \text{ for 0-1M time bucket} \tag{4.11}$$

where:

LAB liquid asset buffer (quite often known as the counterbalancing capacity of a bank);

TI total net inflows over a predefined time period;

TO total net inflows over a predefined time period;

m threshold set up by a financial institution which must be compliant with the regulatory liquidity requirements and therefore set up at a minimum of 100% or higher.

$$(TI + LAB)/TO \geq 80\% \text{ for 1-3M time bucket} \tag{4.12}$$

$$(TI + LAB)/TO \geq 60\% \text{ for 3-6M time bucket} \tag{4.13}$$

The 100% risk tolerance threshold in Eq. (4.5) is established by the Board of Directors of a bank, while 80% and 60% are examples of the warning thresholds (they could be higher).

By general definition *cash inflows* represent incoming cash flows within a predetermined time horizon put in place with parties outside the bank. Inflows arise from the maturity of assets, the use of irrevocable credit lines (liabilities), from the sale of the marketable activities, and positive components of income.

Cash outflows represent the outgoing cash flows within a predetermined time horizon put in place with parties outside the bank. Outflows arise from maturing liabilities, from the use of irrevocable lines of credit, and from negative income components.

Counterbalancing capacity (liquid assets buffer) represents the sum of items used by the bank to meet its liquidity needs in the case of stress scenario. The characteristics of a liquidity buffer are subject to the criteria established by Basel III as high-quality level 1 and level 2 assets.

The funding risk is defined as the risk that a firm does not have stable sources of funding in the medium and long term to enable it to meet its financial obligations, such as payments or collateral calls as they fall due, either at all or only at excessive cost. The risk appetite for the funding risk drives the funding strategy of a bank which is based on well-defined principles. An example of the funding strategy principles for internationally active banks could be:

- Management of the funding position at the country/currency level to ensure countries remain self-sufficient.
- Funding client assets predominantly using client liabilities/deposits to minimise the reliance on other funding sources that may not be available in a stress scenario (e.g. wholesale funding).

■ Maintenance of a client funding base diversified by product type, maturity, region, and industry segment.

Structural liquidity risk is defined as the potential for actual or opportunity loss because the bank cannot pursue its desired business strategy or growth objectives due to suboptimal balance sheet composition. The structural limit shows the extent of the maturity transformation of a bank. It requires the maintenance of a stable funding profile in relation to the composition of the balance sheet and, consequently, the reduction of funding risk over a longer time. The main objective of this metric is to ensure the bank is funding its activities with sufficiently stable sources of funding to mitigate the risk of future funding stress. The items without deterministic maturity are allocated to their respective time buckets according to the outcome of the behavioural analysis. The best market practice sets this ratio to be 100% or higher.

The structural liquidity is measured through different metrics. Below is a brief overview of the most common metrics adopted by banks in Europe.

Structural limit:

$$(\Sigma\,TO_{T>1Y} + Tier\ 1\ capital)/(\Sigma\,TI_{T>1Y}) \geq n\% \qquad (4.14)$$

where:

$TI_{T>1Y}$	represents all cash inflows occurring beyond 1 year;
$TO_{T>1Y}$	represents all cash outflows occurring beyond 1 year;
Tier 1 *capital*	considered as a source of stable funding given its portion is used to fund risk-sensitive assets;
n	threshold set up by a financial institution to limit the extent of maturity transformation.

This ratio aims to guarantee the structural balance between assets and liabilities under a time horizon beyond 1 year. The cash projections for different time buckets are allocated through the maturity ladder. For items without contractual maturity, it is expected to model their corresponding cash flow profile through quantitative/behavioural models.

$$\frac{A}{D} \leq l\% \qquad (4.15)$$

where:

A   total outstanding of loans and advances to customers;
D   total outstanding of customer liabilities;
l   threshold set up by a financial institution. The best market practice consists in setting it up lower than 80%.

The *A/D* ratio ensures that the bank remains largely client funded and does not become excessively reliant on wholesale funding. It is a simple metric but easily understandable, and provides a sense check for the structural integrity of the balance sheet. However, this metric does not differentiate for the quality or tenor of deposits nor the effect of the ongoing improvement initiatives and hence needs frequent re-evaluation.

A ratio greater than 100% reflects the extent to which customer assets are funded by sources other than customer deposits, such as debt issuance, interbank funds, and capital. Consequently, it describes corporate and retail loans as a percentage of corporate and retail deposits. The contractual funding ratio is described as follows:

$$\frac{CMTF}{CMTA} > a\% \tag{4.16}$$

where:

CMTF	the amount of contractual maturity funding beyond 1Y;
CMTA	the amount of contractual maturity assets beyond 1Y;
a	threshold set up by a financial institution reflecting the appetite for the maturity transformation on contractual basis.

The ratio above, known as the funding ratio (FR), reflects the extent to which contractual medium-term assets are funded by contractual medium-term liabilities. The bank must ensure that the asset base can be supported throughout its entire life on the bank's balance sheet. This includes securing an adequate level of funding, and/or identifying avenues for rolling off assets.

The contractual FR is intended to highlight the bank's ability to roll over contractually short-term liabilities to fund medium-term assets based on the bank's contractual obligations.

Medium-term assets are defined as assets with residual contractual or behavioural maturity of greater than or equal to 1 year. Medium-term liabilities are defined similarly. One year is chosen as the threshold to allow time to correct any structural imbalance in funding before the imbalance becomes a major risk to the bank's liquidity profile. Given that the maturity of incoming/outgoing cash flows is determined based on the contractual maturity, the threshold of this ratio is always less than 100%. Also, in this case, capital is included in the contractual FR calculation, as it does provide a long-term funding source.

Some banks set up their own behavioural medium long-term ratio, in addition to the NSFR. The behavioural FR is similar to the structural liquidity ratio as it intends to highlight whether the country's business/product mix and balance sheet structure in a business as usual (BAU) environment is sustainable over time.

The behavioural FR is calculated as follows:

$$\frac{BTF}{BTA} > g\% \tag{4.17}$$

where:

BTF	the amount of stable funding with residual, behavioural maturity lower than 1Y;
BTA	the amount of stable balances of assets with residual, behavioural maturity lower than 1Y;
g	the threshold set up by a financial institution reflecting the appetite for the maturity transformation on behavioural basis.

The liquidity metrics presented above are based on the best practice observed by the author across banks located in Europe (mainly the UK and Italy). Nevertheless, the

Date	Buckets	Cash in	Cash out
02/12/2013	15M	46.73	−41.22
28/02/2014	18M	48.04	−39.51
02/06/2014		47.95	−42.59
01/09/2014	24M	45.67	−7.30
01/12/2014	27M	39.41	−9.95
02/03/2015	30M	37.86	−19.21
01/06/2015	33M	36.27	−6.16
31/08/2015	36M	35.45	−6.09
31/08/2016	4Y	110.55	−23.37
31/08/2017	5Y	52.15	−14.62
02/09/2052	>5Y	197.26	−62.91
TOTAL		**697**	**−273**

FIGURE 4.1 Example of behavioural *maturity ladder*.
Source: own elaboration.

liquidity metrics all around the world are set up to measure the liquidity and funding risk. Consequently, those metrics can be considered universal, even though there can still be some exercise of discretion defined by the local regulator related to their set up and thresholds.

As already mentioned, the NSFR is a regulatory metric to monitor the maturity mismatch across the whole balance sheet on a behavioural basis. It went live as a regulatory requirement on 1 January 2018, and many banks consider an addition of this metric in the suite of current metrics as an opportunity to enhance their own liquidity management framework and its simplification.

Figure 4.1 shows the behavioural *maturity ladder* applied in the liquidity analysis over a time horizon of 6 months. The cash projections for the different time buckets are a function of maturity or, alternatively, for items without contractual maturity, it is expected to assess their corresponding cash flow profile through quantitative/behavioural models.

Interest rate risk in the banking book (IRRBB) is another risk category which is included in the constraints suite of the decision model.

According to the European Banking Authority (EBA), interest rate risk arising from non-trading book activities is an important financial risk for credit institutions, which is considered under SREP Pillar 2 and therefore as a part of the internal capital adequacy assessment process (ICAAP). IRRBB is measured by two complementary metrics: the first one, known as the earnings perspective metric, is focused on the interest rate risk over the short-term horizon, while the second one covers the duration of the whole banking book. Earnings-based measures look at the expected increase or reduction in NII over a shorter time horizon resulting from interest rates movements that are composed of either a gradual or a one-time large interest rate shock. The change in NII is the difference in the expected NII between a base scenario and an alternative, more stressful, scenario. Therefore, this metric is commonly used to assess the ability of a bank to generate stable earnings over a medium-term horizon, which will allow for payment of a stable level of dividends and reduce the beta on its own equity price. In order to be able to calculate changes in the expected earnings under different interest rate shocks and stress scenarios, an institution is expected to model earnings under three different states:

a) Run-off balance sheet: existing assets and liabilities are not replaced as they mature, except to the extent necessary to fund the remaining balance sheet.
b) Constant balance sheet: total balance sheet size and shape maintained by assuming *like for like* replacement of assets and liabilities as they run off.
c) Dynamic balance sheet: incorporating future business expectations, adjusted for the relevant scenario in a consistent manner.

Under an economic value approach, the measure of IRRBB is a theoretical change in the net embedded market value of the whole banking book. Applying the concept of EV to the whole balance sheet of a bank is more challenging: the banking book contains assets and liabilities that are accounted for at held-to-maturity valuation, and for which there may not be observable market prices (e.g. loans and receivables are not as readily marketable and their market value cannot be determined directly). Moreover, there may be embedded under- and overvaluations in the book on a mark-to-market basis, representing income or costs that will emerge in future reported earnings. In addition, margins on loans may be very heterogeneous, thus making determination of an appropriate discount rate problematic, and the cash flows that are being valued are subject to variation depending upon customer behaviour in response to rate changes (and customers may not behave as might rationally be expected). Finally, there may be structural positions (e.g. assets held to stabilise return on non-maturity deposits and/or equity) which will produce a significant change in value. Interest rate risk is in the banking book under EV measurement, but where the risk measured is a direct corollary of risk reduction from an earnings volatility perspective. To avoid the complexity of measuring total EV, banks typically therefore focus on measuring the level of change to the net present value of the relevant balance sheet items, based on existing or adjusted cash flows that are revalued in line with the interest rate shock and stress scenarios. The change in the valuation is a measure of the level of IRRBB, and can be compared with the current value of equity to determine the change to the economic value of equity (EVE) [BCBS, 2016].

In the case studies analysed in this book, only the earnings sensitivity has been analysed and built into the model in the constraint functions. This is driven by the fact that the optimisation exercise is performed over a 6-month time period, so the main driver of the interest rate risk is the repricing risk (defined in Chapter 2). The different repricing frequency between assets and liabilities over 6 months affects the Net Interest Income of the bank in case of fluctuations of the interest rate curve. The interest rate risk analysis, in the case studies, was performed using the static *Maturity gap* and +/– 200 bps instantaneous parallel shock of the interest rate curve. The items without deterministic maturities (current accounts) have been allocated to time buckets according to their rate sensitivity and balance volatility assumptions (Modelling of Customers' Deposits – Liabilities Side). For the assessment of the –200 bps curve decrease, for some products a floor of 0% has been put in place preventing the interest rate curve going into negative interest rate territory.

This is driven by the fact that, on the assets side, especially for commercial loans, it is very common to have an embedded automatic interest rate option (floors in case of the downward movements of the curve) included in the loan contract, which protect a bank from negative rates. Likewise, for the same reason, on the retail deposit side, a bank may decide to keep the customer deposit rate at zero in order not to charge depositors the negative rates. This decision is mostly driven by commercial reasons (otherwise depositors would choose another bank which offers better economic conditions). A bank's exposure to the interest rate risk, on the short end of the interest rate curve, is measured through the Net Interest Income sensitivity (known as impact on earnings) under a predefined interest rate shift scenario, in this example, +/– 200 bps parallel shift. The decision to apply +/– 200 bps is driven by the approach adopted by the supervisor, i.e. the European Central Bank (ECB) in the case of the eurozone. The ECB, in updated guidelines, imposes calibration of the magnitude of the parallel interest rate shock by currency. For the euro currency, it is exactly +/– 200 bps. The earnings sensitivity metric is calculated under an assumption related to the constant balance sheet, i.e. it is assumed that the maturing positions are replaced by items with the same financial characteristics (known as the like to like assumption). It means that the new business projections are not included in the model. The NII sensitivity is calculated using the *maturity gap* approach where the impact on the interest margin resulting from the movements of the interest rates is calculated as a product between the changes in the interest rates and the difference between an interest rate risk sensitive asset (RSA) and liabilities (RSL) through Eq. (2.1) in Chapter 2. In the decision model, a bank's tolerance for earnings sensitivity is set up in terms of the following metric:

$$\frac{\Delta NII}{NII} > -c\% \qquad (4.18)$$

where:

ΔNII represents the impact of the parallel shift of interest rates by +200 bps and –200 bps on the expected net interest income over a 6-month horizon;

NII expected net interest income of the bank from t_0 to t_6;

c threshold set up by a financial institution.

As already mentioned, the *maturity gap* considers only the transactions existing in the banking book at the date of analysis. In addition, it is pointed out that this technique, in general, disregards different maturities of the transactions which expire or reset their rates within the same time buckets (all transaction falling in the same time bucket have the same risk profile) and it allows for the estimation the impact on the NII caused only by the parallel shifts of the curve. More details on the methodological approach for earnings sensitivity are provided in Interest Rate Risk in the Banking Book – Measurement and Management in Chapter 2.

Figure 4.2 shows the illustrative *maturity gap* analysis of a commercial bank over a 12-month gapping period.

Diversification of the funding base is another imperative for a financial institution in order to remain profitable and reduce funding risk. As such, it is proposed to include the concentration metric into the suite of constraint functions. The concentration metric aims to limit the excessive reliance on one source of funding and, consequently, encourages the diversification of the funding portfolio. It is expressed as a simple inequality which sets up the maximum threshold in terms of the share of the single funding source in the total funding base. In some cases, a financial institution, with the aim to pursue its business strategy, decides to make sure that a certain product will be a part of the funding base even though the product does not produce a positive net

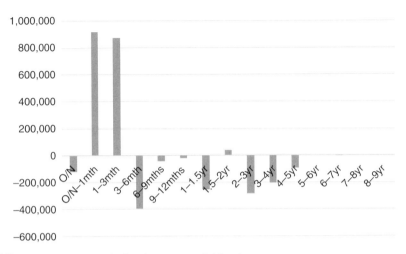

FIGURE 4.2   Maturity gap analysis of a commercial bank.
Source: own elaboration.

interest margin. It is driven very often by the fact that such products are offered to clients as a cross-product initiative; for example, a mortgage linked to a current account, or structured time deposits.

Another important metric which needs to be considered in the optimisation of the assets side is the credit riskiness for every asset category and, consequently, the allocation (absorption) of the risk capital in front of the asset class.

The *capital adequacy ratio* (CAR) is the ratio of a bank's capital to its risk-weighted assets. National regulators track a bank's CAR to ensure that it can absorb a reasonable amount of loss and complies with statutory capital requirements. It is a measure of a bank's capital adequacy and is expressed as a percentage of a bank's risk-weighted credit exposures.

The CAR measures the amount of a bank's core capital expressed as a percentage of its risk-weighted asset and is defined as follows:

$$\frac{Tier\ 1\ capital + Tier\ 2\ capital}{RWA} > b\% \qquad (4.19)$$

where:

Tier 1 capital	(paid up capital + statutory reserves + disclosed free reserves) – (equity investments in subsidiary + intangible assets + current losses);
Tier 2 capital	undisclosed reserves + general loss reserves + hybrid debt capital instruments and subordinated debts;
Risk-Weighted Assets (RWA)	fund-based assets, such as cash, loans, investments, and other assets. The degrees of credit risk, expressed as percentage weights, have been assigned by the national regulator to each asset category;
b	threshold set up by a financial institution in order to comply with the regulatory requirements.

Since different types of assets have different risk profiles, the CAR primarily adjusts for assets that are less risky by allowing banks to 'discount' lower risk assets. The specifics of the CAR calculation vary from country to country, but general approaches tend to be similar for countries that apply the Basel Accords. In the most basic application, government debt is allowed a 0% 'risk weighting' – that is, they are subtracted from total assets for the purposes of calculating the CAR. Under the standardised approach, local regulations establish that cash and government bonds have a 0% risk weighting, and residential mortgage loans have a 50% risk weighting. All other types of assets (loans to customers) have a 100% risk weighting. The bank applies the standardised approach for the calculation of the risk-weighted assets (RWA) in the situation that they didn't develop their own internal ratings-based approach approved by the local regulator.

A bank must calculate the value of all exposures that it faces and then apply a risk weighting depending on the type of asset. In simple terms, the Basel framework requires that a certain amount of the bank's regulatory capital must be allocated (at least notionally) to every loan advanced, or commitment made, by that bank. That allocation therefore restricts the amount of business that a bank may enter into or forces it to raise fresh capital. Therefore, the capital adequacy requirements of any loan carry an implicit cost to the bank advancing it. The capital adequacy cost of a loan depends on the amount of capital by which it has to be backed. This amount is often referred to as the capital charge.

It is interesting to highlight the evolution in the regulatory framework related to the capital adequacy of financial institutions. Since 1992 (when Basel I was first implemented), the minimum requirement is that a bank should have total regulatory capital (i.e. Tier 1, Tier 2, and Tier 3) equal to at least 8% of its RWA; 8% is a minimum figure: it is possible that a bank's regulator may require a higher percentage to be applied.

However, the original Basel Accord was relatively rudimentary in the way it allocated capital to risk. Basel II adopted a different approach and sought to match the amount of capital required to be held by an institution more closely to the exposures that it faces. Within that guiding idea, the main changes introduced by Basel II included:

- More sophisticated methodology for risk-weighting loans advanced by an institution depending on the type of counterparty (e.g. a sovereign as opposed to a corporate); the counterparty's credit rating; and the type of risk mitigants in place (e.g. collateral or guarantees).
- Special regimes to deal with areas such as project finance and commodities finance.
- Alternative calculation methods (the internal ratings-based model) to allow sophisticated financial institutions to use, within the supervisory framework, their own models to evaluate exposures.
- Emphasis on supervisory review (Pillar 2 in Basel II terminology) and disclosure (Pillar 3).

The intention was that the capital requirements set in Basel II are minimum levels, which were fine-tuned through dialogue with the supervisors and disclosure. One consequence of the introduction of Basel II was that the capital charge for any loan could vary during its life. Fluctuations in the credit rating of the borrower or the loan-to-value ratio of eligible collateral would affect the cost to the lenders of keeping the facility open, as would changes in law affecting the enforceability of the collateral. Similarly, a change in the regulatory regime could also impact the risk weighting given to a loan and so too its capital charge.

The basic 8% minimum ratio of capital to RWA remains under Basel III. However, whilst Tier 1 capital under Basel II could be constructed of both common equity and other capital instruments, common equity performed best in absorbing losses throughout the crisis. The Basel Committee has focused on this and notes that the minimum requirement currently is that banks issue common equity equal to 2% of RWA. Basel III has proposed to increase this requirement to 4.5% of RWA.

Basel III has also introduced stricter regulatory deductions (e.g. for minority interests) for calculating Tier 1 capital and tighter requirements for capital instruments which are not common equity to form part of Tier 1 capital.

On the second point, the Basel Committee has acknowledged that certain innovative features have been introduced to Tier 1 capital over the years (e.g. margin step-ups) to lower the cost of raising Tier 1 capital but has stated that those features are to be phased out. In addition to strengthening Tier 1 capital, two capital buffers were added – a capital conservation buffer equal to 2.5% of RWA and a countercyclical buffer of up to an additional 2.5% of RWA. Both buffers must be raised through common equity. The broad basis for this proposal comes from the observation that some institutions with heavy losses and depleted capital from the crisis still made distributions to shareholders. The Basel Committee argues that this should not occur and that banks that suffer losses should rebuild their capital by retaining earnings and raising new capital. The guiding principle is to shift the risk as much as possible from depositors to shareholders and employees of banks. As such, the buffers are not additional, minimum capital requirements. Instead, if an institution does not have the required capital buffers, Basel III will restrict the institution's ability to distribute earnings. Of the two types of buffer, the capital conservation buffer is intended to be large enough to enable banks to maintain capital levels above the minimum requirement throughout a significant sector-wide downturn. The countercyclical buffer is an additional requirement which is implemented by national supervisors when there is excess credit growth in their economy, with the intention of dampening such credit growth (Enthofer and Haas 2016).

The CAR promotes stability and efficiency of the worldwide financial systems and banks. The capital to risk-weighted assets ratio for a bank is usually expressed as a percentage. The current minimum of the total capital to risk-weighted assets, under Basel III, is 10.5%. As already mentioned, some assets are riskier than others. A risk weight is assigned to each asset according to how risky it is, resulting in RWAs. This allows banks, investors, and regulators to consider the risk-weighted capital ratio, which is a bank's capital as a share of its RWAs. Another way of thinking about this approach is to consider a different capital requirement for each asset, depending on its risk category.

The objective function for the asset side aims to maximise the interest income produced by assets in the banking book. Such an optimisation exercise consists of the maximisation of the objective function subject to the constraints described herein. It takes the form of a multivariable equality function which describes the total income of the asset base with variables representing the proportions of different asset classes in the total asset structure. The model searches for the maximum value of such a function which is subject to the certain constraints:

$$f(w_{asset1}, w_{asset2}, w_{asset3}, \ldots, w_{assetj}) = w_{asset1} {}^* A {}^* \sum_{i=1}^{6} r_{asset_{1i}}/12 + w_{asset2} {}^* A$$

$$^* \sum_{i=1}^{6} r_{asset_{2i}}/12 + w_{asset3} {}^* A {}^* \sum_{i=1}^{6} r_{asset_{3i}}/12 + \ldots + w_{assetj} {}^* A {}^* \sum_{i=1}^{6} r_{asset_{ji}}/12$$

$$(4.20)$$

where:

$w_{asset1}, w_{asset2} \ldots w_j$ the proportions of the asset classes in the total asset base;

$r_{asset1i}, r_{asset2i}, \ldots r_{asset ji}$ the annual yield for the corresponding asset class j in i^{th} month of the observation period;

A total amount of the asset base.

The objective function for the liability side aims to minimise the total funding cost of a bank. It is a multivariable equality function which describes the total cost of funding with variables representing the proportions of different sources of funding in the total liabilities structure. The model searches for the minimum value of this function subject to certain constraints.

The minimisation function can be written as follows:

$$f(w_A, w_B, w_C, \ldots, w_j) = w_A {}^* L {}^* \sum_{i=1}^{6} c_{A_i}/12 + w_B {}^* L {}^* \sum_{i=1}^{6} c_{B_i}/12$$

$$+ w_C {}^* L {}^* \sum_{i=1}^{6} c_{C_i}/12 + \ldots + w_j {}^* L {}^* \sum_{i=1}^{6} c_{j_i}/12 \qquad (4.21)$$

where:

$w_A, w_B \ldots w_j$ the proportions of the funding opportunities in the total funding base;

$c_{Ai}, c_{Bi}, \ldots c_{ji}$ the annual cost of funding for the respective funding opportunity j in i^{th} month of the observation period.

In the case studies analysed in this book, the optimisation exercise is subject to the following assumptions:

- The analysis is performed over precise time horizon (for example, the period of 6 months, from t_0 to t_6).
- The maturity profile of assets is determined as being based on the constant balance sheet scenario, i.e. it is assumed that the amortising or maturing assets and liabilities are renewed as *like for like* (by assets and liabilities with the same financial characteristics); however, any different assumption can be easily included into the model.
- The external rate of assets includes the interest rate component, liquidity premium component which represents the risk perception of a bank in the market (known

as the FTP rate), and the commercial spread reflecting the creditworthiness of the asset class.

▪ The contingent liquidity costs are not included in the pricing of assets. This choice is driven by the fact that banks still very often charge the indirect liquidity cost to the business unit through a separate process.

Finding the proportions that satisfy the objective function addresses the question of what the target profile of a bank should be considering the initial structure of the banking book, assumptions listed above, and pricing unchanged for the period of the next 6 months. The shorter the period of analysis, the more precise the model outcome is because there is less uncertainty in the external market conditions.

There is a *non-negativity* condition that must be maintained (the model does not allow the proportions to be set at zero). This is driven by the fact that the optimisation model is not meant to change the business model of the financial institution through excluding certain asset or liability classes. Instead, it is meant to change the relative proportions of the existing items in the total asset/funding base with the objective to maximise (for assets)/minimise (for liabilities) the objective function.

The *non-negativity* condition for assets is written as follows:

$$w_{asset1} + w_{asset2} + \ldots + w_{assetj} = 1 \qquad (4.22)$$

$$w_{asset} > 0 \qquad (4.23)$$

The *non-negativity* condition for liabilities is described below:

$$w_A + w_B + w_{C+\ldots+}w_j = 1 \qquad (4.24)$$

$$w_{funding} > 0 \qquad (4.25)$$

The optimisation model, based on the interior point method, has been run for two different financial institutions and with different sets of constraint functions. This reflects, as already mentioned earlier, a variety of risk measurement metrics used by banks based across Europe.

The constraint functions include the concentration limits for all funding sources where it is assumed that the proportion of the certain funding source cannot be higher than 80%. It is an important constraint set up to limit the overreliance on one particular source of funding.

$$0 \leq w_A \leq 0.8 \qquad (4.26)$$

For both the asset and funding side, the risk appetite of the financial institution to IRRBB, in the decision model, has been set up through the equation:

$$\frac{\Delta NII}{NII} > \text{-4\% over 6M horizon} \qquad (4.27)$$

where 4% represents the potential negative impact on the expected NII in case interest rates move instantaneously by 200 bps. This limit is illustrative; however, it reflects IRRBB developments in the recent regulatory landscape (EBA 2018).

The exposure to the liquidity and funding risk has been limited through the following constraint functions:

$$(TI + LAB)/TO >= 100\% \text{ in the next 30 days} \tag{4.28}$$

$$(\Sigma TO_{T>1Y} + Tier\ 1\ capital)/(\Sigma TI_{T>1Y}) \geq 100\% \tag{4.29}$$

$$\frac{A}{D} \leq 80\% \tag{4.30}$$

$$\frac{CMTF}{CMTA} > 35\% \tag{4.31}$$

$$\frac{BMTF}{BMTA} > 100\% \tag{4.32}$$

For the asset side, there is an additional constraint related to the capital absorption:

$$\frac{Tier\ 1\ capital + Tier\ 2\ capital}{RWA} > 12\% \tag{4.33}$$

As shown above, the decision model works based on a set of assumptions and risk metrics provided as the model input. In addition, the regulatory requirements across all banks, especially in Europe, are aligned through the European regulation (CRD IV/ CRR II). Consequently, it is expected that all those constraints similar and set up at the same levels will be seen. There is a clear trend in the banking industry which consists of the standardisation of the approach towards risk management. The optimisation process contributes to the achievement of this standardisation through building the framework around liquidity, funding, and interest rate risk metrics and improvement of the economic results of a financial institution. This chapter shows that optimisation can be used as the universal approach for all commercial and retail banks because all banks need to comply with the regulatory and internal metrics. The internal limits need to encompass fully the regulatory requirements, and, in most cases, they are even more restrictive than the regulatory ones. In addition, all banks aim to minimise funding costs and increase asset profitability in order to remain competitive. This is driven by the fact that a heavily regulated landscape, competitive market, and low or negative interest rates compress the NII and make it more difficult to meet the shareholders' expectations. From the other side, there is always a risk that, in search of higher returns, banks start to undertake riskier business to fight compressed margins. This would certainly have some negative impacts on the health of the whole banking industry. This is why it is so important to find 'safe' solutions for gaining additional profitability and reduce funding cost. The good thing, in the author's view, is that the application of the optimisation model does not impose a radical change in the business model of a financial institution, where the decision is taken by the board of directors. Instead, it attempts to increase the profitability of a financial institution through rebalancing existing asset and funding base proportions and taking advantage of the numerical optimisation techniques applied to the whole banking book.

THE IMPORTANCE OF MODEL SENSITIVITY ANALYSIS

Before analysing the output of the optimisation model under base and a number of additional scenarios, I would like to introduce briefly the concept of model risk. This is extremely important as the optimisation exercise brings in the model risk, and the higher model risk implies higher probability of being challenged by the regulatory authority and even being charged additional capital against the model risk. The author's view is that the more parsimonious the model, the better it is. This does not mean the author promotes rudimentary models being put in place. It means that unnecessary model sophistication increases the model risk and introduces complexity within the model management, calibration, and validation.

In recent years, there has been a trend in financial institutions towards greater use of models in decision-making, driven in part by regulation but manifesting in all areas of risk management. In this regard, many senior management decisions are automated through models (whether statistical algorithms or a set of rules). To some extent, the use of models is encouraged by the Basel regulations; for example, the allocation of capital for the credit risk is performed through advanced models which estimate the probability of default of the client or develop statistical profiles of delinquent customers in order to apply different recovery strategies. The use of valuation models for products and financial instruments has become widespread in financial institutions, in both the markets and the ALM fields. Other examples include models for the quantification of the bank's liquidity position, projected under different scenarios, the projection of the balance sheet and income statement, and the use of stress-testing models. The recent BCBS Standards on IRRBB (published in April 2016) require development of quantitative models for the ΔEVE, ΔNII, automatic and behavioural options, and credit spread risk in the banking book (CSRBB).

The term 'model' refers to a quantitative algorithm, system, or approach that applies statistical, economic, financial, or mathematical theories, techniques, and assumptions to process input data into quantitative estimates (OCC, FED 2011–2012). There are at least three components of the model in the author's view:

- The inputs, which introduce hypotheses and assumptions into the model.
- A method to transform the input into estimates. This method will generally rely on calculations to produce quantitative estimates.
- A reporting component that converts the estimates into useful business information.

The sources of model risk can be classified into three different groups:

- Data deficiencies in terms of both availability and quality, including data errors, lack of historical depth, errors in the feeding of variables, or insufficient sample size.
- Estimation uncertainty or model error in the form of simplifications, approximations and flawed assumptions, or incorrect model design.
- Model misuse, which includes using the model for purposes other than those for which it was designed and not recalibrated for a long time.

The use of models brings undoubted benefits such as:

- Automated decision-making, which in turn improves efficiency by reducing analysis and manual decision-related costs.

- Objective decision-making, ensuring that estimated results are the same in equal circumstances and that internal and external information is reused, thus leveraging historical experience.
- Ability to synthetise complex issues, such as a bank's aggregate risk.

Model risk is defined as the potential for adverse consequences based on incorrect or misused model output and reports and is considered an important risk, which has only recently captured the attention of regulators and institutions, whose approach ranges from mitigation via model validation to the establishment of a comprehensive framework for active model risk management. There has been little regulatory activity on model risk until now.

The first guidelines were published in 2011 and 2012 in the 'Supervisory Guidance on Model Risk Management', which define model risk and provides a set of guidelines establishing the need for entities to develop a Board approved framework to identify and manage this risk (though not necessarily quantify it). These guidelines cover all phases of a model life cycle: development and deployment, use, validation, governance policies, and documentation as the most important factor in the model validation. The main requirement from this regulatory paper emphasises the need to address the model risk with the same importance as any other risk. Consequently, this risk category can be only mitigated (and not removed) through critical analysis and effective challenge. In addition, models should be continuously improved though expert modelling and robust model validation, necessary elements in model mitigation. There is a need to establish a clear distinction between model ownership, control, and compliance roles, and the specific framework set up remains an important task for the institution. The ultimate responsibility for approving the model framework for model risk management (MRM) lies with the board of directors. Finally, regulators emphasise that the fundamental principle in model risk management is 'effective challenge', understood as a critical analysis by objective, qualified people with experience in the line of business in which the model is used, who are able to identify model limitations and assumptions and suggest appropriate changes. Model risk can have a very significant quantitative impact that can result in management making poor decisions and underestimating risks the bank runs on its books. It is therefore important and desirable to have a MRM framework in place and, where appropriate, develop robust model risk estimation techniques aimed at implementing suitable mitigation techniques. Model validation is a key element in model mitigation and its purpose is the effective and independent challenge of the decision made under the model development. All models that may involve risks should undergo the model validation process and there is no single standardised validation method for all institutions and models. Each institution needs to set standards using its own criteria and these standards should be commensurate with model risk. The model validation function itself must be reviewed by Internal Audit, which needs to analyse its work and implement controls as well as give its opinion on the degree of actual independence of this unit.

The author's experience is that the model validation is usually divided into several parts:

1. Assessment of the outcome of the model under the view that it provides the solution in line with our expectation.

2. Assessment of the assumptions used in the model under the view that they are appropriately applied and aligned with the objective of the model.
3. Assessment of the methodology applied in the model.
4. Assessment of the potential risks related to the model feeding and data gathering process.

DEFINITION OF THE SENSITIVITY PARAMETERS FOR THE OPTIMISATION MODEL

The concept of the model risk and underlining its importance in the construction of any model has been introduced. This section now attempts to set up a number of either external or internal parameters which could, potentially, affect the results obtained through the application of the optimisation techniques.

The intention of this analysis consists of the application of the predetermined scenarios to calculated funding structure and the determination of the impact which those scenarios have on the results obtained by the optimisation model. The outcome of *'what if'* analysis helps to understand which factors are the most significant and could represent a driver in the determination of the banking book structure of the bank.

The analysis is performed under the following scenarios:

- *Base scenario* – based on the prevailing rates and the initial (pre-optimised) structure of the banking book.
- *Changes in the interest rates* scenarios – impact on the target structure.
- *Changes in the output of deposit characterisation model* – changes in the balance volatility and balance sensitivity rate (changes in the behaviour of depositors).
- *Inclusion of the prepayment rate of loans* – inclusion of the prepayment rate in the fixed rate asset base (in analysed case studies, under base scenario, only contractual characteristics of loans have been taken into account).
- *Changes in initial asset base* – changes in the initial structure of floating and fixed rate assets.

'Significant Changes in Interest Rates' Scenario

Under this scenario, the target structure for both the asset and funding base is calculated under a set of extreme yet plausible moves in interest rates across all portfolios. The scenario is built to stress the level of interest rates. The expectation is to observe the change in the target profile of the banking book based on the various interest rate scenarios. A number of *event-driven* scenarios which are calibrated on previous financial shocks have been identified for this set of scenarios. This involves defining stress scenarios that replicate relative changes in interest rates for selected historical events. A far from exhaustive list of examples, on which potential interest rate changes could be based, is listed below.

- October 1973 – First OPEC Oil crises;
- 1979 – Iranian Revolution and Second OPEC Oil Shock;
- August 1982 – Mexican Debt Crises;
- September 1985 – The Plaza Accord to weaken the USD;
- October 1987 – Black Monday in US Stocks;

- September 1992 – Speculative Attack on the European ERM;
- February 1994 – Dramatic Federal Reserve Tightening;
- July 1997 – Asian Currency Crisis;
- August 1998 – Russian Default – Emerging Market Debt Crisis;
- September 1998 – Long Term Capital Management Failure;
- 2000–2001 – Dot.com Bust;
- January 2002 – Argentine Peso Devaluation;
- March 2008 – Bear Stearns Rescue;
- September 2008 – Lehman, AIG, FNMA, and FHLMC Collapse;
- April 2010 – Greece Sovereign Downgrade – Euro Crisis;
- February 2014 – Ukraine/Crimea Crisis.

The following scenarios have been examined to assess the sensitivity of the optimisation model.

Oil Supply Crisis In 1973, the global economy was rocked by an oil crisis caused by an OPEC oil embargo, which dramatically cut the available oil supply and significantly increased world oil prices. The oil supply crisis simulates the shocks of another oil supply crisis to test the impact on the market. The number presented below represents only the EUR curve and USD curve, given that the case studies presented in the final section of the book analyse banks with banking book items denominated in EUR and USD.

The scenario is defined in terms of the upward movements of the curve (in bps) (see Table 4.1).

HY/LBO/Default Risk High yield/leverage buyout/default risk refers to the risk posed by less stable entities and the resulting affect their default could have on the market rates.

The scenario is defined in terms of the downward movements of the curve (in bps) (see Table 4.2).

Inflation Expectation Inflation expectations play a significant role in interest rates and their perceived 'real' value. Environments with high inflation lead to lower returns on nominal interest rates, as inflation erodes interest rates. Greater expected inflation will lead to lower expected returns.

TABLE 4.1 Interest rate shocks under the *Oil supply* crisis scenario.

Oil Supply Crisis	0.25	0.5	0.75	1	2	3	4	5	6	7	8	9	10	15	20	30
EUR Scenario	16	9	23	35	47	53	53	53	53	53	47	40	34	37	37	37
USD Scenario	24	14	35	53	71	80	80	80	80	80	71	60	51	55	55	55

Source: own elaboration.

TABLE 4.2 Interest rate shocks under the *HY/LBO/Default risk* scenario.

HY/LBO/Default Risk	0.25	0.5	0.75	1	2	3	4	5	6	7	8	9	10	15	20	30
EUR Scenario	−8	−16	−18	−18	−21	−21	−21	−23	−22	−21	−18	−16	−14	−14	−14	−14
USD Scenario	−13	−24	−26	−28	−32	−32	−32	−34	−34	−32	−28	−24	−21	−21	−21	−21

Source: own elaboration.

TABLE 4.3 Interest rate shocks under *the Inflation expectation* scenario.

Inflation Expectation	0.25	0.5	0.75	1	2	3	4	5	6	7	8	9	10	15	20	30
EUR Scenario	37	37	37	37	37	41	47	50	52	53	53	53	53	47	47	47
USD Scenario	55	55	55	55	55	62	70	75	78	80	80	80	80	70	70	70

Source: own elaboration.

The scenario is defined in terms of the upward movements of the curve (in bps) (see Table 4.3).

The selected above scenarios examine how changes in asset profitability and cost of funding resulting from the interest rate curve movements impact the target structure of the asset and funding base.

The shock is instantaneous and applied at t_0 for the whole period of the analysis. The forward rates are calculated based on the shocked spot rates. It is assumed there are no impacts on either the percentage of the volatile and core part of current accounts or the prepayment rate resulting from the changes in interest rates.

Changes in the Initial Proportions of the Asset Base

The purpose of this analysis is to examine the impact of the initial structure of the asset base on the target structure of the bank.

It is assumed, under this scenario, that there is a change in a bank's strategy where the funds coming from the amortising floating rate assets are no longer extended to clients under the form of loans but instead are invested in the high-quality liquid assets portfolio. This situation could happen if the intention of a bank's treasurer is to strengthen the counterbalancing capacity of a bank.

Changes in the Output of the Deposit Characterisation Model – Balance Volatility, Balance Sensitivity, and Average Life of the Product

This scenario assumes that there is a change in the behaviour of the CASA clients resulting in an increased proportion of the stable part of the product. Such a change would increase earnings volatility as a higher portion of the product is allocated over medium long-term time buckets (see time bucket sensitivity analysis in Chapter 2 under the section 'Interest Rate Risk in the Banking Book – Measurement and Management'). The purpose of this scenario is to see the impact of the increased earnings sensitivity on both the asset and funding base.

Introduction of the CPR into the Model

The *Base* scenario does not include the impact of early redemption of clients' loans. It is a well-known phenomenon that clients in certain market circumstances decide to prepay partially or completely their loan and refinance it through another bank. This could be driven either by the external market condition (financial prepayments) or individual necessity of the client itself (structural prepayments).

Under the 'prepayment scenario' the constant prepayment rate is 7% and refers only to fixed rate assets. The introduction of the CPR in the model has significant impact both on the IRR structure of the banking book (in terms of *delta NII*) and liquidity metrics, given the additional amount of liquidity which needs to be reinvested.

Practical Example of the Optimisation Process and Quantification of the Economic Impact under Base and Stress Scenarios

This chapter provides the reader with an illustrative analysis of the optimisation process performed for a small-sized European bank (Bank 1) and international bank based in UK (Bank 2). With this purpose, the funding costs for Bank 1 and Bank 2 have been calculated before and after the application of the optimisation model. The reduction in the overall funding cost has been driven by the rebalancing of the proportions of the funding sources. In fact, all calculations have been performed both at the single funding source level and for the whole funding base in order to see the contribution of each component to the total funding cost. The same algorithm has been applied for the asset side. The first analysed scenario is related to the *business as usual* situation, i.e. there is no change in the underlying model assumptions (interest term structure, liquidity profiling, and behavioural assumptions). Thus, it is a baseline scenario.

In order to assess the sensitivity of the model to a number of external and internal assumptions (herein factors) the optimisation exercise is run multiple times under different scenarios (herein sensitivity scenarios) both for Bank 1 and Bank 2. The objective of this analysis consists of the assessment of the sensitivity of the model to those factors and in understanding which factor has an impact on the model outcome and to what extent.

The case study is performed for financial institutions based in Europe. The analysed institutions are typical commercial banks, i.e. they have a well-diversified funding structure consisting of debt issuance and a significant amount of customer funding, such as current accounts and time deposits. The asset side is composed of a liquidity buffer and commercial loans, mainly at floating rate. The process of the selection of institutions has included careful analysis of the size of the risk sensitive assets (RSA) and risk sensitive liabilities (RSL). The intention was to examine banks of significantly different sizes. Bank 1 represents a small-sized institution and Bank 2 represents an international bank, active in different countries.

The major part of the chapter quantifies the profitability derived from the application of the optimisation model and on the analysis of the sensitivity factors. There are follow up observations which have emerged after deeper analysis of the risk metrics.

CASE STUDY: ECONOMIC IMPACT FROM THE OPTIMISATION MODEL UNDER BASELINE AND SENSITIVITY SCENARIOS FOR BANK 1

It will be assumed that Bank 1 has EUR3.4bn of risk sensitive assets and most of them are made up of lending to corporate customers at a floating rate. The remainder constitutes customers lending at a fixed rate and liquidity buffer. The corporate loans are indexed to EURIBOR 1 M, while liabilities are mainly indexed to EURIBOR 3 M and 6 M. Also, it will be assumed for the optimisation exercise that EURIBOR rates will follow the market expectation for the movement of EURIBOR rates onwards (in particular, the forward rate for EURIBOR 1 M, 3 M, and 6 M).

The liquidity buffer of this bank contains liquid assets which could be easily sold out at little or no loss of value. According to the new regulatory landscape (Basel III), banks must keep an appropriate amount of these assets (known as high-quality liquid assets, or HQLA) in order to meet unexpected cash outflows. The liquidity buffer of Bank 1 contains government bonds at a fixed rate which are considered as level 1 assets according to the Basel definition. A further assumption is that Bank 1 is mainly funded by the revolving credit lines (RCA) provided by the parent company, which is based in the US. These revolving lines are 5-year loans at a floating rate indexed to EURIBOR 1 M, 3 M, and 6 M. In addition, some portion is represented by the corporate current accounts which are linked to the *project finance* lending. A small portion of funding is represented by short-term time deposits. The bank also funds itself by a small portion of unsecured senior debt issuance (see Figure 5.1). The total amount of RSL amounts to EUR2.7bn. As in the case of the asset side, the funding rate represents an external rate paid to customers. The current accounts have been behaviouralised between stable and non-stable parts according to the deposit characterisation model described in Chapter 3. The behaviouralisation of items without deterministic maturity (such as current and savings accounts) has crucial importance for all models employed by the bank. The behavioural liquidity metrics and interest rate risk metrics are based on the analysis of this kind of non-maturing deposit (NMD). The decision model is not an exception and it appears that the model is significantly sensitive to the behavioural assumptions. In the case of Bank 1, the current accounts have shown high balance volatility as only 35% of these products have been considered as stable. The remainder portion of balances is volatile and sensitive to the changes in external and idiosyncratic factors. Thus, it is assumed that current accounts, both from the liquidity perspective and interest rate perspective, have been allocated to the short-term buckets, i.e. O/N for IRRBB and 1 M for liquidity.

The main model assumption is that the financial characteristics, such as maturity, pricing, and risk factors, remain unchanged throughout the optimisation exercise, i.e. 6 months (see Figures 5.2 and 5.3). Moreover, it has to be remembered that the optimisation changes the related proportions of the assets and liabilities components in the banking book and does not assume the introduction of any new products.

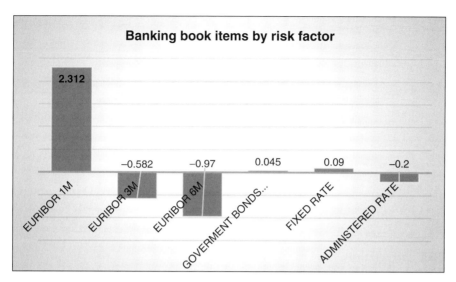

FIGURE 5.1   The breakdown of banking book items by risk factor for Bank 1 (numbers in euro/millions).
Source: own elaboration based on the banking book of Bank 1.

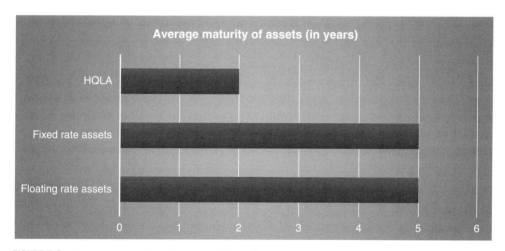

FIGURE 5.2   Average maturity of assets of Bank 1.
Source: own elaboration base on the numbers of the banking book of Bank 1.

Table 5.1 shows the optimisation results for assets in terms of the weighted average income generated by the total asset base split by the single portfolio basis. It shows the weighted average income before the implementation of the optimisation model based on Eq. (4.21). Subsequently, we recalculate the optimisation outcome for each scenario (i.e. baseline and sensitivity scenarios). The change (delta) in the asset income under each scenario is calculated as a difference between the total income achieved after optimisation and the total income from the asset side before the optimisation. The reported numbers are in euro/millions and show the income for the next 6 months starting from

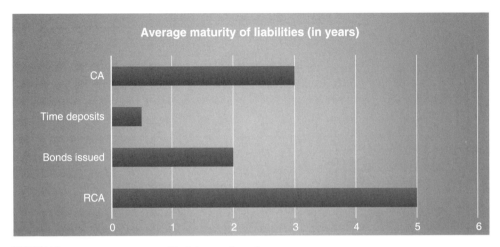

FIGURE 5.3 Average maturity of liabilities of Bank 1.
Source: own elaboration base on the numbers of the banking book of Bank 1.

the date of analysis which, for this particular example, is assumed to be 31 March 2016 (*cut-off* date). As already mentioned, the table also states the split by asset portfolio in order to show the optimisation impact at the total and portfolio level. The calculations are performed through the application of the numerical optimisation toolbox in MATLAB, *fmincon*. It can be seen that, in the case of Bank 1, the weighted average income has improved for all scenarios and the delta between the results before and after optimisation varies from EUR3.8m to EUR7.63m depending on the scenario applied. It can be observed that the highest delta is achieved for the *Change in the asset structure* (7.63m). These results, displayed in the table, lead to the confirmation of our expectation, i.e. they confirm that the introduction of numerical optimisation techniques for the banking book has a positive impact on the bank's profitability in terms of the weighted average income (remember that income has been chosen as a criteria for the optimisation exercise).

Bank 1 has improved its total weighted income under the baseline scenario from EUR68.15m to EUR72.11m, changing the proportion of asset classes. As already mentioned, the highest result (improvement) is achieved under the *Change in the asset structure* scenario (from EUR64.48m to EUR72.10m). Those numbers could be interpreted in the following way. Assuming the change in the total asset structure (increase of HQLA and decrease of the portion of the floating rate assets) there is an immediate impact on the total income comparing to the baseline scenario (with no change in the initial asset proportions). This seems a logical result because HQLA usually earn less (in the case of the European bank) and procure a negative net interest margin (NIM) for the bank. However, when we optimise the HQLA level (decreasing its amount to the level imposed by the constraint functions) and focus on the asset classes which generate the higher income for the bank, this result looks obvious. Similarly, under the *Oil supply crisis* scenario the economic result before the application of the optimisation is equal to EUR71.23m. The model optimises the total asset base through a rebalance of the asset proportions which results in increased total income by EUR7.45m (from 71.23m to 78.68m).

TABLE 5.1 Results in terms of the average income of assets achieved before and after application of the optimisation model for Bank 1.

Weighted average income generated by the total asset structure in euros/millions before the application of the decision model and at the portfolio level

Numbers in euros/millions	Base scenario	Inflation expectation	HY – LBO – Default risk	Oil supply crisis	Change in the deposit characterisation model assumption	Change in the asset structure	Downgrade of the bank by one notch
Total asset portfolio	68.15	74.89	65.18	71.23	68.15	64.48	76.65
Fixed rate assets	15.89	17.64	15.08	17.75	15.89	15.64	17.64
Floating rate assets	52.19	57.18	50.03	53.41	52.19	48.47	58.94
HQLA	0.07	0.07	0.07	0.07	0.07	0.37	0.07

Weighted average income generated by the total asset structure in euros/millions after the application of the decision model and at the portfolio level

Numbers in euros/millions	Base scenario	Inflation expectation	HY – LBO – Default risk	Oil supply crisis	Change in the deposit characterisation model assumption	Change in the asset structure	Downgrade of the bank by one notch
Total asset portfolio	72.11	79.79	68.65	78.68	73.36	72.10	80.46
Fixed rate assets	20.48	22.29	19.64	20.82	19.46	20.64	23.02
Floating rate assets	51.46	57.33	48.84	57.69	53.80	51.29	57.27
HQLA	0.17	0.17	0.17	0.17	0.10	0.17	0.17

TABLE 5.1 (*Continued*)

Change in the asset income resulting from the application of the decision model

Numbers euros/millions	Base scenario	Inflation expectation	HY – LBO – Default risk	Oil supply crisis	Change in the deposit characterisation model assumption	Change in the asset structure	Downgrade of the bank by one notch
Total asset portfolio	3.97	4.91	3.48	7.45	5.21	7.63	3.82
Fixed rate assets	4.59	4.65	4.56	3.07	3.57	5.00	5.38
Floating rate assets	−0.73	0.15	−1.19	4.28	1.61	2.82	−1.67
HQLA	0.11	0.11	0.11	0.11	0.03	−0.19	0.11

Source: own elaboration.

The model calculates the new proportions of the different asset classes to increase overall portfolio profitability and, at the same time, to maintain compliance with the internal and regulatory limits. At this point, it is important to highlight that the optimisation exercise indicates, potentially, the target profile of the analysed portfolio subject to a certain set of assumptions. The process of reshaping of the portfolio, in order to achieve the desirable structure, is another side of the optimisation process in the sense that it takes time to shape the balance sheet, as it cannot be done overnight.

In the tables, HY–LBO stands for high-yield–leveraged buyout.

The analysis of results for the funding base produces similar results as for the asset side, i.e. the application of the optimisation model is beneficial for the financial institution and results in a reduction in funding costs.

We observe cost reduction under all scenarios except one: *Inflation expectation*. Under the *Inflation expectation* scenario the total funding cost has slightly increased (from EUR34.37m to EUR34.88m). However, it is fully explained by the fact that Bank 1, before the implementation of the optimisation model, was not compliant with the short-term cumulative liquidity ratio set at 100% (see Table 5.2). Consequently, the constrained optimisation process imposes such a structure, in terms of liabilities, which complies with the liquidity requirement (and short-term cumulative liquidity ratio). Given significantly higher interest rates under this scenario, compliance with the short-term cumulative liquidity ratio resulted in the increase in overall funding costs in comparison to the structure which is not compliant with the liquidity requirements. For this reason, the benefits from the optimisation model, for this particular bank (which was not compliant with liquidity requirements at the beginning of the analysis), is lower, compared to the situation where the bank was compliant with the short-term cumulative liquidity ratio.

Under the baseline scenario, the rebalancing of the funding base leads to a reduction of funding costs from EUR30.79m to EUR30.49m. The highest reduction in the funding costs, after the optimisation exercise, is achieved under the *Change in the asset structure* scenario. This is because under this scenario there is a change in the bank's commercial strategy as the expiring cash flows of amortising floating rate assets are no longer extended to clients under the form of loans but, instead, they are invested in the HQLA portfolio. This situation could potentially happen if the intention of a bank's treasurer (and other members of the board of directors) is to strengthen the counterbalancing capacity of the bank and disinvest from one asset class. The expectation is to see a decrease in the profitability of the asset base and a lower cost of funds. Consequently, the impact of the application of the decision model is expected to be higher under this scenario.

The high impact on the profitability of Bank 1 after the implementation of the optimisation model can be seen under the *Change in the deposit characterisation model assumptions* scenario as the funding costs decrease from EUR30.79m to EUR29.85m. This is an interesting result leading to the conclusion that optimisation calibrates the target proportions of the funding base following the changing behaviour of clients. In this particular case, under the analysed scenario, there is an assumption that there is increased stability of NMD balances, as the volatile part of the product decreases from the 65% to 40%. This result indicates the importance of the behavioural assumption in the reduction of funding costs and high sensitivity of the optimisation model to this factor. In addition, the sensitivity to behavioural assumptions on the liability side appears to be higher than on the asset side.

TABLE 5.2 Results in terms of the average funding costs achieved before and after application of the optimisation model for Bank 1.

Weighted average cost of funding generated by the total funding structure in euro/millions before the application of the decision model and at the portfolio level

Numbers in euros/millions	Base scenario	Inflation expectation	HY – LBO – Default risk	Oil supply crisis	Change in the deposit characterisation model assumption	Change in the asset structure	Downgrade of the bank by one notch
Total cost of funding	30.79	34.37	29.17	31.78	30.79	30.79	36.97
Corporate current account	0.01	0.01	0.01	0.01	0.01	0.01	0.01
Corporate time deposits	0.18	0.26	0.15	0.21	0.18	0.18	0.18
Bond issued	7.97	7.97	7.97	7.97	7.97	7.97	9.39
Revolving credit lines	22.63	26.14	21.04	23.60	22.63	22.63	27.38

Weighted average cost of funding generated by the total funding structure in euros/millions after the application of the decision model and at the portfolio level

Numbers in euros/millions	Base scenario	Inflation expectation	HY – LBO – Default risk	Oil supply crisis	Change in the deposit characterisation model assumption	Change in the asset structure	Downgrade of the bank by one notch
Total cost of funding	30.49	34.88	28.50	31.73	29.85	26.06	36.57
Corporate current accounts	0.00	0.00	0.00	0.00	0.01	0.02	0.00
Corporate time deposits	0.94	1.33	0.76	1.08	1.01	1.18	0.94
Bond issued	3.73	3.73	3.73	3.72	3.01	0.00	4.38
Revolving	25.82	29.82	24.01	26.92	25.82	24.86	31.24

Change in the cost of funds resulting from the application of the decision model							
Numbers in euros/millions	Base scenario	Inflation expectation	HY – LBO – Default risk	Oil supply crisis	Change in the deposit characterisation model assumption	Change in the asset structure	Downgrade of the bank by one notch
Total change in funding costs	−0.30	0.51	−0.66	−0.06	−0.94	−4.73	−0.40
Corporate current accounts	−0.01	−0.01	−0.01	−0.01	0.00	0.01	−0.01
Corporate time deposits	0.76	1.07	0.62	0.87	0.83	1.00	0.76
Bond issued	−4.24	−4.24	−4.24	−4.25	−4.96	−7.97	−5.01
Revolving credit lines	3.19	3.68	2.97	3.33	3.19	2.23	3.86

Source: own elaboration.

Tables 5.3 and 5.4 summarise the internal metrics related to the exposure to the liquidity and interest rate risk before and after optimisation. Bank 1 breaches the short-term cumulative liquidity ratio under all scenarios before the implementation of optimisation model. However, this limit is respected after optimisation. Additionally,

TABLE 5.3 Internal thresholds (limits) for assets – Bank 1.

		Small-sized bank (Bank 1) – asset side				
		Liquidity metrics		IRRBB metrics		Capital Adequacy Ratio
		Cumulative short-term ratio	Structural liquidity ratio	NII sensitivity +200	NII sensitivity −200	CAR
Base scenario	Before implementation of the decision model	59%	92%	78%	4%	26%
	After implementation of the decision model	100%	94%	−4%	−0.2%	22%
Inflation expectation	Before implementation of the decision model	57%	92%	72%	4%	26%
	After implementation of the decision model	100%	94%	−4%	−0.2%	22%
HY – LBO – Default risk	Before implementation of the decision model	59%	92%	78%	4%	26%
	After implementation of the decision model	100%	94%	−4%	−0.2%	22%
Oil supply crisis	Before implementation of the decision model	60%	92%	71%	4%	26%
	After implementation of the decision model	100%	94%	−4%	−0.2%	22%
Change in the deposit char-acterisation model assumption	Before implementation of the decision model	92%	94%	81%	4%	26%
	After implementation of the decision model	100%	94%	−4%	−0.2%	21.5%
Inclusion of the prepayment rate	Before implementation of the decision model	62%	94%	79%	4%	26%
	After implementation of the decision model	100%	99%	−4%	−0.2%	22%
Change in the asset structure	Before implementation of the decision model	201%	98%	76%	4%	28%
	After implementation of the decision model	100%	94%	−4%	−0.2%	22%
Downgrade of the bank by one notch	Before implementation of the decision model	60%	92%	73%	4%	26%
	After implementation of the decision model	100%	94%	−4%	−0.2%	22%

Source: own elaboration.

TABLE 5.4   Internal thresholds (limits) for liabilities – Bank 1.

		Small-sized bank (Bank 1) – liability side			
		Liquidity metrics		IRRBB metrics	
		Cumulative short-term ratio	Structural liquidity ratio	NII sensitivity +200	NII sensitivity −200
Base scenario	Before implementation of the decision model	59%	92%	78%	4%
	After implementation of the decision model	100%	90%	70%	4%
Inflation expectation	Before implementation of the decision model	60%	92%	72%	4%
	After implementation of the decision model	100%	90%	64%	3%
HY – LBO – Default risk	Before implementation of the decision model	60%	92%	72%	4%
	After implementation of the decision model	100%	90%	65%	3%
Oil supply crisis	Before implementation of the decision model	60%	92%	71%	4%
	After implementation of the decision model	100%	90%	64%	3%
Change in the deposit characterisation model assumption	Before implementation of the decision model	92%	94%	81%	4%
	After implementation of the decision model	100%	90%	70%	3%
Inclusion of the prepayment rate	Before implementation of the decision model	62%	94%	79%	4%
	After implementation of the decision model	100%	90%	69%	3%
Change in the asset structure	Before implementation of the decision model	201%	98%	76%	4%
	After implementation of the decision model	100%	90%	57%	3%
Downgrade of the bank by one notch	Before implementation of the decision model	60%	92%	73%	4%
	After implementation of the decision model	100%	90%	66%	3%

Source: own study.

there is lower sensitivity of the IRRBB metric since the volatility of NII under parallel shock has been reduced.

Consequently, we observe improvement in all the internal metrics of Bank 1, in terms of:

- Improvement in the short-term cumulative ratio, indicating higher CBC of the bank (the short-term liquidity ratio is at the requested level).

- Improvement in the NII sensitivity metrics, indicating a reduction in the NII sensitivity for both the +200 bps and –200 bps scenario.
- Optimisation of the CAR ratio.

As already mentioned, for both the asset side and liabilities side there is a breach in the internal limit before optimisation. This indicates a situation where the short-term liquidity ratio is below the required threshold, i.e. 100%, and the bank must undertake mitigation actions to increase the level of HQLA. The reason for the limit breach by Bank 1 is not investigated in this case study. It is worth pointing out, at this stage, that the application of the optimisation allows for compliance with this internal limit and to keep it stable at 100% for all scenarios (the required level of HQLA).

The optimisation benefits are quantified in Tables 5.1–5.4 through the application of the optimisation algorithm and are subject to inequality constraints. The model calculates the weighted average income from assets and overall cost of funds before and after the optimisation, as per the example in Figure 5.4.

Subsequently, the optimised funding structure is calculated by the optimisation model as per the example in Figure 5.5.

The comparison between the total cost before and after implementation of the optimisation model, under the *Base* scenario, is presented in Figure 5.6.

A similar analysis for all scenarios for Bank 1 is presented in Appendix 1.

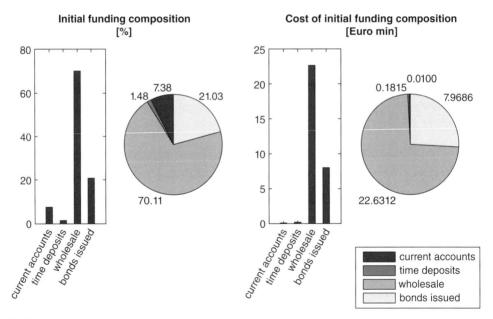

FIGURE 5.4 Initial composition of funding structure of Bank 1 and corresponding funding costs before the implementation of the optimisation model under the *Base* scenario.
Source: own study.

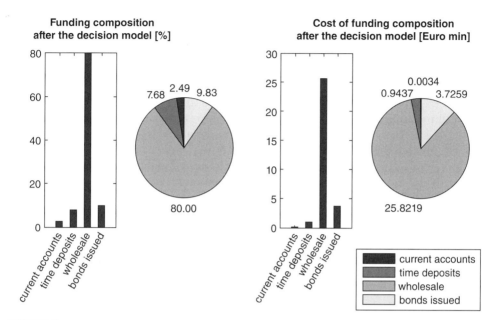

FIGURE 5.5   Optimised composition of the funding base and resulting funding costs for Bank 1 under the *Base* scenario.
Source: own elaboration.

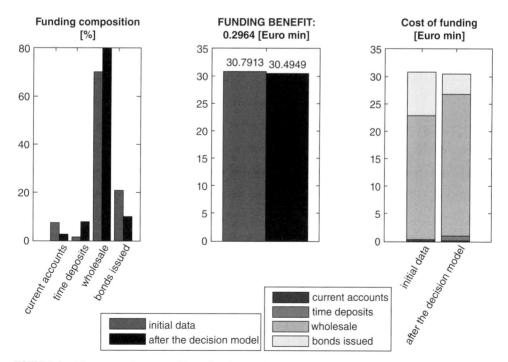

FIGURE 5.6   The quantification of benefits for Bank 1 under the *Base* scenario.
Source: own elaboration.

CASE STUDY: ECONOMIC IMPACT FROM THE OPTIMISATION MODEL UNDER BASELINE AND SENSITIVITY SCENARIOS FOR BANK 2

The objective of this case study is to quantify the economic impact deriving from the application of the optimisation model in an international bank based in the UK and named, for the purpose of this analysis, Bank 2. Similarly to the case study of Bank 1, the impact of the application of the optimisation model is calculated under a base scenario and under sensitivity scenarios. Also, in this case, the model is applied separately to the asset side and liability side. Bank 2 represents a typical large bank based in the UK and, therefore, it reflects the common features of banks located in the UK, i.e. most assets are represented by floating rate loans, short-term fixed rate trade loans, and administered rate products (administered rate products have an important financial characteristic, where it is at the discretion of the bank to adjust rates paid by clients). The administered rate products are highly correlated to the Bank of England base rate. In our case study we assume that the asset base is composed of USD109bn of retail assets, USD178bn of corporate client assets, USD202bn of financial market assets, and USD60bn of HQLA. In total, the RSA amounts to USD549bn. The majority of assets are short-term fixed-rate trade finance loans which are classified by the counterparty type, i.e. loans to banks and loans to non-bank financial institutions. The retail assets are mainly administered rate, which is a common feature in the UK market. The remainder is composed of floating rate assets indexed to LIBOR 1 M and 3 M. The bank holds a buffer of marketable securities that can be converted quickly into cash or pledged as collateral to meet outflows in a liquidity stress and deposits at the central bank. It has the following composition:

a) Central bank cash – 40%.
b) Marketable short-term securities – 40%.
c) Sub 1M ALM assets – 20%.

The client base is distributed between:

a) Retail assets – mortgages.
b) Corporate client assets extended to mid-sized clients.
c) Banks and non-bank financial institutions.

The average maturity of Bank 2 assets is presented in Figure 5.7.
It can be noticed that the average maturity of the assets of Bank 2 is significantly lower in comparison to the maturity of assets in Bank 1. The shorter average maturity of assets is driven by significant reliance on short-term trade finance assets.
The distribution by risk factor is presented in Figure 5.8.
The bank is funded through:

- Retail deposits – current accounts collected from retail clients. Current accounts are largely non-interest bearing or low interest bearing.
- Transactional banking products (cash management and payment) – products without deterministic maturity (products which do not have any contractual maturity). The product covers both corporate clients and banks. Corporate client accounts are considered highly stable, as the corporate clients need a bank account to manage their business's operational transaction activities.
- Senior debt issuance represents floating rate debt with residual maturity of 5 years.

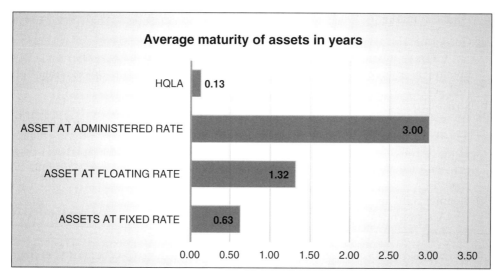

FIGURE 5.7 Average maturity of the asset side of Bank 2.
Source: own elaboration.

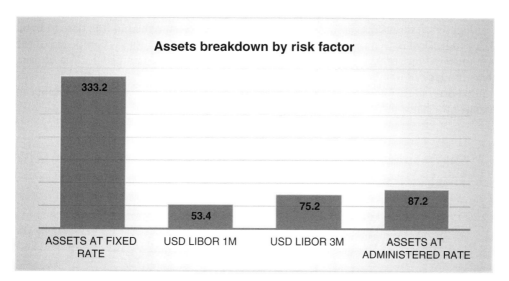

FIGURE 5.8 Breakdown of assets by risk factor (in USD/billions).
Source: own elaboration.

- Financial market products – this product delivers a variety of risk management, financing, and investment solutions for clients, offering capabilities across origination, structuring, sales, and trading. This category offers customers a suite of solutions ranging from short-term vanilla deposits to longer term structured products to match customers' strategic investment needs or operational cash requirements.

Financial market products include:

a) Corporate Time Deposits (CTDs).

   CTDs represents a significant pillar of Bank 2's liability base, as they are a key investment avenue for risk averse investors. CTDs tenors range from overnight up to 2 years.

b) Structured Deposits and Structured Notes.

   Structured Deposits are categorised separately from CTDs as they are generally linked to a derivative element, tracking an underlying asset class and offering higher yields to customers. Structured deposits tend to be transacted in longer tenors than conventional CTD. The residual maturity of the structured deposits is around 12 months.

c) Commercial Paper and Certificates of Deposits.

   A supplementary source of funding providing access to incremental pools of liquidity, the average maturity of this product is around 2 years.

Bank 2 has USD492bn of RSL and is mainly funded by current accounts and savings accounts (CASA) products (56% of the funding base is composed of items without deterministic maturity). Given the importance of this product class in the total funding base, it is interesting to understand how the modelling assumptions of this product impact the outcome of the optimisation model. The remainder of the funding base comprises financial market products.

Figure 5.9 shows the distribution of the risk factors across the funding base in Bank 2. It can be clearly seen that the main portion of the bank's liabilities is composed of the administered rate products, a typical situation for banks located in the UK. In addition, there is a lack of liabilities at floating rate, a fact which, in the author's view, represents limited diversification in terms of the risk factors and, consequently, lower flexibility to manage the basis risk for the institution in comparison to Bank 1.

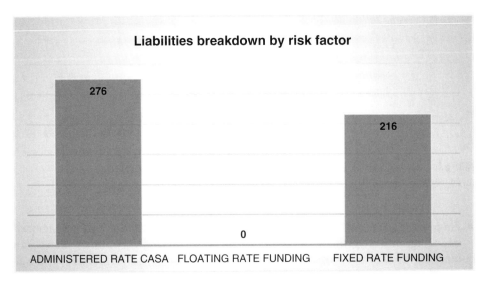

FIGURE 5.9 Liabilities breakdown by risk factors in Bank 2 (in USD/billions).
Source: own elaboration.

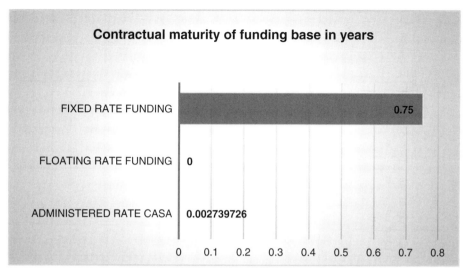

FIGURE 5.10   Average maturity of liabilities of Bank 2.
Source: own elaboration.

Observing the average maturity of the funding base, the significant reliance on the outcome of the behavioural modelling of CASA has emerged. Bank 2, on a contractual basis, has all liabilities with an average maturity lower than 1 year (see Figure 5.10). This structure introduces material model risk embedded in the banking book which is driven by the assumptions and outcomes of the deposit characterisation model described in detail in the Chapter 3 section 'Modelling of Customers' Deposits – Liabilities Side'. This is driven by the fact that products without deterministic maturity (contractual maturity equal to 1 day), for risk management purposes, have to be analysed and modelled.

Let's examine the optimisation applied to the asset side under all sensitivity scenarios which has generated the results shown in Tables 5.5 and 5.6.

Similarly to the case study for Bank 1, for Bank 2 an analysis of the internal limits the bank is subject to is performed, before and after application of the optimisation model, summarised in Tables 5.7 and 5.8.

The analysis of Bank 2, for the asset base, indicates that the highest benefit from the application of the optimisation model was achieved under the *Change in the fixed rate asset structure* scenario, in which case the economic advantage totalled USD1.25bn. This is a very interesting result, as Bank 1 has shown the highest sensitivity to the same factor. The economic benefit, as in the case of Bank 1, has been split by the single portfolio level to provide a better insight into the contribution to the overall result by each product. For example, either the portfolios of corporate assets or floating rate mortgages have seen a significant increase in generated income after the application of the model. The lowest impact can be observed under the *Earthquake* scenario and the *Prepayment inclusion* scenario, although in all cases there is still a benefit which exceeds USD0.25bn.

The extent of the economic benefit has been summarised in Figure 5.11.

TABLE 5.5 Results in terms of the average income on assets achieved before and after application of optimisation for Bank 2.

Weighted average income generated by the total asset structure in USD/billions before the application of the decision model and at the portfolio level

Numbers in USD/billions	Base scenario	Inflation expectation	Earthquake scenario	Oil supply crisis	Change in the deposit characterisation model assumption	Change in the fixed rate asset structure	Downgrade of the bank by one notch	Prepayment inclusion
Total asset portfolio	6.30	7.64	5.86	6.92	6.30	5.33	6.44	6.30
Floating rate mortgages	1.53	1.83	1.50	1.70	1.53	1.53	1.67	1.53
Corporate assets	2.50	3.03	2.36	2.74	2.54	1.43	2.54	2.54
Trade finance	2.11	2.67	1.89	2.37	2.12	2.12	2.12	2.12
HQLA	0.11	0.11	0.11	0.11	0.11	0.26	0.11	0.11

Weighted average income generated by the total asset structure in USD/billions after the application of the decision model and at the portfolio level

Numbers in euros/billions	Base scenario	Inflation expectation	Earthquake scenario	Oil supply crisis	Change in the deposit characterisation model assumption	Change in the fixed rate asset structure	Downgrade of the bank by one notch	Prepayment inclusion
Total asset portfolio	6.58	8.03	6.14	7.29	6.59	6.59	6.83	6.58
Floating rate mortgages	2.06	2.48	2.02	2.30	2.06	2.06	4.38	2.06
Corporate assets	1.99	2.37	1.85	2.15	1.99	1.99	0.00	1.99
Trade finance	2.48	3.14	2.21	2.79	2.48	2.48	2.38	2.48
HQLA	0.05	0.05	0.05	0.05	0.05	0.05	0.07	0.05

Change in the asset income resulting from the application of the decision model								
Numbers in euros/ billions	Base scenario	Inflation expectation	Earthquake scenario	Oil supply crisis	Change in the deposit characterisation model assumption	Change in the fixed rate asset structure	Downgrade of the bank by one notch	Prepayment inclusion
Total asset portfolio	*0.28*	*0.38*	*0.27*	*0.37*	*0.28*	*1.25*	*0.39*	*0.27*
Floating rate mortgages	*0.53*	*0.64*	*0.52*	*0.59*	*0.53*	*0.53*	*2.71*	*0.53*
Corporate assets	*−0.51*	*−0.66*	*−0.51*	*−0.58*	*−0.55*	*0.56*	*−2.54*	*−0.55*
Trade finance	*0.37*	*0.47*	*0.33*	*0.42*	*0.37*	*0.37*	*0.27*	*0.36*
HQLA	*−0.06*	*−0.06*	*−0.06*	*−0.06*	*−0.06*	*−0.21*	*−0.05*	*−0.06*

Source: own elaboration.

TABLE 5.6 Results in terms of the average funding costs achieved before and after application of the decision model for Bank 2.

Weighted average cost of funding generated by the total funding structure in USD/billions before the application of the decision model and at the portfolio level

Numbers in euro/billions	Base scenario	Inflation expectation	Earthquake scenario	Oil supply crisis	Change in the deposit characterisation model assumption	Change in the fixed rate asset structure	Downgrade of the bank by one notch	Inclusion of the CPR in fixed rate assets
Total funding base	2.85	3.44	2.57	3.20	2.85	2.85	2.99	2.85
Retail current accounts	0.01	0.01	0.01	0.01	0.01	0.01	0.01	0.01
Transactional banking current accounts	0.17	0.17	0.17	0.17	0.17	0.17	0.17	0.17
Bond issued	0.64	0.79	0.58	0.69	0.64	0.64	0.78	0.64
Corporate time deposits	1.02	1.30	0.92	1.12	1.02	1.02	1.02	1.02
Structured time deposits	0.33	0.39	0.29	0.39	0.33	0.33	0.33	0.33
Commercial papers and certificates of deposits	0.68	0.78	0.59	0.81	0.68	0.68	0.68	0.68

Weighted average cost of funding generated by the total funding structure in USD/billions after the application of the decision model and at the portfolio level

Numbers in euro/billions	Base scenario	Inflation expectation	Earthquake scenario	Oil Supply Crisis	Change in the deposit characterisation model assumption	Change in the fixed rate asset structure	Downgrade of the bank by one notch	Inclusion of the CPR in fixed rate assets
Total funding base	2.20	2.72	1.98	2.44	2.20	1.98	2.24	2.18
Retail current accounts	0.01	0.01	0.01	0.01	0.01	0.01	0.06	0.01
Transactional banking current accounts	0.06	0.06	0.06	0.06	0.06	0.06	0.01	0.06
Bank issued	0.21	0.27	0.20	0.23	0.21	0.00	0.26	0.20
Corporate time deposits	1.50	1.90	1.35	1.64	1.50	1.50	1.50	1.50
Structured time deposits	0.24	0.28	0.21	0.28	0.24	0.24	0.24	0.24
Commercial papers and certificates of deposits	0.17	0.20	0.15	0.21	0.17	0.17	0.17	0.17

TABLE 5.6 (Continued)

Change in the cost of funds resulting from the application of the decision model								
Numbers in euros/billions	Base scenario	Inflation expectation	Earthquake scenario	Oil Supply Crisis	Change in the deposit characterisation model assumption	Change in the fixed rate asset structure	Downgrade of the bank by one notch	Inclusion of the CPR in fixed rate assets
Total funding base	−0.65	−0.72	−0.59	−0.76	−0.65	−0.87	−0.75	−0.67
Retail current accounts	0.01	0.01	0.01	0.01	0.01	0.00	0.05	0.01
Transactional banking current accounts	−0.11	−0.11	−0.11	−0.11	−0.11	−0.11	−0.16	−0.11
Bond issued	−0.42	−0.53	−0.39	−0.46	−0.42	−0.64	−0.52	−0.44
Corporate time deposits	0.48	0.60	0.43	0.52	0.48	0.48	0.48	0.48
Structured time deposits	−0.10	−0.11	−0.08	−0.11	−0.10	−0.09	−0.10	−0.10
Commercial papers and certificates of deposits	−0.50	−0.58	−0.44	−0.60	−0.50	−0.51	−0.50	−0.50

Source: own elaboration.

TABLE 5.7 Internal ratios for assets of Bank 2.

| | UK bank – asset side | | | | | | |
| | Liquidity metrics | | | | IRRBB metrics | | Capital absorption |
	AD ratio	MTFRcont	MTFRbehav	SH_2M	NII sensitivity +200	NII sensitivity −200	CAR
Before implementation of the decision model	80%	60%	176%	134%	38%	1.9%	12.4%
After implementation of the decision model	79%	60.0%	166%	100%	30%	1.5%	12%
Before implementation of the decision model	80%	60%	176%	134%	31%	1.6%	12.4%
After implementation of the decision model	80%	60.2%	166%	100%	25%	1.2%	12%
Before implementation of the decision model	80%	60%	176%	133%	40%	2.0%	12.4%
After implementation of the decision model	80%	60.2%	166%	100%	32%	1.6%	12%
Before implementation of the decision model	80%	60%	175%	133%	35%	1.7%	12.4%
After implementation of the decision model	80%	60.2%	165%	100%	28%	1.4%	12%
Before implementation of the decision model	80%	60%	176%	134%	31%	1.6%	12.4%
After implementation of the decision model	80%	60%	166%	100%	24%	1.2%	12.0%
Before implementation of the decision model	80%	63%	176%	133%	38%	1.9%	12%
After implementation of the decision model	80%	62%	165%	100%	30%	1.5%	12%
Before implementation of the decision model	58%	82%	215%	214%	73%	3.6%	15.0%
After implementation of the decision model	80%	60%	166%	100%	30%	1.5%	12.0%
Before implementation of the decision model	80%	60%	176%	134%	38%	1.9%	12.4%
After implementation of the decision model	80%	60%	152%	100%	60%	2.9%	14.6%

Source: own elaboration.

Figure 5.12 ranks the sensitivity factors according to their impact on the funding cost reduction obtained by the application of the decision model for Bank 1.

It can be clearly seen that, in both cases, the most important factors are related to the changes in the asset structure (the business strategy of the bank) and changes in the interest rate curve.

As already noted, the impact of the sensitivity factors for Bank 2 has provided similar results as in case of Bank 1, since the highest impact is driven by the interest rate scenarios

TABLE 5.8 Internal ratios for liabilities of Bank 2.

	UK bank – liability side					
	Liquidity metrics				IRRBB metrics	
	AD ratio	MTFRcont	MTFRbehav	SH_2M	NII sensitivity +200	NII sensitivity −200
Before implementation of the decision model	80%	60%	176%	134%	38%	1.90%
After implementation of the decision model	72%	35%	176%	157%	31%	1.52%
Before implementation of the decision model	80%	60%	175%	134%	31%	1.55%
After implementation of the decision model	72%	35%	175%	156%	25%	1.24%
Before implementation of the decision model	80%	60%	176%	134%	40%	1.97%
After implementation of the decision model	72%	35%	176%	157%	32%	1.58%
Before implementation of the decision model	80%	60%	175%	133%	34%	1.74%
After implementation of the decision model	72%	35%	175%	156%	28%	1.39%
Before implementation of the decision model	80%	60%	176%	133%	71%	3.50%
After implementation of the decision model	72%	35%	176%	156%	62%	3.00%
Before implementation of the decision model	80%	59%	176%	133%	65%	3.26%
After implementation of the decision model	72%	35%	175%	156%	55%	2.73%
Before implementation of the decision model	58%	82%	215%	214%	129%	6.40%
After implementation of the decision model	50%	39%	216%	246%	121%	6.08%
Before implementation of the decision model	80%	60%	176%	133%	65%	3.20%
After implementation of the decision model	72%	35%	176%	156%	54%	2.70%

Source: own elaboration.

and change in the asset structure. The difference can be noticed regarding the impact of behavioural modelling on both asset and funding structure after implementation of the decision model. For Bank 2 the *Change in the deposit modelling assumptions* scenario is not amongst the highest impact factors, although still important. The author deduces that this fact can be justified by the size of the bank. Bank 2 is a large international bank which reacts more slowly to changes in modelling assumptions in comparison to Bank 1. The funding and asset base is more diversified, so the impact of changes in behavioural assumptions is subdued by the existence of other items in the banking book.

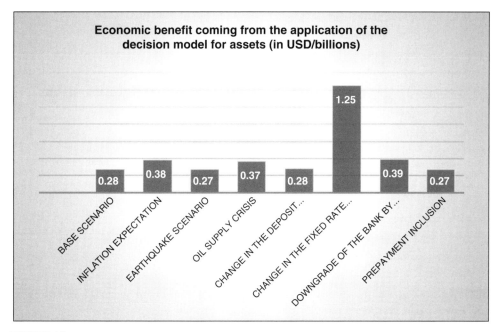

FIGURE 5.11   Economic benefit coming from the application of the decision model for assets for Bank 2.
Source: own elaboration.

Conclusions

The case studies provided in the book aim to analyse the target structure of the banking book before and after the implementation of the optimisation model. As a first stage, the proportions of assets and liabilities have been examined at the initial state for commercial banks based in the eurozone and UK. Thereafter, this structure has been recalculated applying the non-linear optimisation solver in MATLAB, known as *fmincon*. The examined problem has been set up in the form of non-linear objective functions which minimise the cost of funds and maximise the asset income. The minimisation of the funding costs and maximisation of the assets income was articulated as two separate optimisation problems, i.e. it has been run for assets and liabilities separately. In addition, for each optimisation exercise, there are underlying assumptions which are related to the modelling of items without deterministic maturity (for example, the degree of rate sensitivity and balance volatility of CASA); the extent of fixed rate asset prepayments which banks face; the willingness of customers to roll over the time deposits upon their expiration; and the pricing assumptions for both assets and liabilities, i.e. the commercial spread and liquidity premium recognised to liabilities or charged to assets. The differences in the product pricing have to reflect the geographical location of the financial institution and its cost of funding in the local markets, which is based on the FTP curve and all factors included in its construct.

The problem represents the constrained optimisation issue, since minimisation of the cost of funds and maximisation of the assets income are subject to internal limits (constraints) listed in Building the Objective and Constraint Functions in the Optimisation Process of Chapter 4. The constraint functions are both equality and inequality functions, which introduces an additional layer of complexity in the optimisation methodology.

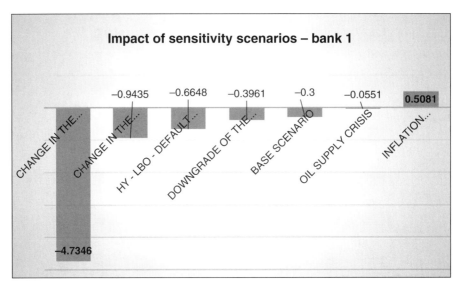

FIGURE 5.12   Impact of the sensitivity factors on the reduction in funding costs achieved by the application of the decision model on liabilities applied to Bank 1.
Source: own elaboration.

In general, this book has addressed the question of whether it is possible, through the application of optimisation techniques, to find the target structure of the banking book which provides the bank with an improved economic result and, at the same time, ensures respect for the internal limits for risks incurred by the bank.

Tables 5.1, 5.2, 5.5, and 5.6 show the results obtained for all scenarios which have been analysed and it can be clearly seen that economic benefit has been achieved under all of them. The magnitude of the economic benefit varies as a function of different factors, such as the level of interest rates in the market, elasticity and volatility of the CASA product, the early redemption rate of fixed rate loans, and, finally, the initial structure of the banking book itself plays an important role in the optimisation process.

Throughout the book we have analysed the application of the optimisation model under the *Base* scenario (known as a *going concern* view), and under a number of scenarios which examine the sensitivity of the model to the external and internal factors described in detail in the Definition of the Sensitivity Parameters for the Optimisation Model of Chapter 4. The results calculated by the optimisation model provide clear evidence of the economic benefit under both the base and sensitivity scenarios. Further, the immediate observation is that the magnitude of this benefit is proportional to the size of the banking book.

Analysing the outcome in terms of the reduction in the cost of funding, it turned out that the most sensitive factor is related to the initial structure of the banking book. The initial composition of the banking book, in terms of assets, seems to determine the level of magnitude of benefit achieved by the application of the model. This could drive towards the conclusion that the optimisation 'works better' for certain structures (compositions) of the banking book than others. This point appears to be valid either for the maximisation of the assets income or the minimisation of the cost of funding. The author goes slightly further with this conclusion and suggests that it could be that some banks are already destined to be more profitable with the optimisation model at the outset, i.e. through their initial structure set up. Another important factor to which the model is sensitive is the term structure of interest rates. Under upwards movement of the curve (scenarios: *Inflation Expectation* and the *Oil Supply crisis*) the reduction in cost of funding is higher than under the base and downward movement of the term structure scenario (the *Earthquake* scenario). Also, under the downgrade event the model seems to drive higher reduction in funding cost in comparison to other factors.

A similar outcome has been achieved through analysing the smaller sized institution (Bank 1). Also, in this case, under all scenarios, economic benefit has been achieved and the highest result has appeared under the *Change in the asset structure* scenario. The application of the decision model demonstrates a strong benefit both for the *Oil Supply crisis* and the *Change in the deposit characterisation model assumption* scenarios. The analysis of the results obtained through the application of the decision model for the funding base provides additional evidence that the *Change in the asset structure* scenario benefits the most. Also, the *Change in the deposit characterisation model assumption* scenario plays a significant role as a factor in the effectiveness of the model.

In one case only, under the *Inflation expectation* scenario, is there no economic benefit. However, this outcome can be easily explained since the analysis of the liquidity ratios of the institution (Tables 5.3 and 5.4) has shown a breach of the short-term cumulative liquidity ratio before the application of the optimisation model.

Consequently, to satisfy the constraints imposed in the model, under a rising interest rate environment, this result can be seen as a minimum cost required to maintain compliance with internal limits. An interesting point emerges in relation to the remainder of the scenarios analysed. As already mentioned, the smaller sized institution (Bank 1) breaches the internal liquidity limit at the initial stage of the optimisation exercise. Nevertheless, the application of the decision model drives the banking book structure towards a composition which satisfies the limit and provides the institution with economic benefit (except in the one case described above). Therefore, it could be easily concluded that if the bank didn't breach the internal limit, the magnitude of the economic benefit would be much higher. In the case of the second financial institution (international bank, Bank 2), there has been no breach of any internal limits.

The above confirms also the second hypothesis that was launched at the outset. The optimisation model improves the management of the interest rate risk and liquidity risk in terms of the better result of internal risk metric in all scenarios applied. It can be clearly seen that in case of the NII sensitivity, the application of the model decreases the interest rate risk sensitivity. The same point is valid for the liquidity risk metrics. It appears that the model also optimises the short-term liquidity metrics, preventing the excess liquidity being kept under the form of a liquidity buffer, and the inefficient management of stable funding. In particular, it refers to the excessive long-term funding the banks have, and as a consequence, limitation of potential profit resulting from the healthy maturity transformation run by the bank.

The final part of this book provides the reader with details of the optimisation process for a bank, i.e. it shows how the objective and constraints functions have been set up. The author has shared the simple optimisation model in Excel.

Additionally, as mentioned in Chapter 3, there are case studies related to the modelling of non-maturing liabilities and structural prepayments. The author has also provided the simple model for the calculation of EVE and NII sensitivity with a brief description of its functionalities.

The content of Appendix 1 and Appendix 2 walks the reader through the optimisation results for each scenario for both asset and liability sides.

Details of the Analysis Performed for Bank 1

APPLICATION OF THE OPTIMISATION MODEL – ASSET SIDE

Base Scenario Under the *Base* scenario, the initial asset structure and their respective income is as follows:

- Floating rate assets – $w_{Asset1} = 78.37\%$
- Fixed rate assets – $w_{Asset2} = 20.31\%$
- Liquid Asset buffer – $w_{Asset3} = 1.31\%$.

The interest income resulting from the asset structure under the *Base* scenario is as follows:

- $income_{Asset1} = $ EUR0.0564bn
- $income_{Asset2} = $ EUR0.0184bn
- $income_{Asset3} = $ EUR0.00001bn.

Total interest income = **EUR0.075bn.**

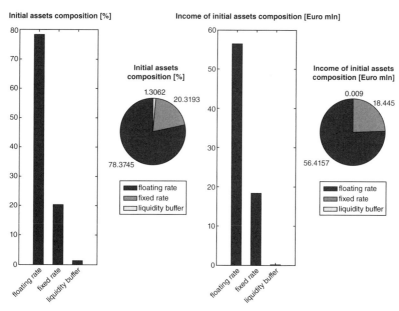

The initial asset structure under the *Base* scenario.
Source: own elaboration.

Under the existing structure, the liquidity and interest rate risk exposure metrics are as follows:

- Cumulative short-term liquidity ratio = 59.7%
- Structural ratio = 91.9%
- Delta $NII_{+200bps}$ = 80.5%
- Delta $NII_{-200bps}$ = 11.62%
- CAR = 26.2%.

After the decision model is put in place, the asset structure changes as follows:

- Floating rate assets – w_{Asset1} = 30.58%
- Fixed rate assets – w_{Asset2} = 66.02%
- Liquid Asset buffer – w_{Asset3} = 3.39%.

The resulting interest income has changed as follows:

- $income_{Asset1}$ = EUR0.022bn
- $income_{Asset2}$ = EUR0.0599bn
- $income_{Asset3}$ = EUR0.00002335bn.

Total interest income = EUR0.0819bn.

The implementation of the decision model resulted in an increase in the interest income over the period of 6 months of **EUR0.069bn.**

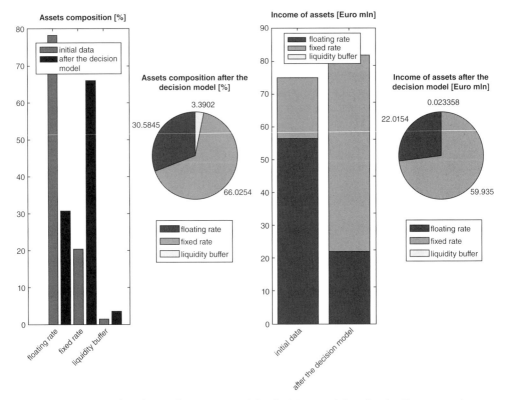

The asset structure after the implementation of the decision model under the *Base* scenario.

Under the target structure, the liquidity and interest rate risk exposure metrics are as follows:

- Cumulative short-term liquidity ratio = 100%
- Structural ratio = 93.9%
- Delta $NII_{+200bps}$ = 4%
- Delta $NII_{-200bps}$ = 7.8%
- CAR = 22%.

Interest Rate Risk Scenarios

Oil Supply Crisis   Under the *Oil supply crisis* scenario, the initial asset structure and their respective income is as follows:

- Floating rate assets – w_{Asset1} = 78.37%
- Fixed rate assets – w_{Asset2} = 20.31%
- Liquid Asset buffer – w_{Asset3} = 1.31%.

The interest income resulting from the asset structure under the *Oil supply crisis* scenario is as follows:

- $income_{Asset1}$ = EUR0.0576bn
- $income_{Asset2}$ = EUR0.0203bn
- $income_{Asset3}$ = EUR0.00001bn.

Total interest income = **EUR0.078bn.**

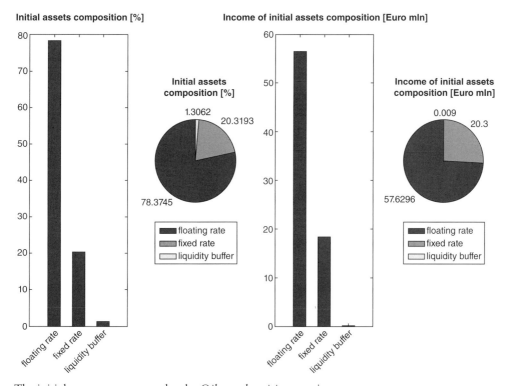

The initial assets structure under the *Oil supply crisis* scenario.

Under the existing structure, the liquidity and interest rate risk exposure metrics are as follows:

- Cumulative short-term liquidity ratio = 59.8%
- Structural ratio = 91.9%
- Delta $NII_{+200bps}$ = 81.5%
- Delta $NII_{-200bps}$ = 11.62%
- CAR = 26.26%.

After the decision model is put in place, the asset structure changes as follows:

- Floating rate assets – w_{Asset1} = 30.62%
- Fixed rate assets – w_{Asset2} = 66.01%
- Liquid Asset buffer – w_{Asset3} = 3.36%.

The resulting interest income has changed as follows:

- $income_{Asset1}$ = EUR0.0225bn
- $income_{Asset2}$ = EUR0.0659bn
- $income_{Asset3}$ = EUR0.0000232bn.

Total interest income = EUR0.08849bn.

The implementation of the decision model resulted in an increase in the interest income over the period of 6 months of **EUR0.01049bn**.

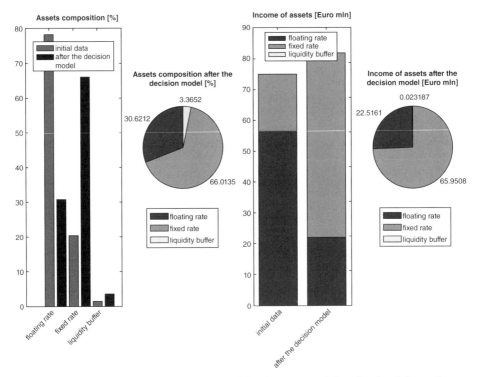

The assets structure after the implementation of the decision model under the *Oil supply crisis* scenario.

Under the target structure, the liquidity and interest rate risk exposure metrics are as follows:

- Cumulative short-term liquidity ratio = 100%
- Structural ratio = 93.9%
- Delta $NII_{+200bps}$ = 4%
- Delta $NII_{-200bps}$ = 7.8%
- CAR = 22%.

Inflation Expectation Under the *Inflation expectation* scenario, the initial asset structure and their respective income is as follows:

- Floating rate assets – w_{Asset1} = 78.37%
- Fixed rate assets – w_{Asset2} = 20.31%
- Liquid Asset buffer – w_{Asset3} = 1.30%.

The interest income resulting from the asset structure under the *Inflation expectation* scenario is as follows:

- $income_{Asset1}$ = EUR0.0614bn
- $income_{Asset2}$ = EUR0.0201bn
- $income_{Asset3}$ = EUR0.00001bn.

Total interest income = **EUR0.0816bn**.

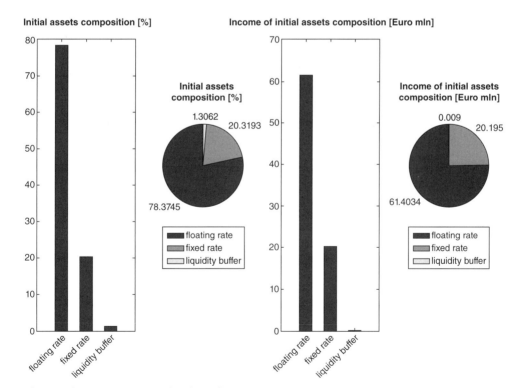

The initial asset structure under the *Inflation expectation* scenario.

Under the existing structure, the liquidity and interest rate risk exposure metrics are as follows:

- Cumulative short-term liquidity ratio = 59.7%
- Structural ratio = 91.99%
- Delta $NII_{+200bps}$ = 85.7%
- Delta $NII_{-200bps}$ = 11.8%
- CAR = 26.2%.

After the decision model is put in place, the asset structure changes as follows:

- Floating rate assets – w_{Asset1} = 30.75%
- Fixed rate assets – w_{Asset2} = 65.87%
- Liquid Asset buffer – w_{Asset3} = 3.37%.

The resulting interest income has changed as follows:

- $income_{Asset1}$ = EUR0.024bn
- $income_{Asset2}$ = EUR0.0654bn
- $income_{Asset3}$ = EUR0.000023bn

Total interest income = **EUR0.0895bn.**

The implementation of the decision model has resulted in an increase in the interest income over the period of 6 months of **EUR0.0079bn.**

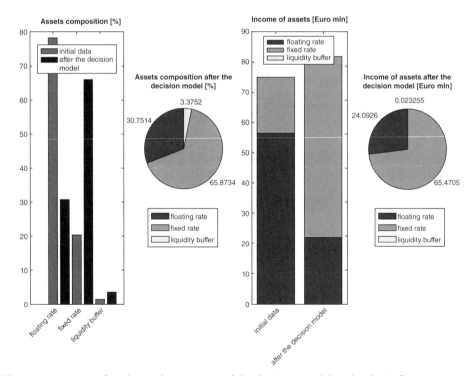

The asset structure after the implementation of the decision model under the *Inflation expectation* scenario.

Under the target structure, the liquidity and interest rate risk exposure metrics are as follows:

- Cumulative short-term liquidity ratio = 100%
- Structural ratio = 93.9%
- Delta $\text{NII}_{+200\text{bps}}$ = 4%
- Delta $\text{NII}_{-200\text{bps}}$ = 7.8%
- CAR = 22.06%.

FUNDING SIDE – BANK 1

Calculation of the target funding profile of the commercial bank based in Milan in Italy under the *Base* scenario provides the following results:

Initial funding structure at t_0:

a) Corporate current accounts – w_A = 7.4%
b) Corporate time deposits – w_B = 1.5%
c) Wholesale funding – w_C = 70%
d) Bonds issued – w_D = 21%.

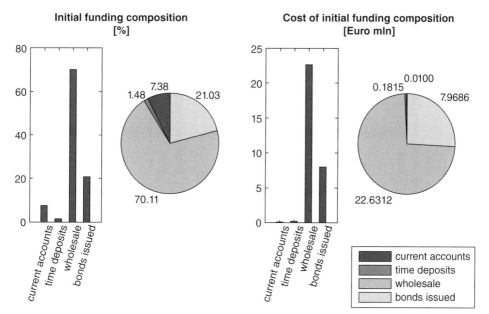

Initial funding structure of the European bank based in Italy under the *Base* scenario.
Source: own elaboration.

The resulting cost of funds of the funding base under the *Base* scenario is equal to **EUR0.03079bn** (EUR30.79m) over a 6-month period.

Under the *Base* scenario, the liquidity risk and interest rate risk metrics are as follows:

- Cumulative short-term liquidity metrics = 59%
- Structural liquidity ratio = 92%
- NII sensitivity$_{+200bps}$ = 78%
- NII sensitivity$_{-200bps}$ = 3.9%.

The bank is breaching the short-term liquidity limit.

After the decision model is put in place, composition of the funding base changes as follows:

a) Corporate current accounts – w_A = 2.5%
b) Corporate time deposits – w_B = 7.67%
c) Wholesale funding – w_C = 79.99%
d) Bonds issued – w_D = 9.8%.

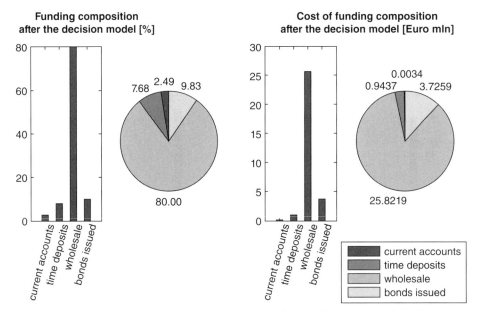

Funding structure of the European bank based in Italy after implementation of the decision model under the *Base* scenario.
Source: own elaboration.

The resulting cost of funds of the funding base under the *Base* scenario is equal to **EUR0.03049bn** (EUR30.49m) over a 6-month period.

After implementation of the decision model, the liquidity risk and interest rate risk metrics are as follows:

- Cumulative short-term liquidity metrics = 100%
- Structural liquidity ratio = 90%
- NII sensitivity$_{+200bps}$ = 70.2%
- NII sensitivity$_{-200bps}$ = 3.5%.

The economic benefit from the implementation of the decision model amounts to **EUR0.2964m** on an annual basis. In addition, the bank respects all limits imposed.

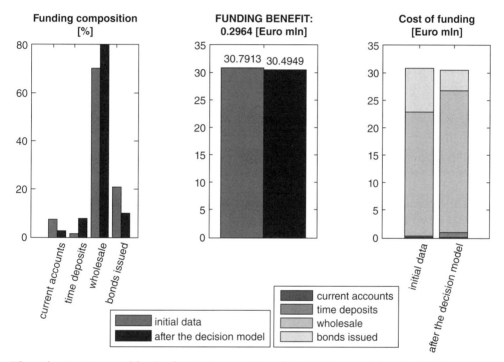

The reduction in cost of funds after implementation of the decision model under the *Base* scenario.
Source: own elaboration.

Interest Rate Risk Scenarios
Oil Supply Crisis Initial funding structure at t_0:

a) Corporate current accounts – $w_A = 7.4\%$
b) Corporate time deposits – $w_B = 1.5\%$
c) Wholesale funding – $w_C = 70\%$
d) Bonds issued – $w_D = 21\%$.

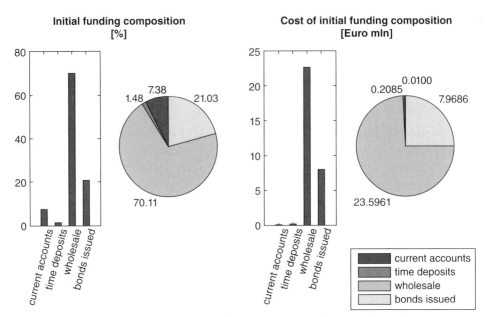

Initial funding structure of the European bank based in Italy under the *Oil supply crisis* scenario. Source: own elaboration.

The resulting cost of funds of the funding base before application of the decision model is equal to **EUR0.03139bn** (EUR31.39m) over a 6-month period.

Under the *Oil supply crisis* scenario, the liquidity risk and interest rate risk metrics are as follows:

- Cumulative short-term liquidity metrics = 59.5%
- Structural liquidity ratio = 92%
- NII sensitivity$_{+200\text{bps}}$ = 71.05%
- NII sensitivity$_{-200\text{bps}}$ = 3.55%.

The bank is breaching the short-term liquidity limit.

After implementation of decision model, the composition of the funding base is as follows:

a) Corporate current accounts – $w_A = 2.53\%$
b) Corporate time deposits – $w_B = 7.65\%$
c) Wholesale funding – $w_C = 79.99\%$
d) Bonds issued – $w_D = 9.8\%$.

The resulting cost of funds of the funding base after application of the decision model is equal to **EUR31.24m** over a 6-month period.

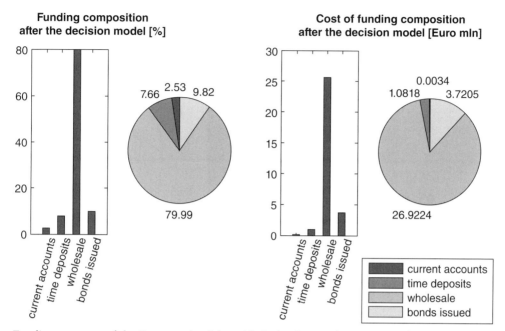

Funding structure of the European bank based in Italy after implementation of the decision model under the *Oil supply crisis* scenario.
Source: own elaboration.

The resulting cost of funds of the funding base under the *Base* scenario is equal to **EUR0.03124bn** (EUR31.24m) over a 6-month period.

After implementation of the decision model, the liquidity risk and interest rate risk metrics are as follows:

- Cumulative short-term liquidity metrics = 100%
- Structural liquidity ratio = 90%
- NII sensitivity$_{+200\text{bps}}$ = 63.8%
- NII sensitivity$_{-200\text{bps}}$ = 3.19%.

The economic benefit from the implementation of the decision model amounts to **EUR0.2812m** on an annual basis.

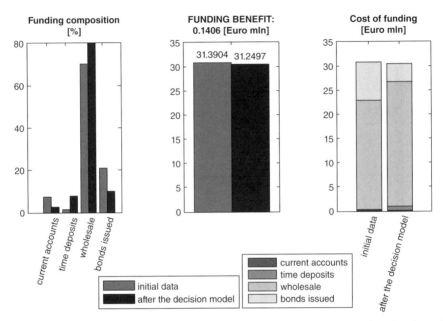

The reduction in cost of funds after the implementation of the decision model under the *Oil supply crisis* scenario.
Source: own elaboration.

HY/LBO/Default Risk   Initial funding structure at t_0:

a) Corporate current accounts – $w_A = 7.4\%$
b) Corporate time deposits – $w_B = 1.5\%$
c) Wholesale funding – $w_C = 70\%$
d) Bonds issued – $w_D = 21\%$.

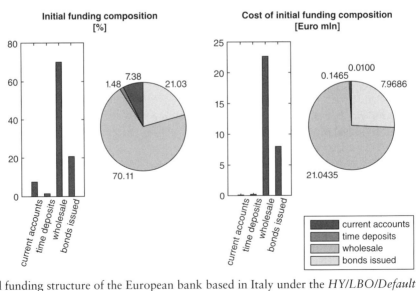

Initial funding structure of the European bank based in Italy under the *HY/LBO/Default risk* scenario.
Source: own elaboration.

The resulting cost of funds of the funding base under the *HY/LBO/Default risk* scenario is equal to **EUR 0.02916bn** (EUR 29.16m) over a 6-month period.

Under the *HY/LBO/Default risk* scenario, the liquidity risk and interest rate risk metrics are as follows:

- Cumulative short-term liquidity metrics = 59%
- Structural liquidity ratio = 92%
- NII sensitivity$_{+200bps}$ = 78.41%
- NII sensitivity$_{-200bps}$ = 3.9%.

The bank is breaching the short-term liquidity limit.

After the decision model is put in place, the composition of the funding base changes as follows:

a) Corporate current accounts – w_A = 2.49%
b) Corporate time deposits – w_B = 7.67%
c) Wholesale funding – w_C =79.99%
d) Bonds issued – w_D = 9.83%.

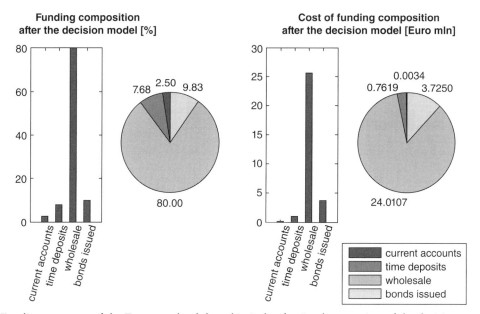

Funding structure of the European bank based in Italy after implementation of the decision model under the *HY/LBO/Default risk* scenario.
Source: own elaboration.

The resulting cost of funds of the funding base under the *HY/LBO/Default risk* scenario is equal to **EUR0.0285bn** (EUR28.5m) over a 6-month period.

After the implementation of the decision model, the liquidity risk and interest rate risk metrics are as follows:

- Cumulative short-term liquidity metrics $= 100\%$
- Structural liquidity ratio $= 90\%$
- NII sensitivity$_{+200bps} = 70.43\%$
- NII sensitivity$_{-200bps} = 3.52\%$.

There is benefit resulting from the implementation of the decision model comparing to the initial structure of funding in t_0. The economic benefit from the implementation of the decision model amounts to **EUR0.6677m** on an annual basis.

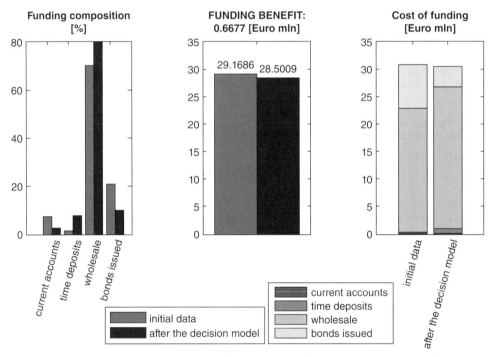

The reduction in cost of funds after the implementation of the decision model under the *HY/LBO/Default risk* scenario.
Source: own elaboration.

Changes in the Deposit Characterisation Model Outcome   Initial funding structure at t_0:

a) Corporate current accounts – $w_A = 7.4\%$
b) Corporate time deposits – $w_B = 1.5\%$
c) Wholesale funding – $w_C = 70\%$
d) Bonds issued – $w_D = 21\%$.

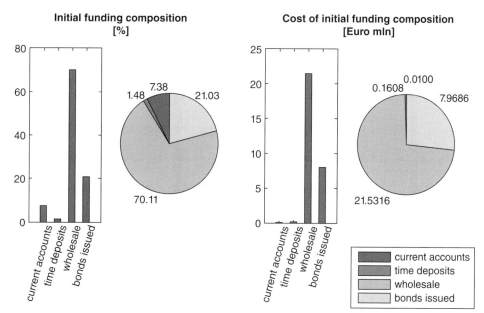

Initial funding structure of the European bank based in Italy under the *Changes in deposit characterisation model outcome* scenario.
Source: own elaboration.

The resulting cost of funds of the funding base under the *Changes in deposit characterisation model outcome scenario* is equal to **EUR0.02967bn** (EUR29.67m) over a 6-month period.

Under the *Changes in deposit characterisation model outcome* scenario, the liquidity risk and interest rate risk metrics are as follows:

- Cumulative short-term liquidity metrics = 91.89%
- Structural liquidity ratio = 93.66%
- NII sensitivity $_{+200bps}$ = 79.36%
- NII sensitivity $_{-200bps}$ = 3.96%.

The bank is breaching the short-term liquidity limit.

After implementation of the decision model, the composition of the funding base changes as follows:

a) Corporate current accounts – $w_A = 3.83\%$
b) Corporate time deposits – $w_B = 8.24\%$
c) Wholesale funding – $w_C = 79.99\%$
d) Bonds issued – $w_D = 7.92\%$.

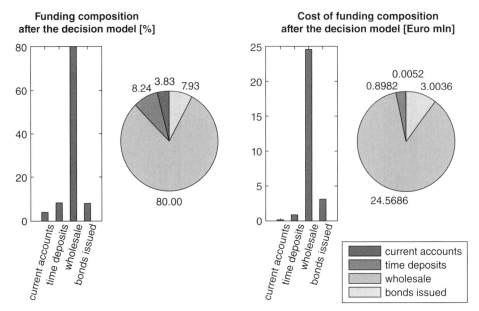

Funding structure of the European bank based in Italy after the implementation of the decision model under the *Changes in deposit characterisation model outcome* scenario.
Source: own elaboration.

The resulting cost of funds after implementation of the decision model under the *Changes in deposit characterisation model outcome* scenario is equal to **EUR0.0284bn** (EUR28.40m) over a 6-month period.

After implementation of the decision model, the liquidity risk and interest rate risk metrics are as follows:

- Cumulative short-term liquidity metrics = 100%
- Structural liquidity ratio = 90%
- NII sensitivity $_{+200bps}$ = 68.71%
- NII sensitivity $_{-200bps}$ = 3.43%.

There is a benefit resulting from the implementation of the decision model compared to the initial structure of funding at t_0. The economic benefit from the implementation of the decision model amounts to **EUR 1.1954m** on an annual basis.

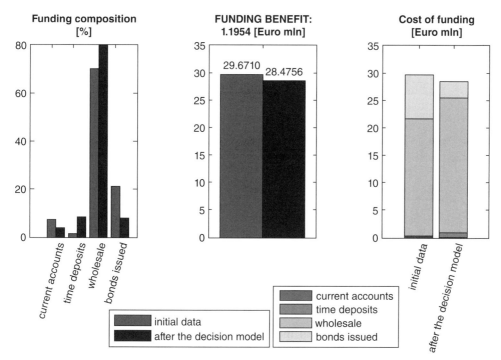

Funding structure of the European bank based in Italy after implementation of the decision model under the *Changes in deposit characterisation outcome* scenario.

Changes in the Initial Proportions of the Asset Base
The proportions of asset portfolio are changed from:

I. $Asset_1 = 78.37\%$
   $Asset_2 = 20.32\%$
   $Asset_3 = 1.31\%$

to:

II. $Asset_1 = 72.8\%$
    $Asset_2 = 20\%$
    $Asset_3 = 7.2\%$.

Initial Funding Structure at t_0

a) Corporate current accounts – $w_A = 7.4\%$
b) Corporate time deposits – $w_B = 1.5\%$
c) Wholesale funding – $w_C = 70\%$
d) Bonds issued – $w_D = 21\%$.

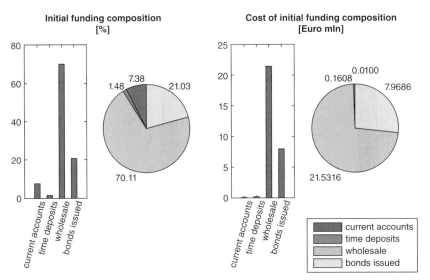

Initial funding structure of the European bank based in Italy under the *Changes in the initial proportions of the asset base* scenario.

The resulting cost of funds of the funding base under the *Changes in the initial proportions of the asset base* scenario is equal to **EUR0.02967bn** (EUR29.67m) over a 6-month period.

After implementation of the decision model, the composition of the funding base changes as follows:

a) Corporate current accounts – $w_A = 13.43\%$
b) Corporate time deposits – $w_B = 9.57\%$
c) Wholesale funding – $w_C = 77.01\%$
d) Bonds issued – $w_D = 0.0002\%$.

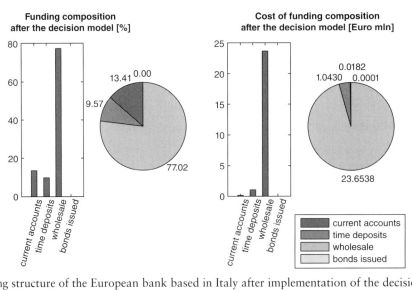

Funding structure of the European bank based in Italy after implementation of the decision model under the *Changes in the initial proportions of the asset base* scenario.
Source: own elaboration.

The resulting cost of funds of the funding base under the *Changes in the initial proportions of the asset base* scenario is equal to **EUR0.0247bn** (EUR24.7m) over a 6-month period.

After implementation of the decision model, the liquidity risk and interest rate risk metrics are as follows:

- Cumulative short-term liquidity metrics = 100%
- Structural liquidity ratio = 90%
- NII sensitivity$_{+200bps}$ = 55.7%
- NII sensitivity$_{-200bps}$ = 2.7%.

There is significant benefit resulting from the change in the initial amounts of asset portfolios compared to the cost of the initial structure of funding (at t_0). The economic benefit from implementation of the decision model amounts to **EUR4.9560m**.

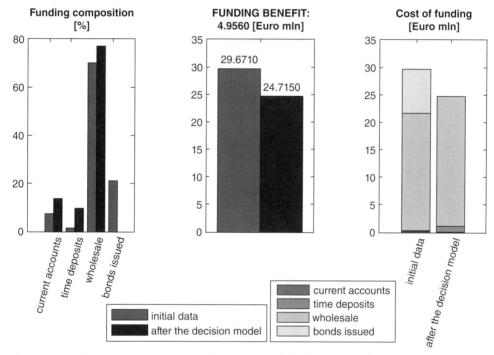

The reduction in cost of funds after implementation of the decision model under the *Changes in the initial proportions of the asset base* scenario.
Source: own elaboration.

Changes in the Initial Proportions of the Asset Base The proportions of the asset portfolio are changed as follows.

Asset base change from:

I. $Asset_1 = 78.37\%$
$Asset_2 = 20.31\%$
$Asset_3 = 1.31\%$

to:

II. $Asset_1 = 83.69\%$
  $Asset_2 = 15\%$
  $Asset_3 = 1.31\%.$

  Initial funding structure at t_0:

  a) Corporate current accounts – $w_A = 7.4\%$
  b) Corporate time deposits – $w_B = 1.5\%$
  c) Wholesale funding – $w_C = 70\%$
  d) Bonds issued – $w_D = 21\%.$

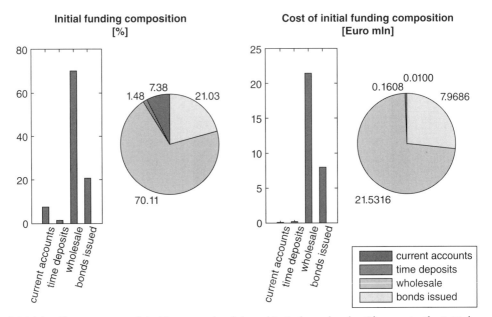

Initial funding structure of the European bank based in Italy under the *Changes in the initial proportions of the asset base* scenario.

The resulting cost of funds of the funding base under the *Changes in the initial proportions of the asset base* scenario is equal to **EUR0.02967bn** (EUR29.67m) over a 6-month period.

Under the *Changes in deposit characterisation model outcome* scenario, the liquidity risk and interest rate risk metrics are as follows:

- Cumulative short-term liquidity metrics = 60.89%
- Structural liquidity ratio = 91.99%
- NII sensitivity$_{+200\text{bps}}$ = 87.76%
- NII sensitivity$_{-200\text{bps}}$ = 4.38%

The bank is breaching the short-term liquidity limit.

After implementation of the decision model, the composition of the funding base changes as follows:

a) Corporate current accounts – $w_A = 2.61\%$
b) Corporate time deposits – $w_B = 7.61\%$
c) Wholesale funding – $w_C = 79.99\%$
d) Bonds issued – $w_D = 9.77\%$.

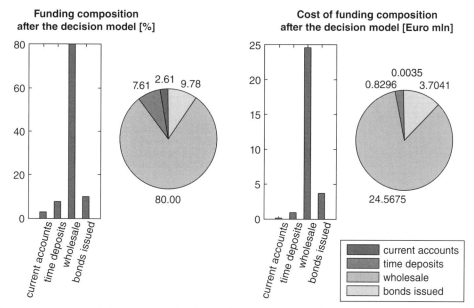

Funding structure of the European bank based in Italy after implementation of the decision model under the *Changes in the initial proportions of the asset base* scenario.
Source: own elaboration.

The resulting cost of funds of the funding base under the *Changes in the initial proportions of the assets base* scenario is equal to **EUR 0.002910bn** (EUR29.10m) over a 6-month time period.

After implementation of the decision model, the liquidity risk and interest rate risk metrics are as follows:

- Cumulative short-term liquidity metrics = 100%
- Structural liquidity ratio = 90%
- NII sensitivity $_{+200bps}$ = 79.7%
- NII sensitivity $_{-200bps}$ = 3.98%.

The economic benefit from the implementation of the decision model amounts to **EUR0.5663m.**

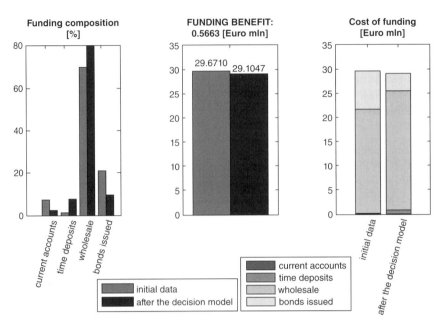

The reduction in cost of funds after the implementation of the decision model under the *Changes in the initial proportions of the asset base* scenario.
Source: own elaboration.

Downgrade of the Bank by One Notch Initial funding structure at t_0:

a) Corporate current accounts – $w_A = 7.4\%$
b) Corporate time deposits – $w_B = 1.5\%$
c) Wholesale funding – $w_C = 70\%$
d) Bonds issued – $w_D = 21\%$.

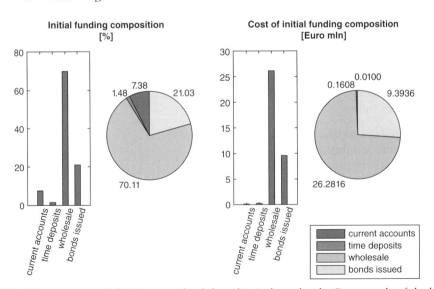

Initial funding structure of the European bank based in Italy under the *Downgrade of the bank by one notch* scenario.

The resulting cost of funds of the funding base under the scenario is equal to **EUR0.03584bn** (EUR35.84m) over a 6-month period.

Under the *Downgrade of the bank by one notch* scenario, the liquidity risk and interest rate risk metrics are as follows:

- Cumulative short-term liquidity metrics = 59.8%
- Structural liquidity ratio = 91.99%
- NII sensitivity$_{+200bps}$ = 72.18%
- NII sensitivity$_{-200bps}$ = 3.6%.

The bank is breaching the short-term liquidity limit.

After implementation of the decision model, the composition of the funding base changes as follows:

a) Corporate current accounts – $w_A = 2.53\%$
b) Corporate time deposits – $w_B = 7.65\%$
c) Wholesale funding – $w_C = 79.99\%$
d) Bonds issued – $w_D = 9.8\%$.

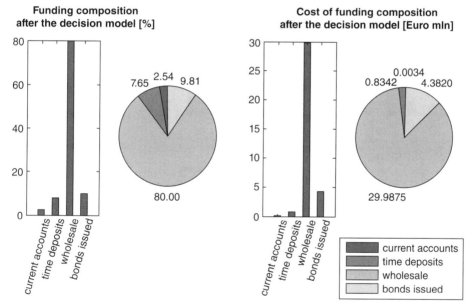

Funding structure of the European bank based in Italy after the implementation of the decision model under the *Downgrade of the bank by one notch* scenario.
Source: own elaboration.

The resulting cost of funds of the funding base under the scenario is equal to **EUR0.0352bn** (EUR35.2m) over a 6-month period.

After the implementation of the decision model, the liquidity risk and interest rate risk metrics are as follows:

- Cumulative short-term liquidity metrics = 100%
- Structural liquidity ratio = 90%
- NII sensitivity $_{+200\text{bps}}$ = 6.8%
- NII sensitivity $_{-200\text{bps}}$ = 3.24%.

The economic benefit from the implementation of the decision model amounts to EUR0.6388m.

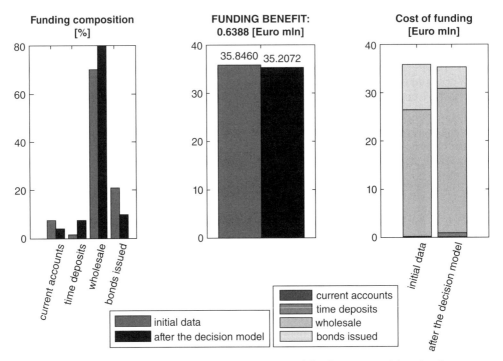

The reduction in cost of funds after the implementation of the decision model under the *Downgrade of the bank by one notch* scenario.
Source: own elaboration.

Inclusion of the CPR for Fixed-Rate Assets   Initial funding structure at t_0:

a) Corporate current accounts – $w_A = 7.4\%$
b) Corporate time deposits – $w_B = 1.5\%$
c) Wholesale funding – $w_C = 70\%$
d) Bonds issued – $w_D = 21\%$.

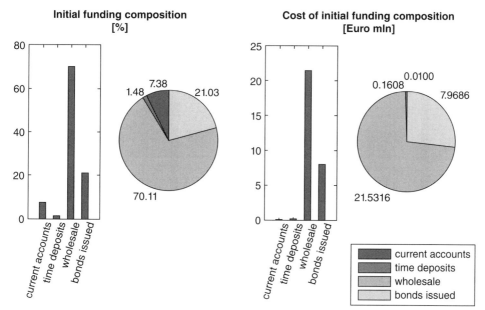

Initial funding structure of the European bank based in Italy under the *Inclusion of the CPR for fixed-rate assets* scenario.
Source: own elaboration.

The resulting cost of funds of the funding base under the scenario is equal to **EUR0.02967bn** (EUR29.67m) over a 6-month period.

Under the *Inclusion of the CPR for fixed rate assets* scenario, the liquidity risk and interest rate risk metrics are as follows:

- Cumulative short-term liquidity metrics = 62%
- Structural liquidity ratio = 94.19%
- NII sensitivity$_{+200bps}$ = 77%
- NII sensitivity$_{-200bps}$ = 3.8%.

The bank is breaching the short-term liquidity limit.

After implementation of the decision model, the composition of the funding base changes as follows:

a) Corporate current accounts – $w_A = 1.84\%$
b) Corporate time deposits – $w_B = 11.12\%$
c) Wholesale funding – $w_C = 79.9\%$
d) Bonds issued – $w_D = 7\%$.

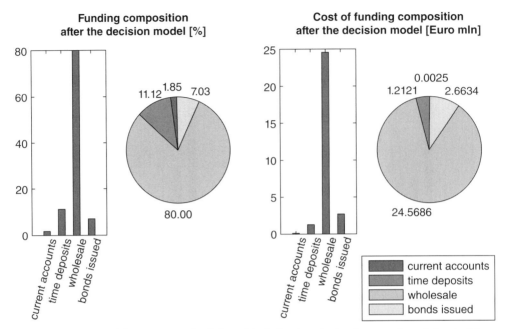

Funding structure of the European bank based in Italy after the implementation of the decision model under the *Inclusion of the CPR for fixed-rate assets* scenario.
Source: own elaboration.

The resulting cost of funds of the funding base under the scenario is equal to **EUR0.02844bn** (EUR28.44m) over a 6-month period.

After the implementation of the decision model, the liquidity risk and interest rate risk metrics are as follows:

- Cumulative short-term liquidity metrics = 100%
- Structural liquidity ratio = 90%
- NII sensitivity$_{+200\text{bps}}$ = 67.68%
- NII sensitivity$_{-200\text{bps}}$ = 3.38%.

The economic benefit from the implementation of the decision model amounts to **EUR1.2244m.**

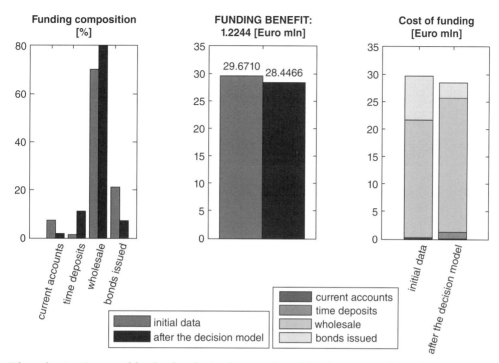

The reduction in cost of funds after the implementation of the decision model under the *Inclusion of the CPR for fixed-rate assets* scenario.
Source: own elaboration.

Details of the Analysis Performed for Bank 2

APPLICATION OF THE OPTIMISATION MODEL – ASSET SIDE

Base Scenario Under the *Base* scenario, the initial asset structure and their respective income are as follows:

- Retail assets – $w_{Asset1} = 19.85\%$
- Corporate Clients assets – $w_{Asset2} = 32.42\%$
- Financial Market assets – $w_{Asset3} = 36.79\%$
  - to Banks – 6 month (20% of $Asset_3$)
  - Non-Bank Financial Institution (NBFI) > 6m – 9 month (40% of $Asset_3$)
  - Non-Bank Financial Institution (NBFI) < 6m – 4 month (40% of $Asset_3$)
- Liquid Asset buffer – $w_{Asset4} = 10.92\%$.

The interest income resulting from the asset structure under the *Base* scenario is as follows:

- $r_{Asset1} = \text{USD1.53bn}$
- $r_{Asset2} = \text{USD2.544bn}$
- $r_{Asset3} = \text{USD2.1158bn}$
- $r_{Asset4} = \text{USD0.1113bn}$.

Total interest income = **USD6.30bn.**

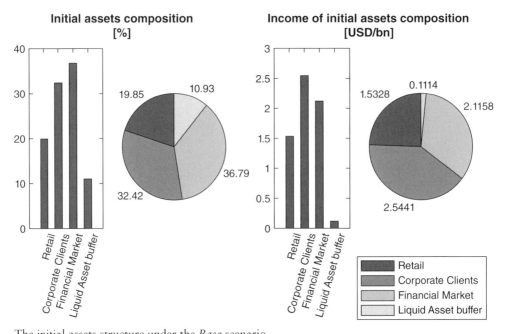

The initial assets structure under the *Base* scenario.

Under the existing structure, the liquidity and interest rate risk exposure metrics are as follows:

- AD ratio = 80%
- MTFR $_{contractual}$ = 60%
- MTFR $_{behavioural}$ = 176%
- SH_2M = 134%
- Delta NII$_{+200bps}$ = 38%
- Delta NII$_{-200bps}$ = 1.9%
- CAR = 12.4%.

After the decision model is put in place, the asset structure has changed as follows:

- Retail assets – w_{Asset1} = 26.76%
- Corporate Clients assets – w_{Asset2} = 25.40%

- Financial Market assets – w_{Asset3} = 43.19%
  - to Banks – 6 month (20% of $Asset_3$)
  - Non-Bank Financial Institution (NBFI) > 6m – 9 month (40% of $Asset_3$)
  - Non-Bank Financial Institution (NBFI) < 6m – 4 month (40% of $Asset_3$)
- Liquid Asset buffer $–w_{Asset4}$ = 4.66%.

The resulting interest income have changed as follows:

- r_{Asset1} = USD2.064bn
- r_{Asset2} = USD1.9935bn
- r_{Asset3} = USD2.4837bn
- r_{Asset4} = USD0.0475bn.

Total interest income = **USD6.588bn.**
The implementation of the decision model has resulted in an increase in the interest income over the period of 6 months of **USD0.2849bn.**

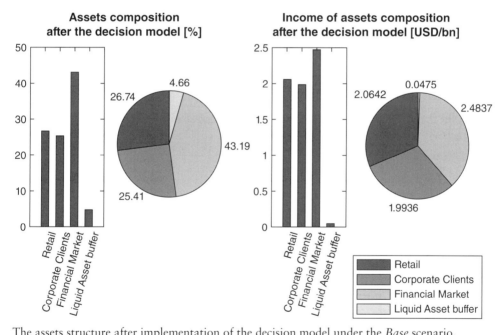

The assets structure after implementation of the decision model under the *Base* scenario.

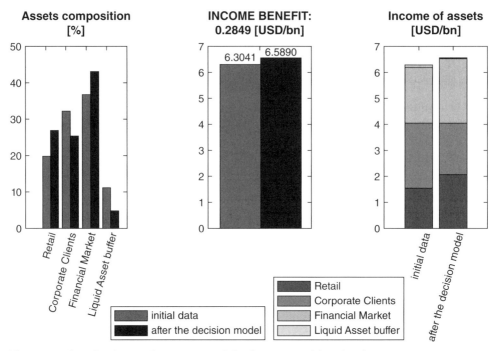

The income benefit after implementation of the decision model under the *Base* scenario.

Under the target structure, the liquidity and interest rate risk exposure metrics are as follows:

- AD ratio = 80%
- MTFR $_{contractual}$ = 60.15%
- MTFR $_{behavioural}$ = 166%
- SH_2M = 100%
- Delta NII$_{+200bps}$ = 30.37%
- Delta NII$_{-200bps}$ = 1.51%
- CAR = 12%.

Interest Rate Risk Scenarios

Oil Supply Crisis Under the *Oil supply crisis* scenario, the initial asset structure and their respective income is as follows:

- Retail assets – w_{Asset1} = 19.85%
- Corporate Clients assets – w_{Asset2} = 32.42%
- Financial Market assets – w_{Asset3} = 36.79%
    - to Banks – 6 month (20% of $Asset_3$)
    - Non-Bank Financial Institution (NBFI) > 6m – 9 month (40% of $Asset_3$)
    - Non-Bank Financial Institution (NBFI) < 6m – 4 month (40% of $Asset_3$)
- Liquid Asset buffer – w_{Asset4} = 10.92%.

The interest income resulting from the asset structure under the *Oil supply crisis* scenario is as follows:

- r_{Asset1} = USD1.7021bn
- r_{Asset2} = USD2.7534bn
- r_{Asset3} = USD2.377bn
- r_{Asset4} = USD0.1113bn.

Total interest income = **USD6.945bn.**

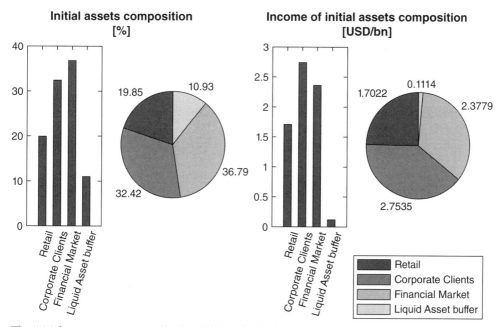

The initial assets structure under the *Oil Supply Crisis* scenario.

Under the existing structure, the liquidity and interest rate risk exposure metrics are as follows:

- AD ratio = 80%
- MTFR $_{contractual}$ = 60%
- MTFR $_{behavioural}$ = 176%
- SH_2M = 134%
- Delta NII$_{+200bps}$ = 35%
- Delta NII$_{-200bps}$ = 1.74%
- CAR = 12.4%.

After the decision model is put in place, the assets structure has changed as follows:

- Retail assets – $w_{Asset1} = 26.78\%$
- Corporate Clients assets – $w_{Asset2} = 25.36\%$
- Financial Market assets – $w_{Asset3} = 43.21\%$
    - to Banks – 6 month (20% of $Asset_3$)
    - Non-Bank Financial Institution (NBFI) > 6m – 9 month (40% of $Asset_3$)
    - Non-Bank Financial Institution (NBFI) < 6m – 4 month (40% of $Asset_3$)
- Liquid Asset buffer $-w_{Asset4} = 4.64\%$.

The resulting interest income has changed as follows:

- $r_{Asset1} = USD2.2962bn$
- $r_{Asset2} = USD2.1537bn$
- $r_{Asset3} = USD2.79287bn$
- $r_{Asset4} = USD0.04728bn$.

Total interest income = **USD7.29bn.**
The implementation of the decision model has resulted in an increase in the interest income over the period of 6 months of **USD0.3452bn.**

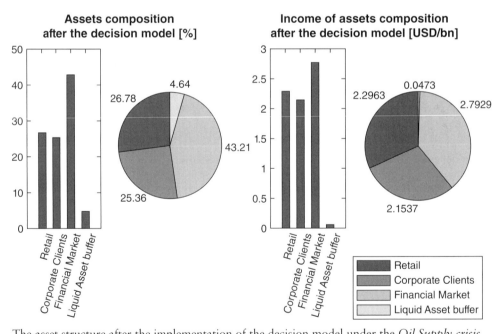

The asset structure after the implementation of the decision model under the *Oil Supply crisis* scenario.

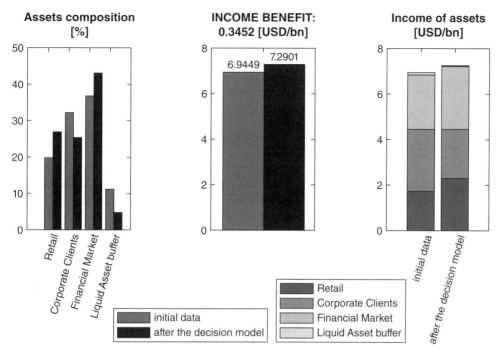

The income benefit after the implementation of the decision model under the *Oil supply crisis* scenario.

Under the target structure, the liquidity and interest rate risk exposure metrics are as follows:

- AD ratio = 79%
- MTFR $_{contractual}$ = 60.15%
- MTFR $_{behavioural}$ = 165.86%
- SH_2M = 100%
- Delta NII$_{+200bps}$ = 27.68%
- Delta NII$_{-200bps}$ = 1.384%
- CAR = 12%.

Earthquake Scenario Under the *Earthquake* scenario, the initial assets structure and their respective income is as follows:

- Retail assets – w_{Asset1} = 19.85%
- Corporate Clients assets – w_{Asset2} = 32.42%
- Financial Market assets – w_{Asset3} = 36.79%
  - to Banks – 6 month (20% of $Asset_3$)
  - Non-Bank Financial Institution (NBFI) > 6m – 9 month (40% of $Asset_3$)
  - Non-Bank Financial Institution (NBFI) < 6m – 4 month (40% of $Asset_3$)
- Liquid Asset buffer – w_{Asset4} = 10.92%.

The interest income resulting from the asset structure under the *Earthquake* scenario is as follows:

- r_{Asset1} = USD1.50bn
- r_{Asset2} = USD2.36bn
- r_{Asset3} = USD1.88bn
- r_{Asset4} = USD0.1113bn.

Total interest income = **USD5.86bn.**

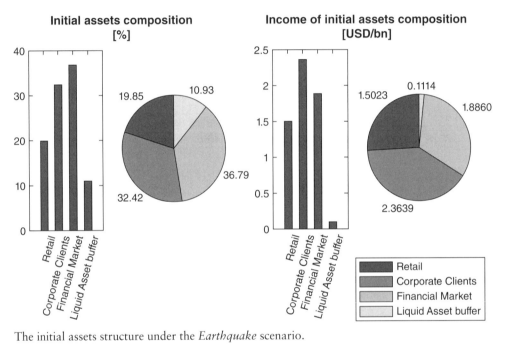

The initial assets structure under the *Earthquake* scenario.

Under the existing structure, the liquidity and interest rate risk exposure metrics are as follows:

- AD ratio = 80%
- MTFR $_{contractual}$ = 60%
- MTFR $_{behavioural}$ = 176%
- SH_2M = 134%
- Delta NII$_{+200bps}$ = 39.5%
- Delta NII$_{-200bps}$ = 1.97%
- CAR = 12.4%.

After the decision model is put in place, the asset structure has changed as follows:

- Retail assets – $w_{Asset1} = 26.8\%$
- Corporate Clients assets – $w_{Asset2} = 25.4\%$
- Financial Market assets – $w_{Asset3} = 43.2\%$
  - to banks – 6 month (20% of $Asset_3$)
  - Non-Bank Financial Institution (NBFI) > 6m – 9 month (40% of $Asset_3$)
  - Non-Bank Financial Institution (NBFI) < 6m – 4 month (40% of $Asset_3$)
- Liquid Asset buffer –$w_{Asset4} = 4.6\%$.

The resulting interest income has changed as follows:

- $r_{Asset1} = $ USD2.022bn
- $r_{Asset2} = $ USD1.85bn
- $r_{Asset3} = $ USD2.21bn
- $r_{Asset4} = $ USD0.0476bn.

Total interest income = **USD6.1365bn.**
The implementation of the decision model has resulted in an increase in the interest income over the period of 6 months of **USD0.2730bn.**

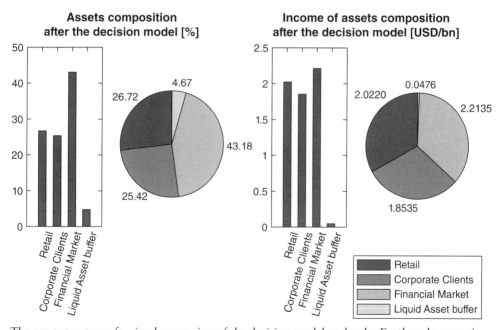

The asset structure after implementation of the decision model under the *Earthquake* scenario.

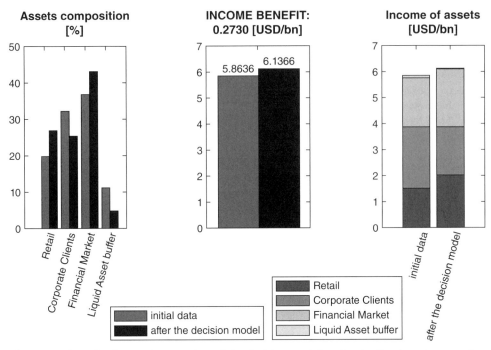

The income benefit after implementation of the decision model under the *Earthquake* scenario.

Under the target structure the liquidity and interest rate risk exposure metrics are as follows:

- AD ratio = 79.9%
- MTFR $_{contractual}$ = 60.15%
- MTFR $_{behavioural}$ = 165.9%
- SH_2M = 100%
- Delta NII$_{+200bps}$ = 31.5%
- Delta NII$_{-200bps}$ = 1.57%
- CAR = 12%.

Inflation Expectation Under the *Inflation expectation* scenario, the initial asset structure and their respective income is as follows:

- Retail assets – w_{Asset1} = 19.85%
- Corporate Clients assets – w_{Asset2} = 32.42%
- Financial Market assets – w_{Asset3} = 36.79%
  - to Banks – 6 month (20% of $Asset_3$)
  - Non-Bank Financial Institution (NBFI) > 6m – 9 month (40% of $Asset_3$)
  - Non-Bank Financial Institution (NBFI) < 6m – 4 month (40% of $Asset_3$)
- Liquid Asset buffer –w_{Asset4} = 10.92%.

The interest income resulting from the asset structure under the *Inflation expectation* scenario is as follows:

- r_{Asset1} = USD1.83bn
- r_{Asset2} = USD3.03bn
- r_{Asset3} = USD2.67bn
- r_{Asset4} = US 0.1113bn.

Total interest income = **USD7.645bn.**

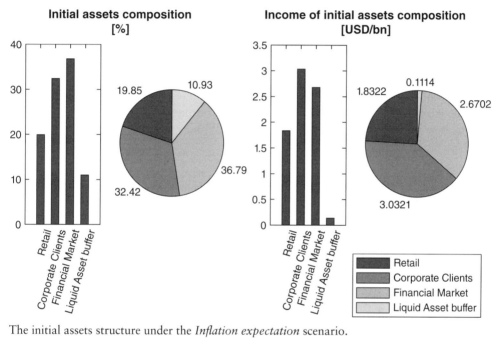

The initial assets structure under the *Inflation expectation* scenario.

Under the existing structure, the liquidity and interest rate risk exposure metrics are as follows:

- AD ratio = 80.2%
- MTFR $_{contractual}$ = 60%
- MTFR $_{behavioural}$ = 176%
- SH_2M = 134%
- Delta NII$_{+200bps}$ = 31.06%
- Delta NII$_{-200bps}$ = 1.55%
- CAR = 12.4%.

After the decision model is put in place the assets structure has changed as follows:

- Retail assets – $w_{Asset1} = 26.8\%$
- Corporate Clients assets – $w_{Asset2} = 25.29\%$
- Financial Market assets – $w_{Asset3} = 43.24\%$
  - to Banks – 6 month (20% of $Asset_3$)
  - Non-Bank Financial Institution (NBFI) > 6m – 9 month (40% of $Asset_3$)
  - Non-Bank Financial Institution (NBFI) < 6m – 4 month (40% of $Asset_3$)
- Liquid Asset buffer –$w_{Asset4} = 4.6\%$.

The resulting interest income has changed as follows:

- $r_{Asset1} = $ USD2.477bn
- $r_{Asset2} = $ USD2.365bn
- $r_{Asset3} = $ USD3.138bn
- $r_{Asset4} = $ USD0.0469bn.

Total interest income = **USD8.0287bn.**
The implementation of the decision model has resulted in an increase in the interest income over the period of 6 months of **USD0.3829bn.**

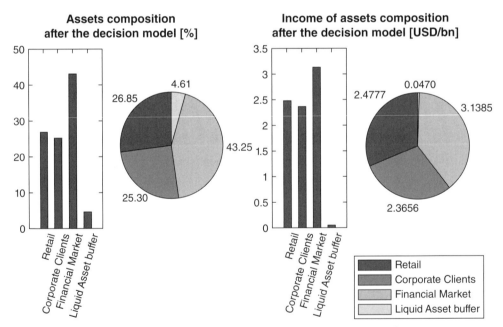

The asset structure after implementation of the decision model under the *Inflation expectation* scenario.

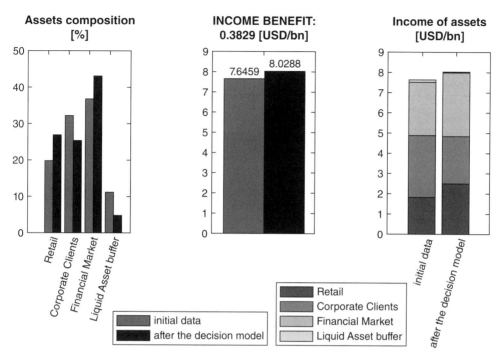

The income benefit after implementation of the decision model under the *Inflation expectation* scenario.

Under the target structure, the liquidity and interest rate risk exposure metrics are as follows:

- AD ratio = 79.9%
- MTFR $_{contractual}$ = 60.15%
- MTFR $_{behavioural}$ = 166%
- SH_2M = 100%
- Delta NII$_{+200bps}$ = 24.64%
- Delta NII$_{-200bps}$ = 1.23%
- CAR = 12%.

Downgrade of the Bank by One Notch Under the *Downgrade of the bank by one notch* scenario, the initial asset structure and their respective income is as follows:

- Retail assets – w_{Asset1} = 19.85%
- Corporate Clients assets – w_{Asset2} = 32.42%
- Financial Market assets – w_{Asset3} = 36.79%
  - to Banks – 6 month (20% of $Asset_3$)
  - Non-Bank Financial Institution (NBFI) > 6m – 9 month (40% of $Asset_3$)
  - Non-Bank Financial Institution (NBFI) < 6m – 4 month (40% of $Asset_3$)
- Liquid Asset buffer – w_{Asset4} = 10.92%.

The interest income resulting from the asset structure under the *Downgrade of the bank by one notch* scenario is as follows:

- r_{Asset1} = USD1.66bn
- r_{Asset2} = USD2.544bn
- r_{Asset3} = USD2.116bn
- r_{Asset4} = USD0.1113bn.

Total interest income = **USD6.44bn.**

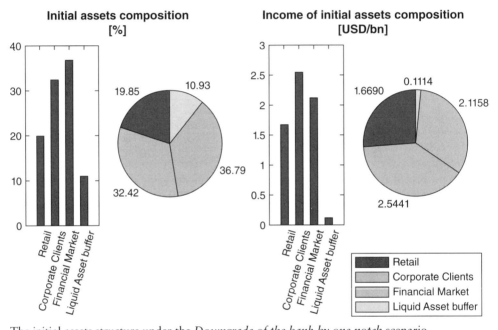

The initial assets structure under the *Downgrade of the bank by one notch* scenario.

Under the existing structure, the liquidity and interest rate risk exposure metrics are as follows:

- AD ratio = 80.2%
- MTFR $_{contractual}$ = 60%
- MTFR $_{behavioural}$ = 176%
- SH_2M = 134%
- Delta NII $_{+200bps}$ = 38.7%
- Delta NII $_{-200bps}$ = 1.9%
- CAR = 12.4%.

After the decision model is put in place, the asset structure has changed as follows:

- Retail assets – w_{Asset1} = 52.14%
- Corporate Clients assets – w_{Asset2} = 0.00011%
- Financial Market assets – w_{Asset3} = 41.46%
  - to Banks – 6 month (20% of $Asset_3$)
  - Non-Bank Financial Institution (NBFI) > 6m – 9 month (40% of $Asset_3$)
  - Non-Bank Financial Institution (NBFI) < 6m – 4 month (40% of $Asset_3$)
- Liquid Asset buffer –w_{Asset4} = 6.38%.

The resulting interest income has changed as follows:

- r_{Asset1} = USD4.3834bn
- r_{Asset2} = USD0.0000085bn
- r_{Asset3} = USD2.38bn
- r_{Asset4} = USD0.065bn.

Total interest income = **USD6.8331bn**

The implementation of the decision model has resulted in an increase in the interest income over the period of 6 months of **USD0.3929bn**.

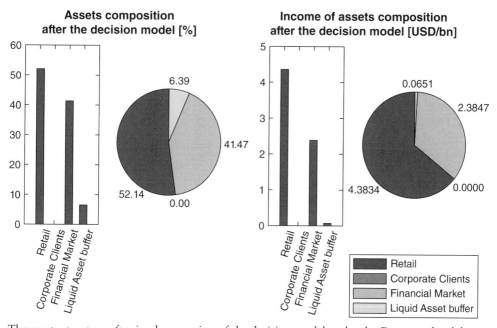

The assets structure after implementation of the decision model under the *Downgrade of the bank by one notch* scenario.

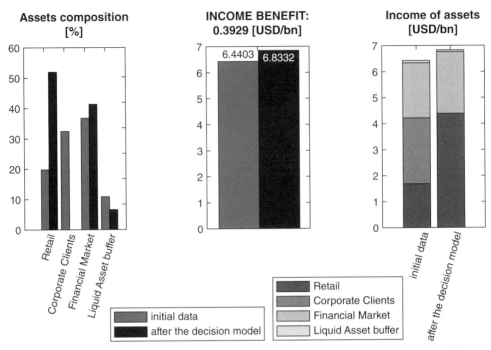

The income benefit after implementation of the decision model under the *Downgrade of the bank by one notch* scenario.

Under the target structure, the liquidity and interest rate risk exposure metrics are as follows:

- AD ratio = 79.9%
- MTFR $_{contractual}$ = 60.15%
- MTFR $_{behavioural}$ = 152%
- SH_2M = 100%
- Delta NII$_{+200bps}$ = 59.9%
- Delta NII$_{-200bps}$ = 2.99%
- CAR = 14.56%.

Inclusion of the CPR for Fixed Rate Assets   Under the *Inclusion of the CPR for fixed rate assets* scenario, the initial asset structure and their respective income is as follows:

- Retail assets – w_{Asset1} = 19.85%
- Corporate Clients assets – w_{Asset2} = 32.42%
- Financial Market assets – w_{Asset3} = 36.79%
  - to Banks – 6 month (20% of $Asset_3$)
  - Non-Bank Financial Institution (NBFI) > 6m – 9 month (40% of $Asset_3$)
  - Non-Bank Financial Institution (NBFI) < 6m – 4 month (40% of $Asset_3$)
- Liquid Asset buffer – w_{Asset4} = 10.92%.

The interest income resulting from the asset structure under the *Inclusion of the CPR for fixed rate assets* scenario is as follows:

- r_{Asset1} = USD1.532bn
- r_{Asset2} = USD2.541bn
- r_{Asset3} = USD2.116bn
- r_{Asset4} = USD0.1113bn.

Total interest income = **USD6.3040bn.**

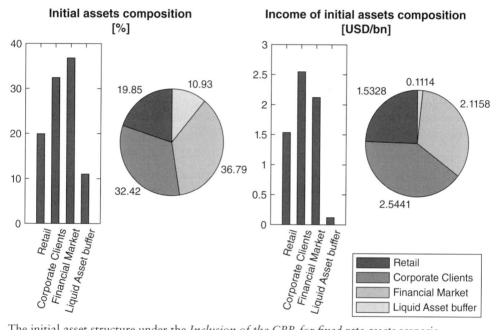

The initial asset structure under the *Inclusion of the CPR for fixed rate assets* scenario.

Under the existing structure, the liquidity and interest rate risk exposure metrics are as follows:

- AD ratio = 80.2%
- MTFR $_{contractual}$ = 60%
- MTFR $_{behavioural}$ = 176%
- SH_2M = 133.8%
- Delta NII$_{+200bps}$ = 38.7%
- Delta NII$_{-200bps}$ = 1.9%
- CAR = 12.4%.

After the decision model is put in place, the asset structure has changed as follows:

- Retail assets – $w_{Asset1} = 26.7\%$
- Corporate Clients assets – $w_{Asset2} = 25.4\%$
- Financial Market assets – $w_{Asset3} = 43.19\%$
  - to Banks – 6 month (20% of $Asset_3$)
  - Non-Bank Financial Institution (NBFI) > 6m – 9 month (40% of $Asset_3$)
  - Non-Bank Financial Institution (NBFI) < 6m – 4 month (40% of $Asset_3$)
- Liquid Asset buffer – $w_{Asset4} = 4.66\%$.

The resulting interest income has changed as follows:

- $r_{Asset1} = \text{USD}2.064\text{bn}$
- $r_{Asset2} = \text{USD}1.9935\text{bn}$
- $r_{Asset3} = \text{USD}2.4837\text{bn}$
- $r_{Asset4} = \text{USD}0.0475\text{bn}$.

Total interest income = **USD6.5889bn.**

The implementation of the decision model has resulted in an increase in the interest income over the period of 6 months of **USD0.2849bn.**

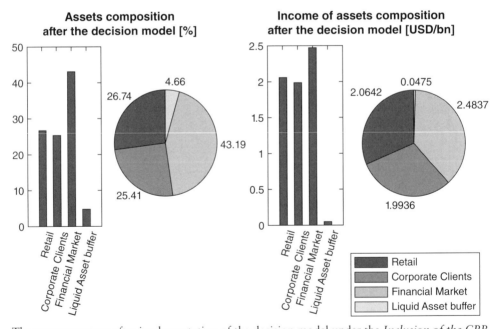

The assets structure after implementation of the decision model under the *Inclusion of the CPR for fixed rate assets* scenario.

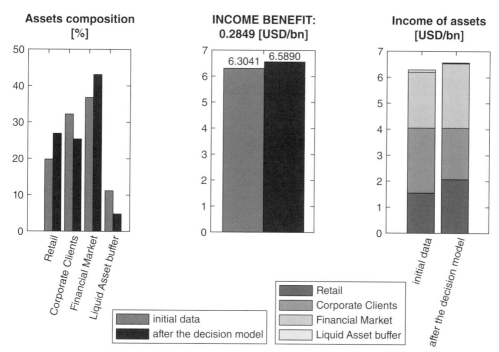

The income benefit after implementation of the decision model under the *Inclusion of the CPR for fixed rate assets* scenario.

Under the target structure, the liquidity and interest rate risk exposure metrics are as follows:

- AD ratio = 79.9%
- MTFR $_{contractual}$ = 62.59%
- MTFR $_{behavioural}$ = 166%
- SH_2M = 100%
- Delta NII$_{+200bps}$ = 30.37%
- Delta NII$_{-200bps}$ = 1.51%
- CAR = 12%.

Changes in the Output of Deposit Characterisation Model, i.e. balance volatility and balance sensitivity Under the *Changes in the output of deposit characterisation model, i.e. balance volatility and balance sensitivity* scenario, the initial assets structure and their respective income is as follows:

- Retail assets – w_{Asset1} = 19.85%
- Corporate Clients assets – w_{Asset2} = 32.42%

- Financial Market assets – $w_{Asset3} = 36.79\%$
  - to Banks – 6 month (20% of $Asset_3$)
  - Non-Bank Financial Institution (NBFI) > 6m – 9 month (40% of $Asset_3$)
  - Non-Bank Financial Institution (NBFI) < 6m – 4 month (40% of $Asset_3$)
- Liquid Asset buffer – $w_{Asset4} = 10.92\%$.

The interest income resulting from the asset structure under *Changes in the output of deposit characterisation model, i.e. balance volatility and balance sensitivity* scenario is as follows:

- $r_{Asset1} = USD1.533bn$
- $r_{Asset2} = USD2.544bn$
- $r_{Asset3} = USD2.116bn$
- $r_{Asset4} = USD0.1113bn$.

Total interest income = **USD6.3040bn.**

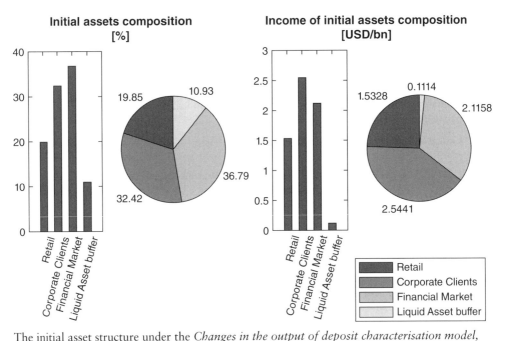

The initial asset structure under the *Changes in the output of deposit characterisation model, i.e. balance volatility and balance sensitivity* scenario

Under the existing structure, the liquidity and interest rate risk exposure metrics are as follows:

- AD ratio = 80.2%
- MTFR $_{contractual}$ = 60%
- MTFR $_{behavioural}$ = 176%

- SH_2M = 133.8%
- Delta NII$_{+200\text{bps}}$ = 31.4%
- Delta NII$_{-200\text{bps}}$ = 1.57%
- CAR = 12.4%.

After the decision model is put in place, the asset structure has changed as follows:

- Retail assets – w_{Asset1} = 26.7%
- Corporate Clients assets – w_{Asset2} = 25.4%
- Financial Market assets – w_{Asset3} = 43.19%
  - to Banks – 6 month (20% of $Asset_3$)
  - Non-Bank Financial Institution (NBFI) > 6m – 9 month (40% of $Asset_3$)
  - Non-Bank Financial Institution (NBFI) < 6m – 4 month (40% of $Asset_3$)
- Liquid Asset buffer – w_{Asset4} = 4.66%.

The resulting interest income has changed as follows:

- r_{Asset1} = USD2.064bn
- r_{Asset2} = USD1.9935bn
- r_{Asset3} = USD2.4837bn
- r_{Asset4} = USD0.0475bn.

Total interest income = **USD6.588bn.**

The implementation of the decision model has resulted in an increase in the interest income over the period of 6 months of **USD0.2849bn.**

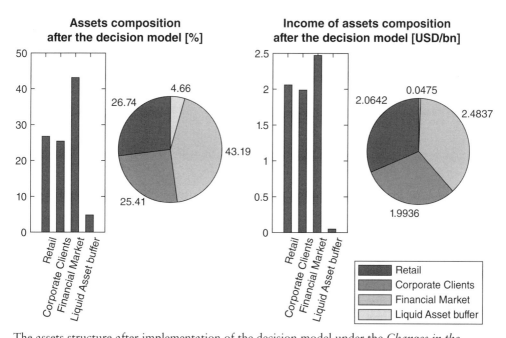

The assets structure after implementation of the decision model under the *Changes in the output of deposit characterisation model, i.e. balance volatility and balance sensitivity* scenario.

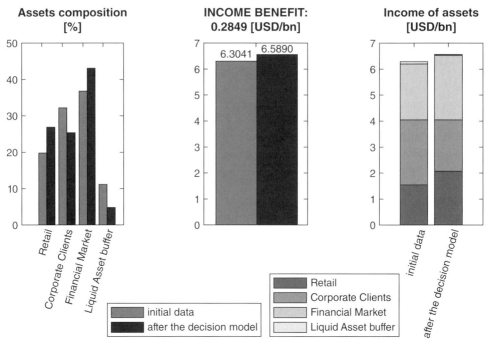

The income benefit after implementation of the decision model under the *Changes in the output of deposit characterisation model, i.e. balance volatility and balance sensitivity* scenario.

Under the target structure, the liquidity and interest rate risk exposure metrics are as follows:

- AD ratio = 79.9%
- MTFR $_{contractual}$ = 60.15%
- MTFR $_{behavioural}$ = 166%
- SH_2M = 100%
- Delta NII$_{+200bps}$ = 24.31%
- Delta NII$_{-200bps}$ = 1.21%
- CAR = 12%.

Changes in the Initial Proportions of the Fixed Rate Assets Under the *Changes in the initial proportions of the fixed rate assets* scenario, the initial asset structure and their respective income is as follows:

- Retail assets – w_{Asset1} = 19.8%
- Corporate Clients assets – w_{Asset2} = 18.21%
- Financial Market assets – w_{Asset3} = 36.79%
  - to Banks – 6 month (20% of $Asset_3$)
  - Non-Bank Financial Institution (NBFI) > 6m – 9 month (40% of $Asset_3$)
  - Non-Bank Financial Institution (NBFI) < 6m – 4 month (40% of $Asset_3$)
- Liquid Asset buffer – w_{Asset4} = 25.13%.

The interest income resulting from the asset structure under the *Changes in the initial proportions of the fixed rate assets* scenario is as follows:

- r_{Asset1} = USD1.532bn
- r_{Asset2} = USD1.429bn
- r_{Asset3} = USD2.115bn
- r_{Asset4} = USD0.2561bn.

Total interest income = **USD5.334bn.**

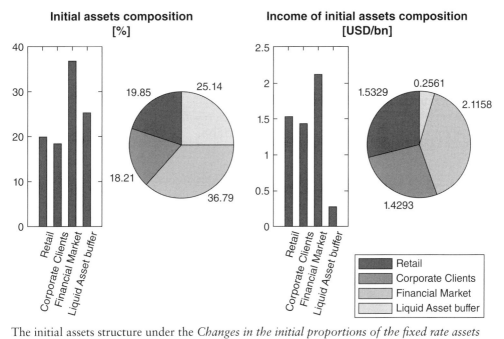

The initial assets structure under the *Changes in the initial proportions of the fixed rate assets* scenario.

Under the existing structure, the liquidity and interest rate risk exposure metrics are as follows:

- AD ratio = 58.4%
- MTFR $_{contractual}$ = 82.39%
- MTFR $_{behavioural}$ = 215%
- SH_2M = 214%
- Delta NII$_{+200bps}$ = 72.8%
- Delta NII$_{-200bps}$ = 3.644%
- CAR = 15.14%.

After the decision model is put in place, the asset structure has changed as follows:

- Retail assets – $w_{Asset1} = 26.7\%$
- Corporate Clients assets – $w_{Asset2} = 25.4\%$
- Financial Market assets – $w_{Asset3} = 43.19\%$
  - to Banks – 6 month (20% of $Asset_3$)
  - Non-Bank Financial Institution (NBFI) > 6m – 9 month (40% of $Asset_3$)
  - Non-Bank Financial Institution (NBFI) < 6m – 4 month (40% of $Asset_3$)
- Liquid Asset buffer – $w_{Asset4} = 4.66\%$.

The resulting interest income have changed as follows:

- $r_{Asset1} = \text{USD2.064bn}$
- $r_{Asset2} = \text{USD1.99bn}$
- $r_{Asset3} = \text{USD2.4837bn}$
- $r_{Asset4} = \text{USD0.0475bn}$

Total interest income = **USD6.588bn.**
The implementation of the decision model has resulted in an increase in the interest income over the period of 6 months of **USD1.255bn.**

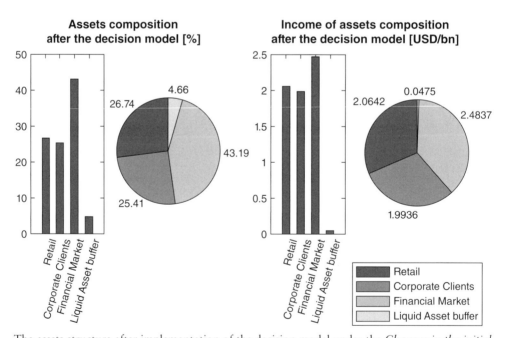

The assets structure after implementation of the decision model under the *Changes in the initial proportions of the fixed rate assets* scenario.

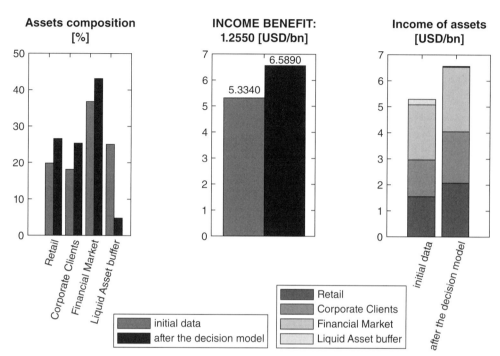

The income benefit after implementation of the decision model under the *Changes in the initial proportions of the fixed rate assets* scenario.

Under the target structure, the liquidity and interest rate risk exposure metrics are as follows:

- AD ratio = 79.9%
- MTFR $_{contractual}$ = 60.15%
- MTFR $_{behavioural}$ = 167%
- SH_2M = 100%
- Delta NII$_{+200bps}$ = 30.37%
- Delta NII$_{-200bps}$ = 1.51%
- CAR = 12%.

LIABILITIES SIDE

Base Scenario The calculation of the target funding profile of the commercial bank based in UK under the *Base* scenario provides the following results:

Initial funding structure at t_0:

- Retail current accounts (CASA) – w_A = 28.3%
- TB current accounts – w_B = 27.8%
- Senior debt issuance – w_C =11.4%

- Corporate time deposits – $w_{D1} = 20.5\%$
- Structured deposits – $w_{D2} = 4.2\%$
- Commercial papers and certificates of deposits – $w_{D3} = 7.8\%$.

The funding costs resulting from the funding structure under the ongoing *Base* scenario:

- c_A = USD0.00695bn
- c_B = USD0.17125bn
- c_C = USD0.6384bn
- c_{D1} = USD1.023bn
- c_{D2} = USD0.333bn
- c_{D3} = USD0.6768bn.

Total cost = **USD2.8493bn.**

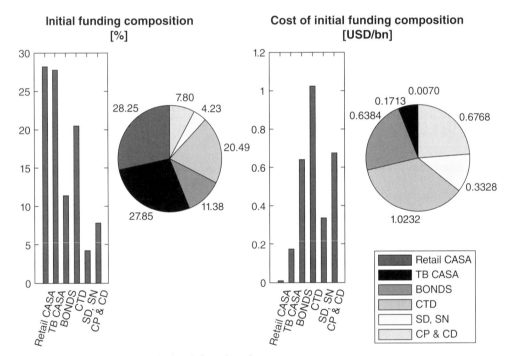

Initial funding structure in the bank based in the UK.

Under the existing structure, the liquidity and interest rate risk exposure metrics are as follows:

- AD ratio = 80.2%
- MTFR $_{contractual}$ = 60%
- MTFR $_{behavioural}$ = 176%
- SH_2M = 133%
- Delta NII$_{+200bps}$ = 65%
- Delta NII$_{-200bps}$ = 3.26%

After the decision model is put in place, the funding structure is changed as follows:

- Retail current accounts (CASA) – $w_A = 51.16\%$
- TB current accounts – $w_B = 10\%$
- Senior debt issuance – $w_C = 3.8\%$
- Corporate time deposits – $w_{D1} = 30\%$
- Structured deposits – $w_{D2} = 3\%$
- Commercial papers and certificates of deposits – $w_{D3} = 2\%$.

The resulting funding costs have changed as follows:

- $c_A = \text{USD}0.0125\text{bn}$
- $c_B = \text{USD}0.0615\text{bn}$
- $c_C = \text{USD}0.2149\text{bn}$
- $c_{D1} = \text{USD}1.4982\text{bn}$
- $c_{D2} = \text{USD}0.2361\text{bn}$
- $c_{D3} = \text{USD}0.1734\text{bn}$.

Total cost = **USD2.1967bn.**

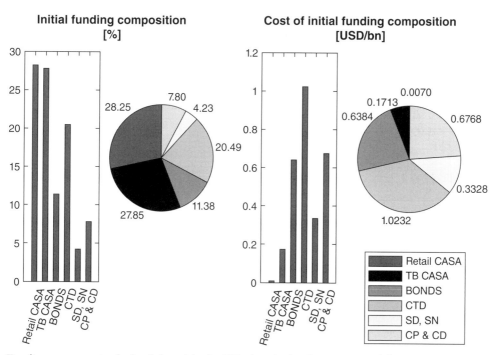

Funding structure in the bank based in the UK after the implementation of decision model.

The implementation of decision model has resulted in a reduction of the funding cost over the period of 6 months of **USD0.6526bn.**

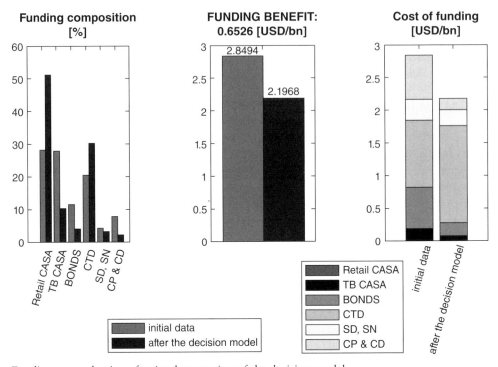

Funding cost reduction after implementation of the decision model.

Under the target structure, the liquidity and interest rate risk exposure metrics are as follows:

- AD ratio = 72%
- MTFR $_{contractual}$ = 35%
- MTFR $_{behavioural}$ = 176%
- SH_2M = 156%
- Delta NII$_{+200bps}$ = 54%
- Delta NII$_{-200bps}$ = 2.7%.

Interest Rate Changes Scenarios

Inflation Expectation Scenario – as per parameters defined in Chapter 4. Under the *Inflation expectation* scenario, the initial funding structure and the respective cost of funding are as follows:

- Retail current accounts (CASA) – w_A = 28.3%
- TB current accounts – w_B = 27.8%
- Senior debt issuance – w_C =11.4%

- Corporate time deposits – $w_{D1} = 20.5\%$
- Structured deposits – $w_{D2} = 4.2\%$
- Commercial papers and certificates of deposits – $w_{D3} = 7.8\%$

The funding costs resulting from the funding structure under the *Inflation expectation* scenario:

- $c_A = \text{USD}0.00695\text{bn}$
- $c_B = \text{USD}0.17125\text{bn}$
- $c_C = \text{USD}0.7916\text{bn}$
- $c_{D1} = \text{USD}1.2989\text{bn}$
- $c_{D2} = \text{USD}0.39\text{bn}$
- $c_{D3} = \text{USD}0.6768\text{bn}.$

Total cost = **USD3.3356bn.**

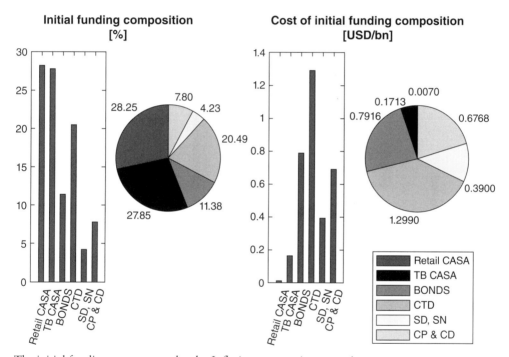

The initial funding structure under the *Inflation expectation* scenario.

After the decision model is put in place, the funding structure has changed as follows:

- Retail current accounts (CASA) – $w_A = 51.16\%$
- TB current accounts – $w_B = 10\%$

- Senior debt issuance – $w_C = 3.8\%$
- Corporate time deposits – $w_{D1} = 30\%$
- Structured deposits – $w_{D2} = 3\%$
- Commercial papers and certificates of deposits – $w_{D3} = 2\%$.

The resulting funding costs have changed as follows:

- $c_A = $ USD0.0125bn
- $c_B = $ USD0.0615bn
- $c_C = $ USD0.2664bn
- $c_{D1} = $ USD1.90bn
- $c_{D2} = $ USD0.2767bn
- $c_{D3} = $ USD0.1734bn.

Total cost = **USD2.6928bn.**

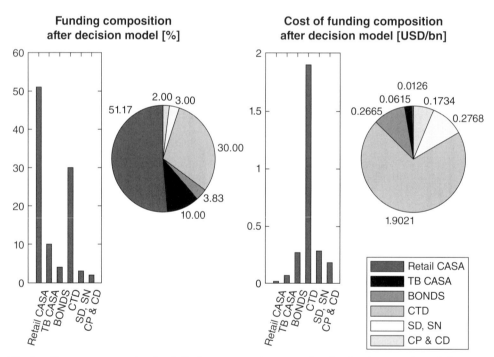

The funding structure under the *Inflation expectation* scenario after implementation of the decision model.

The implementation of the decision model has resulted in a reduction of funding costs over the period of 6 months of **USD0.6428bn.**

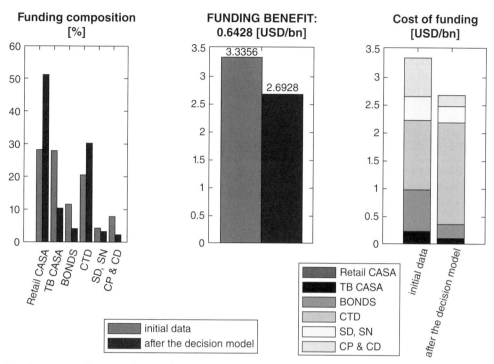

Funding cost reduction after implementation of the decision model under the *Inflation expectation* scenario.

Under the target structure, the liquidity and interest rate risk exposure metrics are as follows:

- AD ratio = 72%
- MTFR $_{contractual}$ = 35%
- MTFR $_{behavioural}$ = 175%
- SH_2M = 156%
- Delta NII$_{+200bps}$ = 49%
- Delta NII$_{-200bps}$ = 2.47%.

Oil Supply Crisis Under the *Oil Supply crisis* scenario, the initial funding structure and the respective cost of funding are as follows:

- Retail current accounts (CASA) – w_A = 28.3%
- TB current accounts – w_B = 27.8%
- Senior debt issuance – w_C = 11.4%
- Corporate time deposits – w_{D1} = 20.5%
- Structured deposits – w_{D2} = 4.2%
- Commercial papers and certificates of deposits – w_{D3} = 7.8%.

The funding costs resulting from the funding structure under the *Oil supply crisis* scenario:

- $c_A = $ USD0.0069bn
- $c_B = $ USD0.1712bn
- $c_C = $ USD0.6938bn
- $c_{D1} = $ USD1.1229bn
- $c_{D2} = $ USD0.3879bn
- $c_{D3} = $ USD0.6768bn.

Total cost = **USD3.0597bn.**

Under the existing structure, the liquidity and interest rate risk exposure metrics are as follows:

- AD ratio = 80%
- MTFR $_{\text{contractual}}$ = 60%
- MTFR $_{\text{behavioural}}$ = 175%
- SH_2M = 133%
- Delta NII$_{+200\text{bps}}$ = 62%
- Delta NII$_{-200\text{bps}}$ = 3.1%.

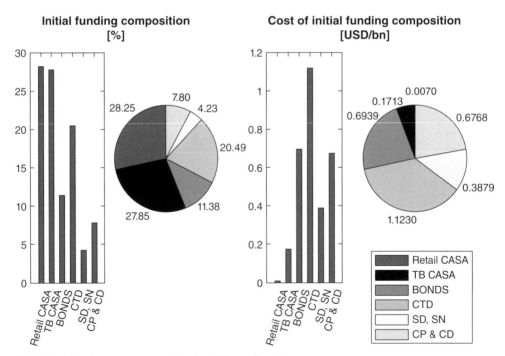

The initial funding structure under the *Oil supply crisis* scenario.

After the decision model is put in place, the funding structure has changed as follows:

- Retail current accounts (CASA) – $w_A = 51\%$
- TB current accounts – $w_B = 10\%$
- Senior debt issuance – $w_C = 3.8\%$
- Corporate time deposits – $w_{D1} = 30\%$
- Structured deposits – $w_{D2} = 3\%$
- Commercial papers and certificates of deposits – $w_{D3} = 2\%$.

The resulting funding costs have changed as follows:

- c_A = USD0.0125bn
- c_B = USD0.0615bn
- c_C = USD0.2335bn
- c_{D1} = USD1.644bn
- c_{D2} = USD0.2752bn
- c_{D3} = USD0.173bn.

Total cost = **USD2.4bn.**

The implementation of the decision model has resulted in a reduction of funding costs over the period of 6 months of USD0.6591bn.

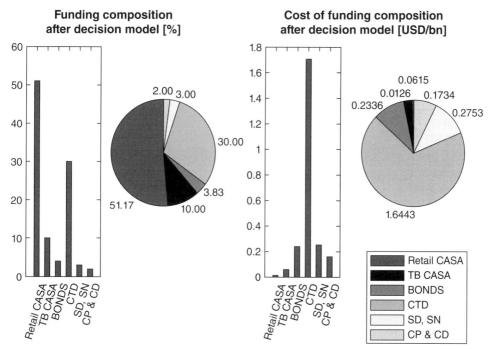

Funding cost reduction after implementation of the decision model under the *Oil supply crisis* scenario.

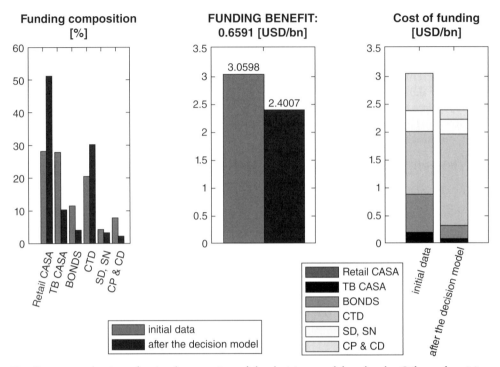

Funding cost reduction after implementation of the decision model under the *Oil supply crisis* scenario.

Under the target structure, the liquidity and interest rate risk exposure metrics are as follows:

- AD ratio = 72%
- MTFR $_{contractual}$ = 35%
- MTFR $_{behavioural}$ = 175%
- SH_2M = 156%
- Delta NII$_{+200bps}$ = 51.7%
- Delta NII$_{-200bps}$ = 2.58%.

Earthquake Scenario Under the *Earthquake* scenario, the initial funding structure and the respective cost of funding are as follows:

- Retail current accounts (CASA) – w_A = 28.3%
- TB current accounts – w_B = 27.8%
- Senior debt issuance – w_C = 11.4%
- Corporate time deposits – w_{D1} = 20.5%
- Structured deposits – w_{D2} = 4.2%
- Commercial papers and certificates of deposits – w_{D3} = 7.8%.

The funding costs resulting from the funding structure under the *Earthquake* scenario:

- c_A = USD0.00695bn
- c_B = USD0.1712bn
- c_C = USD0.5837bn
- c_{D1} = USD0.9246bn
- c_{D2} = USD0.2891bn
- c_{D3} = USD0.6768bn.

Total cost = **USD2.6525bn.**

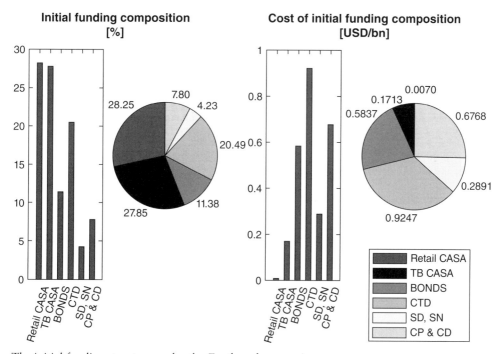

The initial funding structure under the *Earthquake* scenario.

Under the existing structure, the liquidity and interest rate risk exposure metrics are as follows:

- AD ratio = 80%
- MTFR $_{contractual}$ = 60%
- MTFR $_{behavioural}$ = 175%
- SH_2M = 133%
- Delta NII$_{+200bps}$ = 64%
- Delta NII$_{-200bps}$ = 3.2%.

The implementation of the decision model has resulted in a reduction of funding costs over the period of 6 months of USD0.6496bn.

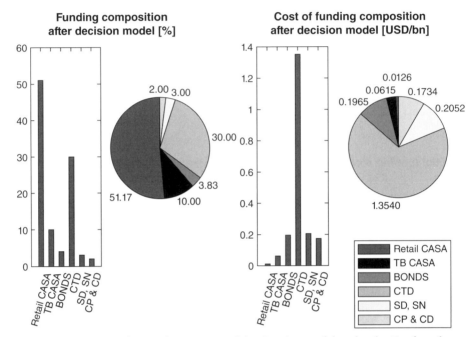

Funding cost reduction after implementation of the decision model under the *Earthquake* scenario.

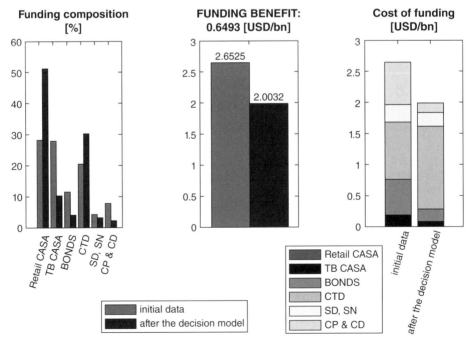

Funding cost reduction after implementation of the decision model under the *Earthquake* scenario.

Under the target structure, the liquidity and interest rate risk exposure metrics are as follows:

- AD ratio = 72%
- MTFR $_\text{contractual}$ = 35%
- MTFR $_\text{behavioural}$ = 175%
- SH_2M = 156%
- Delta NII$_\text{+200bps}$ = 53%
- Delta NII$_\text{-200bps}$ = 2.67%.

Changes in the Output of Deposit Characterisation Model, i.e. balance volatility and balance sensitivity Under the *Changes in the output of deposit characterisation model* scenario, the initial funding structure and the respective cost of funding are as follows:

- Retail current accounts (CASA) – w_A = 28.3%
- TB current accounts – w_B = 27.8%
- Senior debt issuance – w_C =11.4%
- Corporate time deposits – w_{D1} = 20.5%
- Structured deposits – w_{D2} = 4.2%
- Commercial papers and certificates of deposits – w_{D3} = 7.8%.

The funding costs resulting from the funding structure under the *Changes in the output of deposit characterisation model* scenario:

- c_A = USD0.00695bn
- c_B = USD0.1712bn
- c_C = USD0.6384bn
- c_{D1} = USD1.023bn
- c_{D2} = USD0.3328bn
- c_{D3} = USD0.6768bn.

Total cost = **USD2.8493bn.**

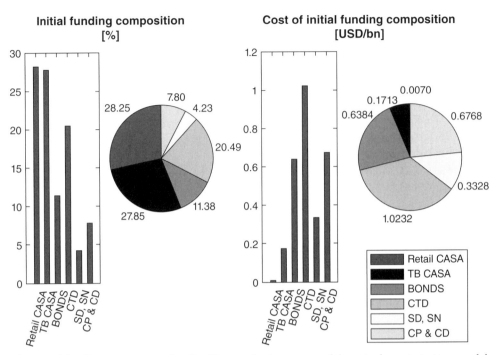

The initial funding structure under the *Changes in the output of deposit characterisation model* scenario.

Under the existing structure, the liquidity and interest rate risk exposure metrics are as follows:

- AD ratio = 80%
- MTFR $_{contractual}$ = 60%
- MTFR $_{behavioural}$ = 175%
- SH_2M = 133%
- Delta NII$_{+200bps}$ = 71%
- Delta NII$_{-200bps}$ = 3.5%.

After the decision model is put in place, the funding structure has changed as follows:

- Retail current accounts (CASA) – $w_A = 51.16\%$
- TB current accounts – $w_B = 10\%$
- Senior debt issuance – $w_C = 3.8\%$

- Corporate time deposits – $w_{D1} = 30\%$
- Structured deposits – $w_{D2} = 3\%$
- Commercial papers and certificates of deposits – $w_{D3} = 2\%$.

The resulting funding costs have changed as follows:

- $c_A = USD0.0126bn$
- $c_B = USD0.0615bn$
- $c_C = USD0.2149bn$
- $c_{D1} = USD1.4982bn$
- $c_{D2} = USD0.2361bn$
- $c_{D3} = USD0.1734bn$.

Total cost = **USD2.1967bn.**
The implementation of the decision model has resulted in a reduction of funding costs over the period of 6 months of **USD0.6526bn.**

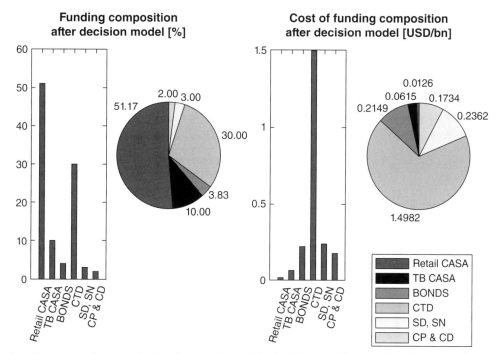

Funding cost reduction after implementation of the decision model under the *Changes in the output of deposit characterisation model* scenario.

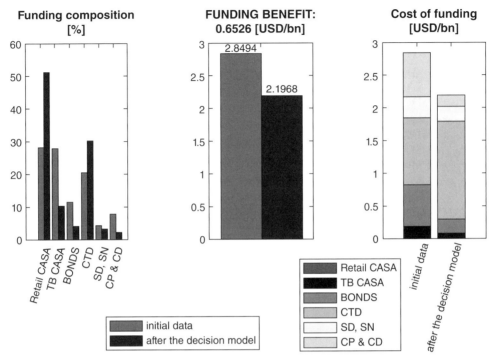

Funding cost reduction after implementation of the decision model under the *Changes in the output of deposit characterisation model* scenario.

Under the target structure, the liquidity and interest rate risk exposure metrics are as follows:

- AD ratio = 72%
- MTFR $_{contractual}$ = 35%
- MTFR $_{behavioural}$ = 176%
- SH_2M = 156%
- Delta NII$_{+200bps}$ = 61.85%
- Delta NII$_{-200bps}$ = 3.09%.

Inclusion of the CPR for Fixed Rate Assets Under the *Inclusion of the CPR for fixed rate assets* scenario, the initial funding structure and the respective cost of funding are as follows:

- Retail current accounts (CASA) – w_A = 28.3%
- TB current accounts – w_B = 27.8%
- Senior debt issuance – w_C = 11.4%
- Corporate time deposits – w_{D1} = 20.5%
- Structured deposits – w_{D2} = 4.2%
- Commercial papers and certificates of deposits – w_{D3} = 7.8%.

The funding costs resulting from the funding structure under the *Inclusion of the CPR for fixed rate assets* scenario:

- c_A = USD0.00695bn
- c_B = USD0.1712bn
- c_C = USD0.6384bn
- c_{D1} = USD1.023bn
- c_{D2} = USD0.3328bn
- c_{D3} = USD0.6768bn.

Total cost = **USD2.8493bn.**

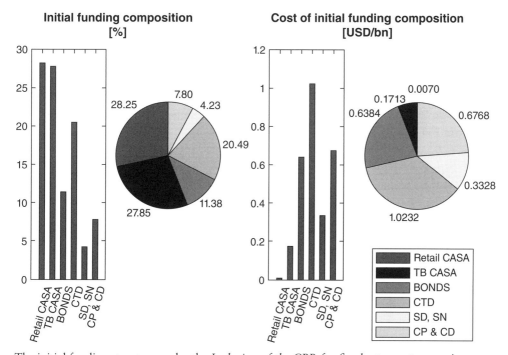

The initial funding structure under the *Inclusion of the CPR for fixed rate assets* scenario.

Under the existing structure, the liquidity and interest rate risk exposure metrics are as follows:

- AD ratio = 80%
- $\text{MTFR}_{\text{contractual}}$ = 59.02%
- $\text{MTFR}_{\text{behavioural}}$ = 175%
- SH_2M = 133%
- Delta $\text{NII}_{+200\text{bps}}$ = 65%
- Delta $\text{NII}_{-200\text{bps}}$ = 3.26%.

After the decision model is put in place, the funding structure has changed as follows:

- Retail current accounts (CASA) – $w_A = 51.47\%$
- TB current accounts – $w_B = 10\%$
- Senior debt issuance – $w_C = 3.52\%$
- Corporate time deposits – $w_{D1} = 30\%$
- Structured deposits – $w_{D2} = 3\%$
- Commercial papers and certificates of deposits – $w_{D3} = 2\%$.

The resulting funding costs have changed as follows:

- c_A = USD0.0127bn
- c_B = USD0.0615bn
- c_C = USD0.1976bn
- c_{D1} = USD1.4982bn
- c_{D2} = USD0.2361bn
- c_{D3} = USD0.1734bn.

Total cost = **USD2.1795bn.**

The implementation of the decision model has resulted in a reduction of funding costs over the period of 6 months of **USD0.6698bn.**

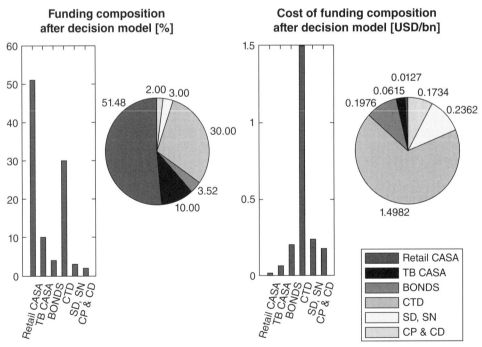

Funding cost reduction after implementation of the decision model under the *Inclusion of the CPR for fixed rate assets* scenario.

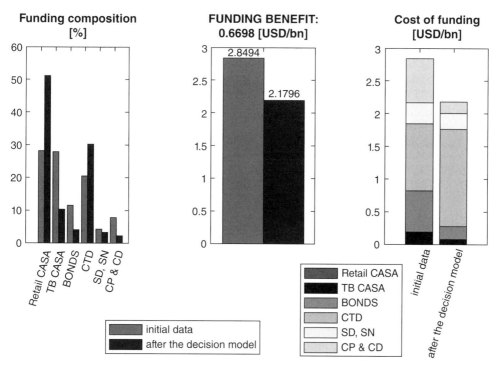

Funding cost reduction after implementation of the decision model under the *Inclusion of the CPR for fixed rate assets* scenario.

Under the target structure, the liquidity and interest rate risk exposure metrics are as follows:

- AD ratio = 72%
- MTFR $_{contractual}$ = 35%
- MTFR $_{behavioural}$ = 175%
- SH_2M = 156%
- Delta NII$_{+200bps}$ = 54.6%
- Delta NII$_{-200bps}$ = 2.73%.

Downgrade of the Bank by One Notch Under the *Downgrade of the bank by one notch* scenario, the initial funding structure and the respective cost of funding are as follows:

- Retail current accounts (CASA) – w_A = 28.3%
- TB current accounts – w_B = 27.8%
- Senior debt issuance – w_C =11.4%
- Corporate time deposits – w_{D1} = 20.5%
- Structured deposits – w_{D2} = 4.2%
- Commercial papers and certificates of deposits – w_{D3} = 7.8%.

The funding costs resulting from the funding structure under the *Downgrade of the bank by one notch* scenario:

- c_A = USD0.00695bn
- c_B = USD0.1713bn
- c_C = USD0.7784bn
- c_{D1} = USD1.0231bn
- c_{D2} = USD0.3328bn
- c_{D3} = USD0.6768bn.

Total cost = **USD2.9893bn.**

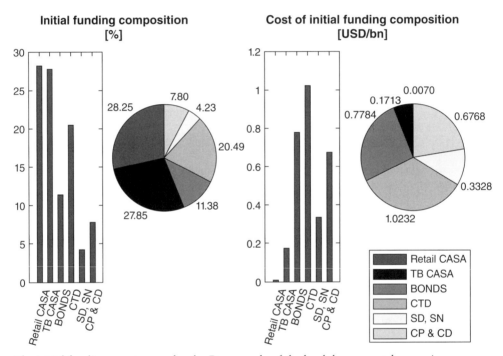

The initial funding structure under the *Downgrade of the bank by one notch* scenario.

After the decision model is put in place, the funding structure has changed as follows:

- retail current accounts (CASA) – $w_A = 51.16\%$
- TB current accounts – $w_B = 10\%$
- senior debt issuance – $w_C = 3.8\%$

- corporate time deposits – $w_{D1} = 30\%$
- structured deposits – $w_{D2} = 3\%$
- commercial papers and certificates of deposits – $w_{D3} = 2\%$.

The resulting funding costs have changed as follows:

- $c_A =$ USD0.0126bn
- $c_B =$ USD0.0615bn
- $c_C =$ USD0.2620bn
- $c_{D1} =$ USD1.4982bn
- $c_{D2} =$ USD0.2361bn
- $c_{D3} =$ USD0.1734bn.

Total cost = **USD2.2439bn.**

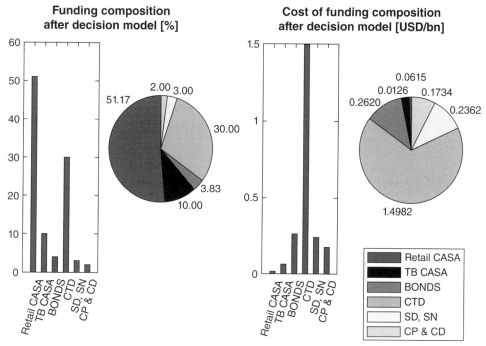

Funding cost reduction after implementation of the decision model under the *Downgrade of the bank by one notch* scenario.

The implementation of the decision model has resulted in a reduction of funding costs over the period of 6 months of **USD0.7455bn.**

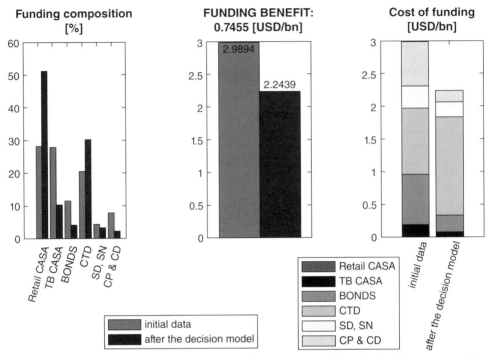

Funding cost reduction after implementation of the decision model under the *Downgrade of the bank by one notch* scenario.

Under the target structure, the liquidity and interest rate risk exposure metrics are as follows:

- AD ratio = 72%
- MTFR $_{contractual}$ = 35%
- MTFR $_{behavioural}$ = 176%
- SH_2M = 156%
- Delta NII$_{+200bps}$ = 54.26%
- Delta NII$_{-200bps}$ = 2.713%.

Changes in the Initial Proportions of the Fixed Rate Assets Under the *Changes in the initial proportions of the fixed rate assets* scenario, the initial funding structure and the respective cost of funding are as follows:

- Retail current accounts (CASA) – $w_A = 28.3\%$
- TB current accounts – $w_B = 27.8\%$
- Senior debt issuance – $w_C = 11.4\%$
- Corporate time deposits – $w_{D1} = 20.5\%$
- Structured deposits – $w_{D2} = 4.2\%$
- Commercial papers and certificates of deposits – $w_{D3} = 7.8\%$.

The funding costs resulting from the funding structure under the *Changes in the initial proportions of the fixed rate assets* scenario:

- c_A = USD0.00695bn
- c_B = USD0.1713bn
- c_C = USD0.6384bn
- c_{D1} = USD1.0231bn
- c_{D2} = USD0.3328bn
- c_{D3} = USD0.6768bn.

Total cost = **USD2.8493bn.**

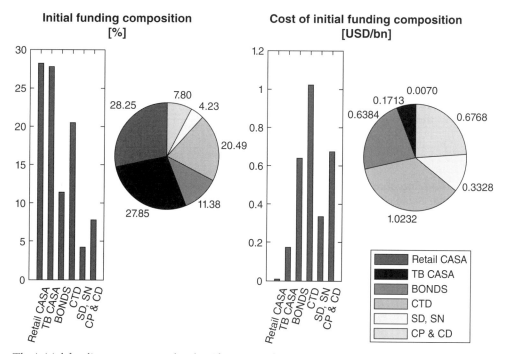

The initial funding structure under the *Changes in the initial proportions of the fixed rate assets* scenario.

Under the existing structure, the liquidity and interest rate risk exposure metrics are as follows:

- AD ratio = 58.40%
- MTFR $_{contractual}$ = 82.39%
- MTFR $_{behavioural}$ = 215%
- SH_2M = 214%
- Delta NII$_{+200bps}$ = 129%
- Delta NII$_{-200bps}$ = 6.4%.

After the decision model is put in place, the funding structure has changed as follows:

- Retail current accounts (CASA) – $w_A = 54.9\%$
- TB current accounts – $w_B = 10\%$
- Senior debt issuance – $w_C = 0.00011\%$
- Corporate time deposits – $w_{D1} = 30\%$
- Structured deposits – $w_{D2} = 3\%$
- Commercial papers and certificates of deposits – $w_{D3} = 2\%$.

The resulting funding costs have changed as follows:

- $c_A = \text{USD}0.0135\text{bn}$
- $c_B = \text{USD}0.0615\text{bn}$
- $c_C = \text{USD}0.000005995\text{bn}$
- $c_{D1} = \text{USD}1.4982\text{bn}$
- $c_{D2} = \text{USD}0.2361\text{bn}$
- $c_{D3} = \text{USD}0.1734\text{bn}$.

Total cost = **USD1.982bn.**

The implementation of the decision model has resulted in a reduction of funding costs over the period of 6 months of **USD0.8666bn.**

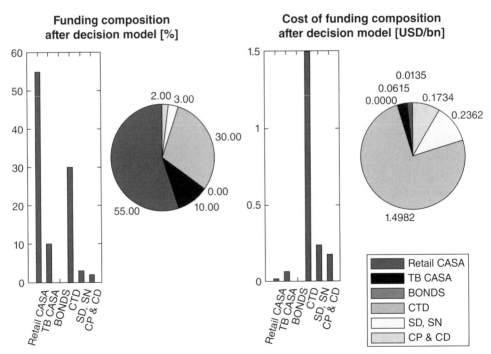

Funding cost reduction after implementation of the decision model under the *Changes in the initial proportions of the fixed rate assets* scenario.

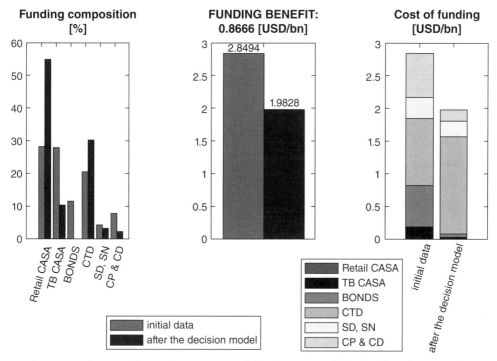

Funding cost reduction after implementation of the decision model under the *Changes in the initial proportions of the fixed rate assets* scenario.

Under the target structure, the liquidity and interest rate risk exposure metrics are as follows:

- AD ratio = 50%
- $\text{MTFR}_{\text{contractual}} = 39\%$
- $\text{MTFR}_{\text{behavioural}} = 216\%$
- SH_2M = 247%
- $\text{Delta NII}_{+200bps} = 121\%$
- $\text{Delta NII}_{-200bps} = 6.08\%$.

Changes in the Initial Proportions of the Floating Rate Assets Under the *Changes in the initial proportions of the floating rate assets* scenario, the initial funding structure and the respective cost of funding are as follows:

- Retail current accounts (CASA) – $w_A = 28.3\%$
- TB current accounts – $w_B = 27.8\%$
- Senior debt issuance – $w_C = 11.4\%$
- Corporate time deposits – $w_{D1} = 20.5\%$
- Structured deposits – $w_{D2} = 4.2\%$
- Commercial papers and certificates of deposits – $w_{D3} = 7.8\%$.

The funding costs resulting from the funding structure under the *Changes in the initial proportions of the fixed rate assets* scenario:

- c_A = USD0.00695bn
- c_B = USD0.1713bn
- c_C = USD0.6384bn
- c_{D1} = USD1.0231bn
- c_{D2} = USD0.3328bn
- c_{D3} = USD0.6768bn.

Total cost = **USD2.8493bn.**

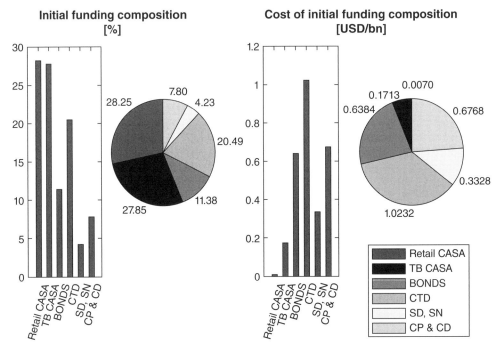

The initial funding structure under the *Changes in the initial proportions of the fixed rate assets* scenario.

Under the existing structure, the liquidity and interest rate risk exposure metrics are as follows:

- AD ratio = 72%
- MTFR $_{contractual}$ = 66.74%
- MTFR $_{behavioural}$ = 193%
- SH_2M = 165%
- Delta NII$_{+200bps}$ = 75.48%
- Delta NII$_{-200bps}$ = 3.77%.

After the decision model is put in place, the funding structure has changed as follows:

- Retail current accounts (CASA) – $w_A = 53.23\%$
- TB current accounts – $w_B = 10\%$
- Senior debt issuance – $w_C = 1.77\%$
- Corporate time deposits – $w_{D1} = 30\%$
- Structured deposits – $w_{D2} = 3\%$
- Commercial papers and certificates of deposits – $w_{D3} = 2\%$.

The resulting funding costs have changed as follows:

- $c_A = $ USD0.0131bn
- $c_B = $ USD0.0615bn
- $c_C = $ USD0.0991bn
- $c_{D1} = $ USD1.4982bn
- $c_{D2} = $ USD0.2361bn
- $c_{D3} = $ USD0.1734bn.

Total cost = **USD2.08bn.**
The implementation of the decision model has resulted in a reduction of funding costs over the period of 6 months of **USD0.6526bn.**

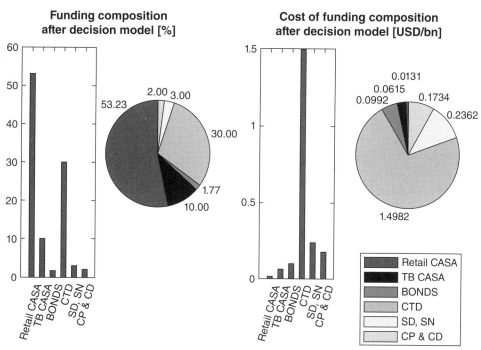

Funding cost reduction after implementation of the decision model under the *Changes in the initial proportions of the floating rate assets* scenario.

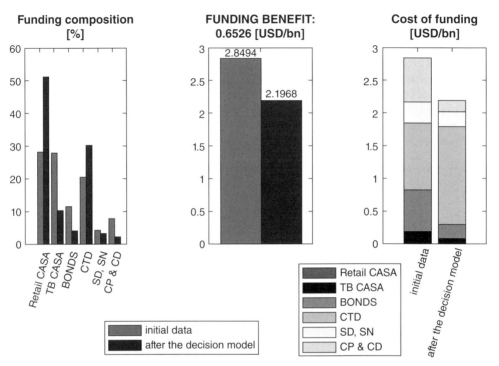

Funding cost reduction after implementation of the decision model under the *Changes in the initial proportions of the floating rate assets* scenario.

Under the target structure, the liquidity and interest rate risk exposure metrics are as follows:

- AD ratio = 63.38%
- MTFR $_{contractual}$ = 35%
- MTFR $_{behavioural}$ = 193%
- SH_2M = 192%
- Delta NII$_{+200bps}$ = 66%
- Delta NII$_{-200bps}$ = 3.30%.

Bibliography

Adam A. (2007). *Handbook of Asset Liability Management: From Models to Optimal Return Strategies*. Wiley, Chichester.

Ahmed J.M. (2015). *A Course in Basel II and III*. CreateSpace Independent Publishing Platform.

Alessandri, P. and Drehmann, M. (2010). An economic capital model integrating credit and interest rate risk in the banking book. *Journal of Banking and Finance* 34: 730–742.

Baldan C., Zen F., and Rebonato T. (2012). Liquidity risk and interest rate risk on banks: Are they related? *The IUP Journal of Financial Risk Management* IX(4): 27–51.

Barfield R. (ed.) (2011). *A Practitioner's Guide to Basel III and Beyond*. Thomson Reuters, Sweet & Maxwell.

Basel Committee on Banking Supervision (1997). Principles for the management of interest rate risk, September.

Basel Committee on Banking Supervision (2004). Principles for the management of interest rate risk, July.

Basel Committee on Banking Supervision (2010). Basel III: International framework for liquidity risk management, standards and monitoring, December.

Basel Committee on Banking Supervision (2011). Basel III: A global regulatory framework for more resilient banks and banking systems – revised version, June.

Basel Committee on Banking Supervision (2013). Basel III: The Liquidity Coverage Ratio and liquidity risk monitoring tools, January.

Basel Committee on Banking Supervision (2014). Basel III: The Net Stable Funding Ratio, January.

Basel Committee on banking Supervision (2016). Standards: Interest rate risk in the banking book, April.

Bergner M., Marcus P., and Adler M. (2014). Bank runs and Liquidity Management Tools. In: Andreas Bohn and Marije Elkenbracht-Huizing (eds), *The Handbook of ALM in Banking*. Risk Books, London.

Bierg G. and Kaufman G.G. (1985). Duration gap for financial institutions. *Financial Analyst Journal* 41(2): 68–71.

Blair S. and Akkizidis I. (2011). Funding liquidity: risk, analysis and management, in: *The PRM Handbook*, Supplementary Papers, PRMIA.

Brigo, D. and Mercurio, F. (2007). *Interest Rate Models – Theory and Practice*. Springer Finance.

Burghardt G. (1994). *The Treasury Bonds Basis*. Irwin, New York, 90.

Cadamagnani F., Harimohan R., and Tangri K. (2015). A bank within a bank: how a commercial bank's treasury function affects the interest rates set for loans and deposits. The Prudential Regulatory Authority, *Bank of England Quarterly Bulletin* Q2 2015, 55(2): 153–164.

CEBS (2008). Technical Advice on Liquidity Management, September.

Choudhry M. (2007). *Bank Asset Liability Management: Strategy, Trading, Analysis*. Wiley, Singapore.

Choudhry M. (2017). Strategic ALM and integrated balance sheet management: the future of bank risk management, *European Finance Journal*, Aug–Sep.

Choudhry M. (2018). *The Moorad Choudhry Anthology*. Wiley, London.

Cornett, M.M., McNutt J.J., Strahan P.E., and Theranian H. (2011) Liquidity risk management and credit supply in the financial crises. *Journal of Financial Economics* 101: 297–312.

Drago D. (1998). Rischio di interesse e gestione bancaria. Modelli e tecniche a confront. Bancaria Editrice, Roma.

Drago D. (2001). *Nuove tendenze dell'Asset Liability management nelle banche*. Giuffre, Milano.

Enthofer H. and Haas P. (2016). *Asset Liability Management Handbook*. Linde.

European Banking Authority (EBA) (2014). Guidelines on common procedures and methodologies for the supervisory review and evaluation process (SREP), December.

European Banking Authority (EBA) (2017a). Guidelines on ICAAP and ILAAP information collected for SREP purposes, February.

European Banking Authority (EBA) (2017b). Consultation Paper, Guidelines on the management of interest rate risk arising from non-trading book activities, October.

European Banking Authority (EBA) (2018a). Final Report, Guidelines on the management of interest rate risk arising from non-trading book activities, July.

European Banking Authority (EBA) (2018b). Final report, Guidelines on the revised common procedures and methodologies for the supervisory review and evaluation process (SREP) and supervisory stress testing, July.

Forsgren A, Gill F.E., and Wright M.H. (2002). Interior methods for nonlinear optimization, *Society for Industrial and Applied Mathematics Rev* 44(4): 525–597.

Gentili G. and Santini N. (2014). Measuring and managing interest rate and basis risk. In: Andreas Bohn and Marije Elkenbracht-Huizing (eds) *The Handbook of ALM in Banking: Interest Rates, Liquidity and the Balance Sheet*. Risk Books, London.

Grundke, P. (2004). Integrating interest rate risk in credit portfolio models. *Journal of Risk Finance* 5: 6–15.

Gualandri, E. (1991). Aziende di credito e rischio d'interesse. In: P.L. Fabrizi (ed.) *La gestione integrata dell'attivo e passivo nelle aziende di credito*. Giuffrè, Milano.

Gualandri, E., Landi, A., and Venturelli, V. (2009). Financial crises and new dimensions of liquidity risk: rethinking prudential regulation and supervision. *Journal of Money, Investment and Banking*, 8: 25–42.

Hauschild A. and Buschmann C. (2014). Strategies for the management of reserve assets. In: Andreas Bohn and Marije Elkenbracht-Huizing (eds), *The Handbook of ALM in Banking: Interest Rates, Liquidity and the Balance Sheet*. Risk Books, London.

Hellemons H.J.A. (2012). Bank balance sheet optimization. Thesis, VU University Amsterdam, Amsterdam.

Hull J. (2012). *Risk Management and Financial Institutions*. Wiley, New York.

Kaufman G.G. (1984). Measuring and managing interest rate risk: A primer, *Economic Perspectives* (Federal Reserve Bank of Chicago) 8(1): 16–29.

Knies K. (1876). *Geld und Credit II, Abteilung Der Credit*. Leipzig.

Lekatis G. (2014). *Understanding Basel III, What is Different After January 2015*. Washington.

Lubinska, B. (2014). Review of the static methods used in the measurement of the exposure to the interest rate risk. *Financial Sciences* 4(21): 25–41.

Lubinska, B. (2017). Balance sheet shaping through decision model and the role of the funds transfer pricing process. In: Krzysztof Jajuga, Lucjan T. Orlowski and Karsten Staehr (eds) *Contemporary Trends and Challenges in Finance*, Springer Proceedings in Business and Economics book series (SPBE). Springer, Cham. 183–193.

Lusignani G. (1996). *La gestione dei rischi finanziari nella banca*. Il Mulino, Bologna.

Lusignani, G. (2004). La gestione dei rischi nella banca. In: M. Onado (ed.) *La banca come impresa*. Il Mulino, Bologna.

McCarthy J. (2015). Liquidity risk. In: *The PRM Handbook, Market Risk, Asset Liability Management and Funds Transfer Pricing*, vol. III, PRMIA.

Memmel, C. (2011). Banks' exposure to interest rate risk, their earnings from term transformation, and the dynamics of the term structure. *Journal of Banking and Finance* 35: 282–289.

Neu P., Widowitz M., and Vogt, P. (2012). In the Center of the Storm: Insights from BCG's Treasury Benchmarking Survey, October. www.bcgperspectives.com/content/articles/financial_institutions_financial_management_budgeting_reporting_center_of_storm_treasury_benchmarking_survey_insights/?chapter=5#chapter5 (accessed 3 October 2012).

Newson P. (2017). *Interest Rate Risk in the Banking Book*. Risk Books, London.

Nocedal, J. and Wright, S.J. (2006). *Numerical Optimization*, Springer Series in Operations Research and Financial Engineering. Springer-Verlag, New York.

OCC, FED (2011–2012). Board of Governors of the Federal Reserve System Office of the Comptroller of the Currency, April. Sound Practices for Model Risk Management: Supervisory Guidance on Model Risk Management. https://www.occ.treas.gov/news-issuances/bulletins/2011/bulletin-2011-12a.pdf.

Parramore K. and Watsham T. (2015a). Numerical methods. In: *The PRM Handbook*, Mathematical Foundations of Risk Management, vol. II, PRMIA.

Parramore K. and Watsham T. (2015b). Regression analysis in finance. In: *The PRM Handbook, Mathematical Foundations of Risk Management*, vol. II, PRMIA.

Resti, A. and Sironi, S. (2007). *Risk Management and Shareholders' Value in Banking: From Risk Measurement Models to Capital Allocation Policies*. Wiley, Oxford.

Resti, A. (2011). Liquidita' e capitale delle banche: le nuove regole, i loro impatti gestionali. (Banks's capital and liquidity in the Basel III framework). *Bancaria* 11: 14–23.

Ryan, R.J. (2013). The Evolution of Asset/Liability Management (a summary). Research Foundation of CFA Institute.

Soulellis G. (2014). The modelling of non-maturity deposits. In: Andreas Bohn and Marije Elkenbracht-Huizing (eds), *The Handbook of ALM in Banking: Interest Rates, Liquidity and the Balance Sheet* (Chapter 5). Risk Books, London.

Staikouras, S. (2006). Financial intermediaries and interest rate risk: II. *Financial Markets, Institutions and Instruments* 15: 225–272.

Widowitz M., Vogt, P., and Neu, P. (2014). Funds transfer pricing in the new normal. In: Andreas Bohn and Marije Elkenbracht-Huizing (eds), *The Handbook of ALM in Banking: Interest Rates, Liquidity and the Balance Sheet*. Risk Books, London.

Zen, F. (2008). *La misurazione e la gestione del rischio del tasso di interesse nel banking book*. Giappichelli Editore, Torino.